CHRISTIANITY —— AND ISLAM:

THE FINAL CLASH

CHRISTIANITY
AND ISLAM:

THE CLASH
FINAL

A Look at the Church, Radical Islam, Israel, and America in End-Time Bible Prophecy

ROBERT LIVINGSTON

Pleasant Word
A Division of WINEPRESS PUBLISHING

Printed in the United States of America

Packaged by Pleasant Word, a division of WinePress Publishing, PO Box 428, Enumclaw, WA 98022. The views expressed or implied in this work do not necessarily reflect those of Pleasant Word, a division of WinePress Publishing. Ultimate design, content, and editorial accuracy of this work are the responsibilities of the author.

Unless otherwise noted, all Scriptures are taken from the New American Standard Bible, © 1960, 1963, 1968, 1971, 1972, 1973, 1975, 1977 by The Lockman Foundation. Used by permission.

ISBN 1-4141-0262-3
Library of Congress Catalog Card Number: 2004096204

Table of Contents

Acknowledgments

There are many individuals that I would like to thank for their support of this project. Thanks to Pat for the map illustrations and also giving extensive feedback on early versions of the manuscript. Thanks to Mark, Danica, John, Nancy, Jeff, Mark my brother, and others for your helpful feedback on the manuscripts and the many various and sundry other ways you helped me out.

I also want to thank my pastors Rick and Mike for their encouragement and friendship. In fact, my church family has been wonderfully supportive throughout this effort as have a number of you outside my local church. Thank you for all your support and prayers.

Many thanks to Derek, and Phil, and Isaiah 6 ministries for their friendship, love for God and the nations, and general support.

Also, thanks to all the folks at WinePress Publishers for your work on this project. Thanks to Harvey of Design Delineations for this book's website (*www.finalclash.com*).

I also want to thank my wife and children for their patience, support, prayers and good ideas. You guys are the best!

Lastly, I want to thank my Lord Jesus Christ for his unfailing love, amazing grace and abiding friendship. What a total privilege, delight and absolute joy it is to serve you! Maranatha!

Foreword

R obert Livingston is a man with a passion to see the gospel advanced in the world today. He is both a missiologist and a missionary. Since first meeting him several years ago, I have increasingly grown to appreciate his indomitable desire to reach the world. His heart, passion, and love for the Lord and His Word is contagious.

I have eagerly awaited the appearance of Robert Livingston's book *Christianity and Islam: The Final Clash*. It takes a fresh look at Revelation with a non-technical presentation that makes it accessible to the general readership. The study falls generally within the tradition of the futurist interpretation of Revelation. As such, it is filled with current events and historical data that exposes the Islamic agenda of world domination as the Antichrist force that comes of age in the final days. But don't be too quick to pigeonhole the book. Livingston takes some unexpected interpretive turns for those well acquainted with popular dispensational futurism.

Of particular value and interest is Livingston's intimate acquaintance with the Islamic religion and world missions that makes him particularly well suited to expound the vision of John. His optimism and conviction is exciting as he looks toward the triumph of Jesus Christ in the mission of the Church. The thoughtful reader is compelled to grapple with the profound insights that the author unfolds.

I commend this book to anyone who wonders about the possible links of our times with the Last Days. Whether you agree with Livingston's conclusions or not, you will find yourself with a renewed desire to be part of the "Great Completion" of the Great Commission. It is a book worthy of thoughtful consideration.

Paul Brown, M.Div., Gordon-Conwell Theological Seminary
Founder and Director of the Timothy Center
PO Box 5
Madrid, NY 13660
www.thetimothycenter.org

Prologue

It was a typically beautiful day during the summer of 1996 in this bustling Middle-Eastern City. The sun was shining brightly through the dusty windows, but not as brightly as the speaker's face. I listened intently as I watched her excited brown eyes dancing with joy. Fatima (not her real name) was bubbling over with a new-found excitement as she stood in the front of our makeshift church sanctuary. Her flowing dark hair was still covered by a headscarf. Having been raised in a religious Muslim home, she still only felt comfortable in public with a scarf on.

Speaking through tears of joy she described how she first ran across a Bible at a book fair. It was the only book on sale that she could afford. She had often been curious about it anyway. After all, the Koran frequently mentioned it. Taking home her first copy of the Bible, she was careful to immediately place it high on her shelf and not on the table where it might accidentally be knocked off. It would be a shameful thing to allow Allah's word to touch the ground.

While it is true that Muslims believe that Allah sent the Gospel and books of Moses (the Torah) and David (the Psalms), they have also been told that Jews and Christians have corrupted the text. Still, corrupted or not, portions of it probably contained truth she reasoned, as do many other Muslims. Out of respect for Allah, she handled it with care. After eating lunch, she began reading it from the end. After all, she believed God's revelations were first written in Arabic. Since Arabic is read from right to left, she assumed the first part of the Bible must start in Revelation.

As she began to read the book of Revelation, she was quickly astonished. She was shaken to the very core of her being. Suddenly the scales fell off her eyes as she began to understand that everything she had believed her whole life was radically wrong. The shock was overwhelming, but the message of Revelation was clear to her. It's truth and power was so penetrating she could not avoid the obvious conclusion. She would have to deny Islam and, come what may, become a follower of Jesus Christ. Fatima became one of the growing thousands of Muslims who are finding new life in Jesus Christ.

Attending a religious school for Islamic studies, she was kicked out of her Islamic boarding school when she told her instructor the conclusions she had reached. She made her way back to the book table where she had purchased the Bible. The believers working at the stand were able to provide her with a place to stay while she began her journey with her new Lord and Savior Jesus Christ.

As I listened to her story, I was filled once again with thanksgiving to the Lord Jesus for rescuing another soul from the clutches of Islam. Yet, it was my turn to become astonished. As she mentioned her conclusions about Revelation, I suddenly realized that my Western perspective had quite possibly blinded me from some rather stunning possibilities concerning the book of the Revelation. I had just begun a renewed study of the book of the Revelation. Curious to see whether or not her insights might have merit, I determined to take them into consideration. What I discovered over the next several years astonished me. Examine them for yourself as you read this book.

Months before hearing Fatima's story, I had felt a strong, growing conviction I needed to study the book of the Revelation and all end-time prophecy scriptures. I kept the timetable open to study as long as needed. I sought a consistent theology on this subject of end-time prophecy. I had already read numerous books on the subject over the years. In spite of having read much, I felt there were still important things I had yet to uncover in Revelation and related scriptures. I had a growing urge to find out more.

In Revelation Jesus tells John to write about "the things which are" (Rev. 1:19a). These, of course, refer to the issues addressed in the messages to the seven churches. But John is to also write of "the things which will take place *after* these things" (Rev. 1:19b).

There has historically been disagreement about when events following the message to the seven churches begin their fulfillment. This was one of the initial focal points of my study. What part of Revelation refers to future events? What refers to current truths? And what parts, if any, were fulfilled after John's day, but before today? If many of these events are future, when do we transition from what we see today to what we will see? I am convinced that many answers to these questions unfold in careful study of the text of Revelation itself and related Biblical texts.

Be aware that this book is not particularly complimentary of Islam. There is especially uncomplimentary information about Islamic fundamentalists. They are a zealous minority of Muslims who are avid enemies of the cause of the Gospel. Yet, in no way does that mean I do not have a deep love and affection for Muslim people, including fundamentalists. Even the greatest enemies of the faith, such as the Apostle Paul, can become its greatest proponents. Like Stephen, we should pray for those who persecute us; one of them could end up being the Church's next Paul. Muslims are some of the most wonderful potential followers of Christ I have ever met and lived among. In the future I fully intend to return to live in the Middle East. Middle Eastern cultures are very hospitable and wonderfully friendly. They are honored to have foreigners visit their homes, and they treat their guests like kings. There is a saying in many Muslim cultures that all guests are sent by God himself. You are received accordingly.

It has been my experience that many Muslims are fascinated by the gospel message. They are very curious, and as long as one is respectful and does not directly defame Islam, one can have excellent conversations about the Lord. Even many "secular" Muslims are deeply interested in spiritual things. Muslims frequently bring up the Lord in conversation and often ask questions about Christianity.

Spiritual interest is great. The need for laborers to work with Muslims has never been greater.

Many Muslims are unaware of much that is in the Koran. Many oppose using indiscriminate violence against foreigners. Yet, all share a common fate. They were born in places with little exposure to the Gospel and the message of salvation. They are blind sheep who can be manipulated and easily fall prey to the enemy. We must reach them with the good news of Jesus.

I am convinced a day of harvest is coming in the Muslim world. In fact, it is already beginning. More Muslims have come to faith in Christ in the past 20 years, than all previous history combined. Conversions are happening at an accelerating rate. God is doing a new thing in the Middle East. Allow me to emphasize. *In no way is this book intended to scare Christians from sharing the Gospel with Muslims. On the contrary, it is my sincere hope that greatly increased efforts will be made to take the Gospel to them.*

Some Technical Points

Concerning the Bible verses cited, I have used the 1995, updated version of the New American Standard Bible (NASB) for all quotations taken from the Holy Scriptures. It should be noted the translators of the New American Standard Bible place some words of the text in italics when they are not literally found in the original languages. Those words have been inserted into the English text in order to translate the intended meaning and maintain grammatical and readable English. In some instances, for greater emphasis, I have placed portions of the Bible text in italics. However, the italics I have put in the text of verses found in this book are *only for my emphasis* and have not been done by the translators of the NASB Bible. I have ignored NASB italics when quoting from NASB.

In all cases, unless otherwise cited, the version of the Koran used was the Revised Translation by N.J. Dawood published by Penguin Classics. Unlike most English translations of the Koran, Dawood translates the name of Allah as *God* in English. I have read three different English versions of the Koran and found Dawood's translation particularly helpful. He makes a great effort to cut out ambiguity and aims for clarity of the literal message of the Koran.

Christians who know Arabic have stated that most English translations of the Koran greatly tone down the harsher aspects of its message. The translators sometimes deliberately change the text in spots most likely to offend Western minds. By contrast, I have been told this English translation is the most direct for translating literal meaning. To help maintain a greater Muslim flavor to the verses, I have reinstated *Allah* as the name of God in all the verses. Also, any italics or words in parenthesis are mine and not the translator's. However, the rest of the text is as Dawood translated it.

Also, I intend to eventually write a study guide and post it on this book's website *www.finalclash.com*. This website will also give the reader the opportunity to contact the author and ask questions.

Introduction
Preparing the Bride
(Rev. 1:1–3:22)

Did you ever wonder why Jesus hasn't returned yet? Are Christians mistaken? Are they reading their Bibles wrong? Will there be a literal return of Christ? Didn't many Christians in the past think Mussolini or Hitler was the anti-Christ? Obviously they were wrong, and Jesus hasn't come yet. Later some thought Communism would produce the anti-Christ. Perhaps it would be Stalin, or Kruschev, Breshnev or maybe Gorbachev. Others thought Y2K computer problems would precede his coming. Some unbelievers and liberal "Christians" are increasingly skeptical, mocking those who believe in Christ's literal return. We may chide them for their unbelief. Yet, the fact is that Christ has still not come. Will things just continue along as they always have? Where is this promised coming?

Interestingly, Peter answered this question for us. "Know this first of all, that in the last days mockers will come with their mocking, following after their own lusts, and saying, 'Where is the promise of His coming? For ever since the fathers fell asleep, all continues just as it was from the beginning of creation'" (2Pet. 3:3–4). Peter goes on to assure believers that, indeed, Christ will return. Ironically, mocking Christ's return is itself a fulfillment of prophecy. The more of it we see, the more we can know the time is fast approaching.

Nevertheless, it seems confusion about Christ's coming has never been greater. Some Christians have opted to check out of the confusion. But is it wise to dismiss a large portion of scripture and an extensive teaching of Christ as unimportant? Is it really unimportant? Jesus stated,

> Be on guard, so that your hearts will not be weighed down with dissipation and drunkenness and the worries of life, and that day will come on you suddenly like a trap; for it will come upon all those who dwell on the face of all the earth. But keep on the alert at all times, praying that you may have strength to escape all these things that are about to take place, and to stand before the Son of Man. (Luke 21:34–36)

Laying Out the Scene (Rev. 1:1–8)

To examine this issue, we must look carefully at Revelation. Is a message for the Church found here today? Where are we in the prophetic drama of Revelation? What is this Great Tribulation that Jesus spoke about? Who is the anti-Christ (the Beast as Revelation calls him)? What about the number 666? What might its significance be? What is this worldwide kingdom of the Beast? Might current events be related to passages in the Scriptures in a credible way? What about the war on terrorism? What about Islam? What past history might be spoken of in the prophecies of Revelation? Who are the seven kings of the seven-headed beast? What is the Mark of the Beast the Scriptures warn against taking? Who is the false prophet? Is the United States talked about prophetically in the Holy Scriptures?

This book explores intriguing answers to these questions springing from the pages of the Bible. We will explore a very credible possibility of how end-times prophecy may be fulfilled within our lifetime. Right at the start of Revelation, John receives wonderful promises. He states, "Blessed is he who reads and those who hear the words of the prophecy, and heed the things which are written in it; for the time is near" (Rev. 1:3). The blessing is certainly no less available for us today. More than ever, the study of Revelation is no waste of time. More than ever, we need to renew our eternal perspective. Indeed, we are promised that we will be blessed if we read it. Yet, John doesn't stop there.

This promise is also for those who "*hear* the words." The word *hear* is what the Lord Jesus uses at the end of each prophetic exhortation given to the seven churches. He states, "He who has an ear, let him *hear* what the Spirit says to the churches" (Rev. 2:7, 11, 17, 29, 3:6, 13, 22). But the blessing is not just for those who hear. He says it will come to those who "*heed* the things which are written." Heeding the things that are written means allowing them to have a permanent impact on our lives. Heeding the message unleashes the blessing. There is much valuable insight and instruction waiting to make an impact on our lives in Revelation.

Seeing Jesus in His Glory, the Center of all our Worship

Right from the start of Revelation, grace and peace are extended to us from Jesus Christ (Rev. 1:4). Aren't you glad he always gives us the grace we need? And grace is what we will need to live through the drama of Revelation. Jesus is introduced here as the faithful witness (Rev. 1:5) for he has faithfully revealed the Father to us (John 14:9). It is because of the ministry of Jesus that we can more fully understand the heart of God and be prepared for the days to come. The word used for witness (*martus*) is related directly to the word *martyr*. He carried on his witness of revealing the Father even to the point of death on the cross. He was a faithful martyr, for on the cross Jesus demonstrated his undying love for the Church. He released us from our sins through his selfless sacrifice. What a powerful demonstration of the love of God for us!

It is he—the faithful martyr Jesus Christ—who is the supreme character of Revelation. This last book of the Bible is the story of Jesus Christ's revelation to the entire world, both seen and unseen. Revelation uncovers how Jesus will faithfully cause his kingdom to completely retake planet earth from his adversary the devil. It's true that we see the devil and his lieutenants at their horrific worst. But then we see Jesus Christ, emphatically triumphant in all his magnificence and glory.

We leave Revelation knowing that we can count on him. We rest assured that Jesus Christ, the faithful witness, didn't stop with the cross. He gave death itself a fatal blow by rising from the dead. He is revealed as the firstborn from the dead because all who believe in Jesus Christ will also be resurrected (1Cor. 15:1–57). He is the resurrection and the life. He has made all believers a kingdom of priests, worshipers of God. Revelation prophetically shows us how Jesus, the faithful witness, will faithfully perfect his bride and prepare her for the wedding day.

In order to prepare the earth for his complete takeover, Jesus will begin by cleansing and purifying his Church. As Peter stated, ". . . It is time for judgment to begin with the household of God; and if it begins with us first, what will be the outcome for those who do not obey the gospel of God? And if it is with difficulty that the righteous is saved, what will become of the godless man and the sinner?" (1Pet. 4:17–18). Are we ready for such a shaking? He has been doing it all along, but it will happen all the more as the day approaches (see Heb. 12:26–29).

Jesus Christ alone is rightful ruler of earth (Rev. 1:5). He will be faithful to establish his rule. He will actively defeat the rulers of earth demonically inspired to resist him. John reveals, "He is coming with the clouds, and *every* eye will see Him; even those who pierced Him; and *all* the tribes of the earth will mourn over Him. So it is to be" (Rev. 1:7). Resistance will come from *all* the corners of earth, for *all* tribes will mourn him. But his coming "is to be." There is no stopping it.

When Paul was writing to Timothy, he encouraged him saying, "This command I entrust to you, Timothy, my son, in accordance with the prophecies previously made concerning you, that by them you fight the good fight, keeping faith and good conscience . . ." (1Tim. 1:18). Although Paul was referring to personal prophecy for Timothy, how much more should we as the Church lay hold of prophetic words intended for us, that by them *we* might "fight the good fight, keeping faith and good conscience." Prophetic messages are intended to give direction and encouragement. Ignoring the prophetic word of Revelation increases the risk of wandering aimlessly and losing sight of our marching orders and our corporate destiny as the bride of Christ.

The Tribulation and Kingdom and Perseverance in Jesus

Thus, an important message of Revelation is for us to keep the faith in spite of great difficulties. Did you ever notice how John greets the Church in a most peculiar way at the beginning of Revelation? He tells them he is their "brother and fellow partaker in *the tribulation and kingdom and perseverance which are in Jesus*" (Rev. 1:9). Right away we gain the perspective that those who hold to the word of God and testimony of Jesus will find tribulation in their participation in the kingdom. But, wait a minute. I thought Jesus came to give us an abundant life (John 10:10). Apparently the abundant life includes tribulation.

Tribulation requires perseverance. In our rush to identify the Great Tribulation, the danger is to forget that "all who desire to live godly in Christ Jesus will be persecuted" (2Tim. 3:12). Opposition to true Christians is bound to come in a variety of ways. The history of the Church testifies to this.

Here in the West we can easily forget that for many believers in the world, mere mocking and harassment—often the extent of our persecution—are relatively superficial afflictions. Believers in many places face the possibility of far more serious suffering.

Imprisoned on May 8, 1998, Brother Ranjha Masih was a victim of Pakistan's Law 295c, against blaspheming Muhammad.

> On April 26, 2003, the judge gave Ranjha a sentence of life imprisonment and a fine of $878 US. This is the first time in Pakistan's history that a life sentence has been given. All other 295c convictions have been given the death sentence.

> At a Christian funeral procession, Muslim witnesses claimed that Ranjha threw a rock at an Islamic sign. Ranjha claims he did not. Muslims write to him, 'Accept Islam and we will forgive you.' Ranjha has stated from his cell: 'I am ready to be crucified for Jesus. I will not deny Him.' His wife works as a maid earning $36US a month to support their four children in a one-bedroom house. Just as the Disciples considered imprisonment for Christ an honor, so do Ranjha and his family, even in their sufferings. [1]

Many believers like Brother Ranjha and his family have recognized and embraced the suffering that is theirs in Christ Jesus and like Paul their cry is, ". . . that I may know Him and the power of His resurrection and the fellowship of His sufferings, being conformed to His death . . ." (Phil. 3:10). As John penned words about tribulation, he himself was undergoing deportation and exile. He responded by being in the Spirit. What a great response! God used him powerfully in the midst of his suffering and we have benefited to this day.

The Lord gave John messages for the seven churches. But these messages were also intended for those *beyond* these literal seven local churches. John is told at the end of each message, "He *who has an ear, let him hear* what the Spirit says to the *churches*" (Rev. 2:7, etc.). We are instructed to listen to what the Spirit says to the *churches*, not church. Thus, it is reasonable to assume God picked out these seven churches because the issues they faced represent some major issues and problems facing the Church throughout the Church Age.[2]

In the messages to the seven churches we see Jesus perfecting the Church, helping her to focus on the eternal. Jesus encourages certain attitudes and behaviors and warns and rebukes against others. These messages also instruct us how the Lord Jesus will deal (and has dealt) with a wide variety of issues that have confronted the body of Christ during this age. As Tenney stated, "they are seven different types of churches that may be found in any period of the world's history since Pentecost." Unfortunately, the scope of this book will not permit us to delve into these important messages. However, we must understand the seven churches are also representative of the broader Church. Knowing this can help us understand the role of the Church in Revelation.

Seven Golden Lampstands and the Body of Christ

In Revelation 1:12, John turns around to see who is talking. Imagine the intensity of the moment as he turned to see who this magnificent voice was. There, in front of him, are seven golden lampstands and in the center of the lampstands is One who looks like a son of man. But this is not just any person. Overcome and falling down like a dead man (Rev. 1:17), John gives a spectacular description of the glorified Christ. Among other things, in his right hand are seven stars. What incredible brilliance! We are told, in verse 20, that these seven stars are seven angels for the seven churches.[3] Then we learn something else of very great significance; John identifies the seven golden lampstands as being the actual seven churches *themselves*.

Think about that for a minute. The seven earthly churches located in Asia Minor, at the seven cities mentioned, were also present in heaven surrounding the risen Christ. How amazing! How can this be? Fortunately, the Spirit-inspired words of Paul the Apostle help enlighten us. "God being rich in mercy, because of His great love with which He loved us, even when we were dead in our transgressions, made us alive together with Christ . . . and *raised us up with Him, and seated us with Him in the heavenly places in Christ Jesus . . .*"(Eph. 2:4–6).

All of us, not just the literal seven churches are seated with Christ Jesus in heavenly places. Thus, once again we see that these seven churches also likely represent the wider body of Christ. We actually get a picture of ourselves currently seated in heavenly places with Christ Jesus. John got to see this truth for himself and describe it to us. The Holy Spirit of God indwells his people and because of this we are quite literally in God's presence even right here on earth.

What a beautiful corporate illustration of "Christ in you, the hope of glory" (Col. 1:27b)! The indwelling presence of the Holy Spirit in the Church is what John referred to when he talked about the "seven Spirits who are before His throne" (Rev. 1:4). This was not a reference to seven Holy Spirits. This is *the* Holy Spirit, present in the seven churches that also represent the diverse expressions of the whole body of Christ. Lampstands hold lamps. In the same way, the Church is God's ordained structure intended to be, hold and provide support to the lights of the world, believers in Jesus Christ (Matt. 5:14). As we shall see later on, this is important to know in order to understand the role the Church will play in the return of Christ.

He'll Finish What He Started

Importantly, Jesus also reminds us at the beginning of this Revelation that he has started everything and he has the power to finish what he started for he is the "Alpha and the Omega" (Rev. 1:8a). He is not just another religious teacher. He has proven he is so much more, for he has conquered death and is alive forevermore. He saved himself, so he can save others. He himself holds the keys of death and Hades (Rev. 1:18). The reality of the Resurrection is an anchor for the Church to grasp. For Jesus is about to reveal that the process of cleansing the earth of all opposition will be very difficult. It will involve great suffering, even martyrdom, on the part of his people. We will have to trust in his faithfulness. The reality of his complete victory over death and Hades will be essential ammunition for the Church during this time.

In order for the Church to complete the transformation into the glorious bride prepared and ready for her husband, there will be trials and difficulties. A pregnant woman has to go through difficulties and trials during her pregnancy. The most difficult trial often comes just before the birth of the child during the last labor pains. Final labor pains are known medically as the period of "transition." It is the time when the baby is on the verge of being born. It is then when pain is most intense.

So too, the Bible tells us the greatest trial awaits the Church just before the return of Christ. What will happen in the world as we enter this final transition phase before the return of Christ?

. . . .

Chapter 1

The Islamic Beast is Revived (Rev. 13:1–4)

S uicide bombers and Islamic terror cells have become a normal part of the daily news. Even children are pulled into this violent world by the grasping tentacles of hatred and the lies of a false paradise. What has caused the springing up of such apparent madness? And where might it lead? Two thousand years ago, John the apostle was transported into the future. He witnessed the world stunned by the rebirth of an Empire long thought to be dead.

John must have been horrified as he saw this incredible set of future events unfold before his eyes. The shock of what he experienced radiates from the text as he wrote, "I saw one of his heads as if it had been slain, and his fatal wound was healed. And the *whole earth was amazed* and followed after the beast . . ." (Rev. 13:3).

Popularly understood to be a literal head wound of an individual, John actually says that "*one* of his heads" looked slain, but recovered. Since *one* of the seven heads of the seven-headed beast gets healed, this is clearly not a person. Only later is this wound also referred to being connected with an individual (Rev. 13:12,14). The first apparent resurrection refers to the revival of an empire that had appeared to die. But what empire could that be?

After World War I, the Ottoman Empire was dissolved. In 1922, the Muslim Caliphate—the spiritual and political head of Islam stationed in Istanbul—was abolished and lost all authority. This happened at the hand of the founder of the secular Turkish Republic, Kemal Ataturk. It is important to realize the significance of this to the Islamic world. The Caliph was considered the spiritual and political leader of the Islamic World, much as the Pope has been considered the spiritual, and in the past, political leader of Roman Catholics. At one time the Ottoman Empire had been the dominant power in the world. But for hundreds of years it had been on the decline and with the stroke of a pen, it was sent into oblivion.

The Building Storm

When Kemal Ataturk abolished the Caliphate, he abolished the officially recognized political and spiritual leadership of Islam. Muslims around the world were devastated. It would be like getting rid of the office of Pope for Roman Catholics. Ever since the time of Muhammad there had been Caliphs, sometimes more than one, but nevertheless, there had always been at least one. The abolishment of the Caliphate delivered a significant blow to the Islamic dream of world rule and Islamic Empire. It was humiliating.

Nearly all the Islamic World, with the exception of Saudi Arabia, fell under the rule of Western "Christian" nations. It was a very disillusioning time for Muslims and in many ways continues to be. As Dr. Muqtedar Khan, (Director of International Studies at Adrian College) himself a Muslim, stated, "Today the Muslim world suffers from a deep sense of insecurity, largely from the West, which it rightly or wrongly sees as a force determined to separate Muslims from Islam."[4]

Even though Islamic nations have since gained independence from colonial powers, some Muslims feel Islam is reeling from encroaching apostasy. Many feel the West is deliberately out to destroy Islam. Speaking of the United States, Tunisian Islamist Rachid Ghannouci expresses his frustrations. "It (the US) would like to change Islam, secularize it," says Ghannouchi. "It wants to promote Islam with *Sharia* and without *jihad* . . ." He goes on to say, "Why should we have to sacrifice our Islam to have a friendship with America?"[5] He and some other Muslims feel the West is infecting Islam. This is something from which it must be cleansed they believe.

In spite of encroaching modernism, any prediction of fundamentalist Islam's disappearance has always proven shortsighted. The Muslim brotherhood of Egypt was organized in 1928, in part to respond to the outrage of an abolished Caliphate and their humiliation by Western "Christian" Colonialism.

It was decided Islam had become corrupt and far too Westernized, and thus it fell under Allah's judgment. Only a pure Islam could revive the Caliphate and restore true Islam to the world. This torch was picked up by an influential Egyptian cleric, Sayyid Qutb in the 1950's and 1960's. He was a fundamentalist philosopher jailed in Egypt and eventually martyred for his insistence on the necessity of the re-establishment of *Sharia* Law in Egypt and eventually the world. He was entirely supportive of the use of violence to accomplish this goal, citing numerous Koranic texts. It is his writings that inspired Al-Qaeda and many other radicals as well. Will radical Islam be revived and eventually rear its ugly head again in a position of authority?

Some have felt this is not possible since a majority of Muslims are said to support "democracy." In every one of the seventeen Muslim nations in a recent Pew Global Attitudes Survey, a majority in all, except for Indonesia, stated they desired democracy in their country and felt it could work in their country. This has led some people to assume there is widespread support for democracy in the Muslim world and hope for a bright future. Unfortunately, the situation is far more complex.

Democracy Islamic Style

The reality is that the Muslim understanding of democracy often stands at odds with our Western view. For many Muslims, democracy does not mean freedom of religion, as we understand it. To blaspheme Muhammad requires punishment, even under the democracy of secular Turkish law. This divergence in views about the character of democracy is also revealed in the same Pew Survey results. For example, when asked if religion should be allowed to be a personal matter for the individual and remain separate from the government, there is a big discrepancy. Unlike a state-church system as often seen in Europe that has evolved to allow nearly complete freedom of religious practice for individuals, an Islamic state system necessitates restrictions on the practice of freedom of religion, particularly for non-Muslims. Unlike a Western state-church system, a separation of state and mosque would be absolutely essential for true religious freedom in an Islamic nation.

But is that the sentiment of most Muslims? The results of the survey are telling. In Jordan, although 68% felt democracy could work in their country, only 24% felt government policy and religious practice should be separate. In Pakistan, 58% indicate support for democracy, but only 33% believe in a separation of mosque and state. Additionally, significant numbers of Muslims in many countries believe democracy is a Western way of doing things. Ominously, such a view is strongest in the two Muslim nations that have the most democratic political systems in the Muslim world, 53% in Indonesia and 37% in Turkey.[7] In other words, in the Muslim nations where Muslim governments are making a somewhat serious stab at democracy, Muslims are the least satisfied with democracy and view it as a "Western way" of doing things.

Even in Turkey, a supposedly secular Muslim government with separation of mosque and state, and freedom of religion written in the constitution, the secular government spends millions of dollars building mosques and paying the salaries of Islamic clerics and Muslim missionaries to other countries. They also place numerous restrictions on churches that do not exist for mosques. In recent years, the police have been known to shut down church meetings. They have closed some church buildings and not allowed many to open for the most dubious reasons. In general, this freest of Islamic nations has basically harassed and attempted to hinder the free practice and spread of Christianity.

For all Muslim nations combined, 82% of Muslims believe Islam should play a major role in politics. Furthermore, a solid majority in most Islamic nations surveyed believes the role of Islam should increase.[8] As Robert Jordan, former US ambassador to Saudi Arabia has stated if there were elections in Saudi Arabia, "The government that would replace the (current) government of Saudi Arabia would look a whole lot more like the Taliban than a Jeffersonian Democracy."[9]

In a number of Muslim countries there is deep dissatisfaction with the current state of affairs in their nations. As liberal Muslim journalist Yusuf Ibrahim noted, "We are losing the hearts and minds of the secularists who are (traditionally) anti-fundamentalist. There is immense distance between the people and their rulers."[10]

In Pakistan, the one Islamic nation currently with nuclear weapons, the relatively secular and pro-Western general who is running the country, General Perez Musharaf, has been walking a delicate tightrope. He has also been the target of several assassination attempts by Al-Qaeda. He is trying desperately to keep an increasingly restive populace under control while supporting the current American war on terrorism. In the survey, 56% of Muslims in Pakistan believe Islam plays a large role in politics, but 86% believe it should play a larger role. Just 35% think the current role of Islam is very large, but 75% think it should have a very large role.[11]

Many within his nation's spy agency and army and security elements had actually been working actively in support of the Taliban regime right up until September 11, 2001. Most of the Taliban rulers had been trained in the Madrassas (religious Islamic schools) of northern Pakistan where nearly all of the ten-hour school days are spent memorizing the Koran and learning about *jihad* (holy war).[12] The only government in the world that had a Taliban embassy in its nation was Pakistan.

The shock of 9/11 and intense pressure from the United States led to an immediate flip-flop. Still there is a sense that many within the security services are unsupportive of this 180-degree turn. It has also recently come out that Pakistan's nuclear scientists sold nuclear secrets to Libya, Iran and North Korea. Why hasn't Osama bin-Laden been caught? "Some in Washington believe the Pakistanis don't really want him captured," reports *US News & World Report*.[13]

Taliban elements and even perhaps Osama bin-Laden, regularly traverse back and forth between the Afghan frontier and mountainous Pakistani tribal areas across the border to safe houses. Cooperation between Pakistani forces on the Pakistani side of the border and American troops on the Afghan side has often been less than stellar. Also "family ties between members of the Pakistani Eleventh Corps, which has conducted some (anti-terrorist) operations in the tribal areas, and Pashtuns who live in the areas resulted in advance warning of several early raids on sanctuaries (for terrorists) in the borderlands . . ."[14]

In spite of a temporary crackdown after 9/11, Pakistan continues to educate and turn out ideologically committed radicals. These radicals are dedicated to bring Islamic fundamentalist rule. Some are even sent to fight as children to gain experience in warfare. Norval writes "Religious schools (*madrassas*) and Koranic study centers have become the single most important source for recruiting new members into radical Islamic movements and given the huge pool of the young throughout the Muslim world . . . It has deadly future ramifications . . ." [15]

In many cases, anti-Americanism throughout the Muslim world is feeding growing support for Islamic parties that have traditionally been the most virulently anti-American. Recently a Peshawar Pakistani—who had voted for one of the Islamic parties that recently came to power in Peshawar—was upset about restrictions on music placed on Peshawar by these same Islamic parties. He was asked then, why he and many people voted for the government if they are unhappy with the restrictions. He stated, "Some parties supported America. Many people were upset with those parties so they voted for the anti-American Islamists." [16]

In most Islamic nations, support remains high for Osama bin-Laden. In Indonesia, 58% of the population felt Osama bin-Laden could be counted on to "do the right thing regarding world affairs." 55% in Jordan, 49% in Morocco, and 45% in Pakistan felt the same way. Amazingly, 71% of those living under the Palestinian Authority felt that bin-Laden would do the right thing! [17]

Many Muslims view the United-States-led war on terrorism as nothing more than a smoke screen to allow a new crusade against Islam and control of the oil of the Middle East. In nearly every Muslim country surveyed, less than a quarter of the populations support the war on terrorism effort, often much less. Only 16% in Pakistan, 9% in Morocco, 2% in Jordan and 2% in the Palestinian Authority were in favor of such a war. [18]

The Islamic Solution

Why is there growing support for the radicals? Certainly there is continued frustration over the existence of Israel and the Palestinian cause, as well as growing US intervention in the region. But the survey also discovered that "people everywhere also strongly believe that their traditional way of life is getting lost."[19] Sayyid Qutb, a philosophical giant in the terrorist world of Al-Qaeda could not have agreed more. He preached that the modern world has been drifting because it has no way to unite the secular and the spiritual. He believed Christianity was doomed to error ever since it began to apply the idea that one should "give to Caesar what is Caesar's and to God what is God's."[20]

> Qutb knew who to blame. He blamed the early Christians. He blamed (his view of) Christianity's modern legacy, that was the liberal idea that religion should stay in one corner and secular life in another corner. He blamed the Jews. In his interpretation . . . they became craven and unprincipled when powerless, and vicious and arrogant when powerful. And these traits were eternal. The Jews occupy huge portions of Qutb's Koranic commentary—their perfidy, greed, hatefulness, diabolical impulses, never-ending conspiracies and plots against Muhammad and Islam. Qutb was relentless on these themes. He looked on Zionism as part of the eternal campaign by the Jews to destroy Islam.

> And Qutb blamed one other party. He blamed the Muslims who had gone along with Christianity's errors—the treacherous Muslims who had inflicted Christianity's 'schizophrenia' on the world of Islam. And, because he was willing to blame, Qutb was able to recommend a course of action too—a revolutionary program that was going to relieve the psychological pressure of modern life and was going to put man at ease with the natural world and with God.[21]

That revolutionary program involves the re-establishment of true *Sharia* law. First it would be established over the Islamic world, and then by spreading the world of Islam it would fill the entire world. As one British Pakistani Muslim radical recently stated, "We believe the world is on the verge of a pure Islamic state."[22]

Qutb's ideas are not confined to the Al-Qaeda network. They are increasingly widespread. Today even "moderate" Islamic leaders are saying similar things. Recently the Prime Minister of Malaysia, long considered a moderate, was quoted as declaring that the Jews are ruling the world through proxy via the major powers (i.e. The United

States). He also declared that Muslims needed to work hard to rearm themselves and assert their power in the world more forcefully.[23]

Another modern-day disciple of Qutb's ideas, a leader in the Pakistani Islamist Party movement (not known to be part of Al-Qaeda), Mullah Hafez Ali stated, "We inherited this culture from Allah 1400 years ago as a complete way of life. We don't need to follow the West."[24]

Another Islamic leader of a Madrassa school in northern Pakistan put it this way, ". . . we should have the law of the Quran, then everything will be alright."[25] The ideas embraced by Al-Qaeda are reflected in newly forming Islamist groups throughout the Muslim world.[26] Recently, Suleyman Al-Fata, a columnist widely read in Saudi Arabian newspapers admitted that the Saudi government had "confirmed the discovery of two new fundamentalist organizations in Saudi Arabia."[27] Of course, direct connections between some in the Saudi government and terrorists are now also widely believed.

Some hold out the hope that a majority of Muslims would never support *Sharia* Law and thus, such a system will never spread. The hope is that a "democratic" Islamic world will somehow bring peace and contain bloodshed. The problem is that even if truly fair elections were held in all Islamic nations, in nearly every case, strongly anti-American, pro Islamist governments would be installed.[28]

The powerful ability of Islamists to manipulate widespread anti-Americanism to spread their Islamist agenda is well recognized. Even where elements of democracy are being tried many agree that, "the radical mullahs are succeeding through democratic means by exploiting the anti-Americanism in the society."[29] Even within Iraq itself, "there is a growing market for anti-Americanism . . . and politicians are beginning to compete for it."[30]

Iran is often held out as a beacon of hope for potential change because anti-government protests have risen in fervor in recent years demanding more freedom. However, even here, student protesters often state they are not opposed to Islam or Islamic government, but only to the current mullah's way of implementing it. Also, the latest parliamentary elections in early 2004 saw many reformist candidates kicked off the ballots. This resulted in the landslide election of conservative hard-line Muslims. Some *Islamists* in other nations are actually quite willing to temporarily attempt to work through democracy to advance an Islamist agenda that would eventually lead to *Sharia* Law.

Recep Tayip Erdogan, the newly elected Prime Minister of Turkey and a "moderate" Islamist was overwhelmingly elected to the Turkish Parliament with 85% of the vote. His party gained nearly two-thirds of the seats of Parliament with 34.6% of the vote. This was the first time in 15 years that a single party had gained the majority in the Turkish Parliament. He has styled himself as a softly pro-Western, modern Islamist with democratic ideals. Some believe he has genuinely converted to democratic notions from an earlier radical Islamic belief. However, the staunchly secular Turkish military is wary of his true intentions. They are not alone. One American diplomat was quoted as saying, "He's saying all the right things about Europe and moving westward, but I fear he's like a wolf in sheep's clothing."[31]

Just a few years back, while mayor of Istanbul, he declared himself its Imam (spiritual leader). "He never clearly allayed secular concerns, keeping them alive instead with comments like: 'Democracy is a streetcar. When you come to your stop, you get off."[32] In December, 1997, while speaking at a political rally, he stated, "The mosques are our barracks, the domes our helmets, the minarets our bayonets, and the believers our soldiers."[33]

Some believe he is now a true democrat. At the very least, he realizes he cannot yet openly challenge the secular bureaucracy and secular military. Perhaps, for now, he will have to quietly ride the streetcar called democracy. Some believe that through court appointments, changes in the law, and quiet bureaucratic maneuvers he is secretly working for a hidden agenda. That involves working for a day when he or a successor can take Turkey closer to getting off at the next stop of *Sharia* Law.

One potentially alarming reform happened in July 2003. In an "unprecedented move, parliament passed a reform package limiting the role of the country's powerful military in politics. The new law strips the military-dominated National Security Council—a policy-making body that shadows the Prime Minister's cabinet—of its executive powers, making it an advisory body only and also allows for greater parliamentary scrutiny of military spending."[34] The military have always intervened in the past through this council to prevent the country from drifting too Islamic in its policies. They have effectively been stripped of this power.

In any case, democracy is not a necessary element for fundamental Islam to gain power. All that is needed is a fanatical devotion to one's viewpoint, a sufficient number of supporters, and a willingness to use violence to take power. It may be that a weak form of democracy, such as the Turkish model may spread for a time to some Islamic nations. This may help give a little wider opening to Christians to spread the Gospel throughout the Islamic world. We should seize the opportunity while we have it. However, even optimists and liberal Muslims believe any attempted road to stable democracy will be fraught with difficulty and danger.³⁵ Failure could have disastrous results.

Failed Democracies Create the Ripest Soil for Revolution

Even if democracy should begin to gain some ascendancy, this doesn't assure long-term success. Failure of weak democracies have preceded and helped the rise of the most oppressive governments the world has known. Germany, Japan, Italy, Spain, Russia, and China all made failed attempts at representative government early in the twentieth century. These attempted forays into representative government happened after the overthrow of autocratic rulers in the early 1900's, shortly before, during and after World War I. When these fledgling democratic efforts were unable to address strong economic downturns and increasing anarchy, absolutist ideologies stepped in to fill the void. Many people who at first were hesitant to support such ideologues were won over to support dictatorships. Many said, "We tried democracy and it didn't work."

Democracy, or representative government, is not the Gospel and will never be the salvation of man. As the word of God states, "He has promised, saying, 'Yet once more I will shake not only the earth, but also the heavens.' This expression, 'yet once more' denotes the removing of those things which can be shaken, as of created things, so that those things which cannot be shaken may remain'" (Heb. 9:26b–27). Representative government is a temporary invention of man, even if it does line up with a few Biblical principals in a couple of areas. Certainly, it has often proved helpful in the spread of the Gospel. However, when Jesus returns, he will not set up a democracy. Therefore, we can be sure that democracy too will be shaken and found wanting.

Post-World-War-I Germany, although newly democratic, in a few years saw the rise of the Nazi Party and Adolph Hitler seizing power through parliamentary maneuvering, bribery and intimidation. Italy was also newly democratic, but in even fewer years than Germany, it soon also saw the rise of the dictator Benito Mussolini, who as many Italians were fond of saying, managed "to get the trains to run on time."

Spain's brief post-World-War-I attempt at democracy also descended into brutal civil war and came out the other end with the fascist dictatorship of Francisco Franco. Russia overthrew the Russian monarchy with a liberal democratic socialist government that believed in representative government, only to be violently replaced itself about eight months later by the more radical Bolshevik communists.

Japan, also newly democratic after World War I, replaced its parliamentary democracy with a military government ostensibly serving the "divine" Emperor Hirohito. The result of these failed attempts in democracy was the most violent war of the twentieth century.

Will democracy really come to the Middle East? Perhaps, for a time, there will be a temporary increase of democracy in the Middle East, maybe even a temporary subsiding in the feverish hatred of Western governments. Nevertheless, with freedom will come a greater spread of the Gospel and a greater spread of immoral Western culture that will only serve to further aggravate, irritate and radicalize the devout Muslim. He will grow even more convinced he is under assault from the West.

In the mind of many Muslims, incredible as it may seem, immoral Western culture and Christianity are often linked as one and the same. I can remember a religious Muslim chiding me with a straight face because of all the alcohol drinking and drunkenness that took place at Church services where they served wine every Sunday. Also, in the mind of the radical Muslim, representative government leads to nothing more than free sex and alcohol. In fact, there is some truth to that.

Before Saddam's downfall, X-rated movie theaters, movies and pornography were banned in Iraq. Today, under American occupation the laws against these things are not enforced and stores that sell these products and the theaters that show them are multiplying, especially in Baghdad. The spread of Western ways, whether through immorality or a growth in the number of Christian converts, will further impress on the devout Muslim's mind, that there is no choice but *jihad* to preserve and spread Islam.

Who can Wage War Against Them?

How did we survive the great nuclear danger of the cold war with Communism? Ultimately, it was the desire for self-preservation on both sides that allowed for the defense doctrine of MAD, mutually assured destruction.[16] This policy held the nuclear powers at bay during the Cold War. Each side feared annihilation, even as it pointed its nuclear weapons at the other.

In most cases, the revolutionary ideologies that supported these absolutist regimes of the twentieth century were largely secular in outlook and materialistic in their goals. There was no promise of eternal heaven for the Nazi or communist fanatical martyr. Communism openly despised, hated and sought to eradicate such ideas of an afterlife. Thus, even in their fanaticism, there was a natural check on their ambitions due to the natural desire of self-preservation. Yet, even then, many were willing to gladly give their lives in causes they deeply believed in.

Fundamentally, Islam does not suffer from the restraints of secular ideology. The doctrine of MAD is meaningless to a devout Muslim. Death in the cause of Allah is the one sure guarantee of heaven. The concept of *jihad* and the assurance Islam will one day conquer the whole world are deeply planted in a devout Muslim's mind and culture.

Representative government has no place in fundamental Islam. This is well explained by the Pakistani Islamic teacher Sayyid Abul Ala Maududi (1903–1979), an important non-Arab theorist and propagandist in the Sunni Muslim world.

He believed the character of social order flowed from the top to bottom, and thus, to change society one must change the thinking of its leaders. Ideas of democracy, however, were not among the concepts to be used to change the thinking of Muslim leaders.

Maududi believed democracy, in particular Western democratic forms of government, were evil devices of Satan through which men satisfy their whims and evil desires. Islam, on the other hand, is a monolithic system in which Allah alone legislates. God, not man, has given us the law, and it is found in the holy texts of Islam. The divine rule of Maududi's is the rule of the Ayatollahs in Iran, or the bin Ladens of Islamic fundamentalism, not the representative democracy of the United States and her Western allies.

The militant Islamic fundamentalist revolutionary, in order to succeed, still needs the support of the population but instead of allowing his vision of the future to compete in the market place of ideas, he resorts to force, intimidation, armed propaganda and subversive organization.

Intimidation uses terror tactics to coerce the people into following the militant's revolutionary program.[37]

The fact is that many experts are openly pessimistic and believe a showdown with Islam is likely. The continued rise of fundamental Islam in the Muslim world is likely to be an unstoppable trend in the long run. Indeed, if Islam is the final ideology of the Beast's kingdom, only the return of Jesus himself will defeat it.

Even now as this book prepares to go to press in June of 2004, the future of Iraq and the Middle East remains uncertain. Followers of radical Islamist Muktadar Al-Sadr, known as the Mahdi's army, were fighting with coalition forces for control of several cities. Will the US and its tentative allies be able to contain the rebellion? Even if the US succeeds temporarily, will Al-Sadr or others like him eventually take control at a future time? How long can these forces be contained? And to where might they spread? Even if there is a temporary respite, it is only a matter of time before radical Islam explodes.

The World will be Stunned

The "whole earth" will be amazed at the resurrection of an Empire and eventually follow after the Beast (Rev. 13:3). Could this resurrected kingdom be a revived Islamic Empire? As Norval cogently stated, "As the power of Islamic states declined, the concept of *jihad* didn't just whither away like the mythical Marxist state. *Jihad* just became dormant, awaiting the opportunity to rise again and once again become a force within the Muslim community." Certainly the whole earth will be dumbfounded and shocked if fundamentalist Islam overtakes and unites the Muslim world.

Will military power really be able to prevent an eventual takeover? "We've been very successful in killing or capturing members of the al Qaeda command structure," says terrorism consultant Peter Probst, a former CIA officer. "But we've failed to come to grips with the fact that al Qaeda is much more than an organization of a network. It is a movement."

World takeover is the goal of the *Islamists* and not just Osama bin-Laden. As Yugoslavia fell apart in the early 90s, even "before the first shots were fired, Bosnian Muslim leader Alija Izetbegovic proudly proclaimed his "Islamic Declaration" that "there can be no peace or coexistence between the Islamic faith and the non-Islamic societies and political institutions." He encouraged his fellow Muslims that "the Islamic movement should and must start taking power as soon as possible as it is morally and numerically strong enough not only to overthrow the existing non-Islamic power structure, but also to build a great Islamic federation spreading from Morocco to Indonesia, from tropical Africa to Central Asia."

Several groups in Central Asia have been gaining growing influence within the Central Asian populations. Although not traditionally considered hotbeds of radicalism, that is changing. Some are even seeking to unite the Islamic world through peaceful means. This includes the group called the Party of Islamic Liberation that has declared *jihad* on the governments of Central Asia through peaceful means if possible only to use violence later against non-Muslims. This party, ". . . seeks to reunite the Central Asian republics and eventually the whole Muslim world . . . with the eventual aim of establishing a caliphate similar to that established after the death of the Prophet Muhammad in seventh-century Arabia."[41]

Another group is known as the Islamic Movement of Uzbekistan (IMU). It originated in Uzbekistan, but has become a transnational group. Its goal is to violently topple the regime of Uzbekistan's President Islam Karimov ". . . as part of a *jihad* that will reach across Central Asia."[42] It was this group that was responsible for the first ever suicide bombings that hit the capital Tashkent in March 2004.

After the collapse of Communism and the break up of the Soviet Union, Christian missionaries were not the only newcomers to Central Asia. New visitors also included Islamic missionaries from Pakistan, Saudi Arabia, Iran, Turkey and many other places. They helped build thousands of new mosques and distributed the Koran freely. They taught unlearned Muslims their brand of Islam that was often fundamental in nature.

For example, in the newly independent Republic of Tajikistan there were only eighteen mosques at the time the Soviet Union collapsed. However, today, there are over two thousand. In the capital, Dushanbe, several Muslim countries are funding a huge mosque construction project. Iran is broadcasting messages of fundamental Islam into the area daily. Via Afghanistan, books, tapes, and videos that espouse a return to traditional Islam are flooding the country. Although many Tajiks do not identify themselves with radical Islam, there is a sense of growing pressure to conform.[43] Similar pressures are being felt throughout Central Asia.

In nearby Kyrgyzstan, there were only thirty-three mosques in 1991. Today Saudi Arabian, Pakistani and Turkish missionaries of Islam have built over one hundred twenty mosques and over two thousand Muslim prayer houses.[44]

Support is building for the radicals. Rashid reports that "whilst poverty and unemployment increase, and economic opportunities decrease, Central Asia's debt-ridden societies are ripe for any organization or party that offers hope for a better life."[45] Al-Qaeda's global network links these organizations to the politics of global radical Islam. In what may be an attempt to placate radical groups, many "moderate" Islamic states have allowed private funding to flow through their banks to these *jihadi* organizations.

So-called moderate states such as Saudi Arabia and Dubai have been key players in this game. They have allowed charities that promote Wahhabiism (Saudi Arabia's homespun fundamentalist brand of Islam), to provide ". . . missionaries, scholarships, and Islamic literature, including millions of copies of the Koran translated into the native languages" to flow to Central Asia.[46] Ironically, many radicalized Saudis, like Osama bin-Laden, are now openly advocating the overthrow of the corrupt Saudi regime. Only in the past year or two has the Saudi government finally awakened to the threat. Rashid reports that "Saudi Arabia is in danger of becoming another Algeria, where hundreds of militants who fought in Afghanistan in the 1980s returned to fight the civil war of the 1990s."[47]

Saudi Arabia is becoming increasingly vulnerable to revolution. It has experienced a sustained economic contraction of massive proportions over the past decade leading to higher levels of unemployment and ever-lowering wages. Wages have fallen from a per capita income that peaked at about $27,000 in 1989, to a current level of barely more than $6,000.[48] That's a 450% decrease in personal income in just 14 years. Some estimates place unemployment among 20–24 year olds at levels of about 30%.[49]

Economic hopelessness and boredom from idleness has exposed the massive corruption and graft in the system. There is growing resentment of the Saudi government. Many are increasingly disgusted with their government's continual support of Western economies and governments at the expense of Islam.

Saud Al-Faheed is a leading Saudi dissident and reformer living in London, England. He is the leader of the Movement for Islamic Reform. Daily he hosts a radio show broadcast live into Saudi Arabia that is trying to undercut the current Saudi regime and establish a pure Islamic state. He believes that opening up reform in Saudi Arabia will empower the silent majority in Saudi Arabia who agree with the Wahhabi (strict and supportive of literal holy war) interpretation of Islam. In his view, the Saudi regime has been too liberal on social issues. He believes that religious leaders should be chosen to govern the country, unlike the current absolute monarchy governed by a ruling family. He states that "Religious authorities would not lose their privileged position, *but have more of a direct political role"* not unlike that seen currently in Iran.⁵⁰

This Islamic revolutionary goes on to say,

> Unfortunately, the departure of the regime (Saudi ruling house of Saud) is inevitable. Nobody can avoid the impending clash within the country. The time will come when they (the people) have nothing to lose. (There is) 40% unemployment. Sixty percent of oil revenue goes to the royal family. Thirty percent of the people are in abject poverty. People will have nothing to lose. People will start enjoying sacrifice. It will become prestigious to join the protest.⁵¹

He states, that

> the momentum within the people is so strong against the United States . . . The United States has a strategic link with the royal family and they will end-up with nothing. The only thing the regime can give us is support from America." But "Islam doesn't allow people to obey a corrupt, despotic regime. Our major role is to tell real Islam to the people. The regime cannot change the environment that causes Al-Qaeda to grow. The regime's resistance to change guarantees support for Al-Qaeda to grow.⁵²

In the view of retired CIA analyst Robert Bayer, increasingly sophisticated terrorist attacks on oil companies and foreigners in Saudi Arabia are indicators that the Saudi regime is growing more and more unstable.⁵³

Fauz Gerges, author of *Islamists and the West* and a professor at Sarah Lawrence College, believes the battle for control of the Islamic world is well underway. He is convinced the terrorists of today will be extremely hard to stop. In an interview on the PBS *Newshour* he stated:

> Al Qaeda has become highly decentralized. Corporate *jihad* has become very fluid and broad and hard to contain. The attacks in Saudi Arabia and Morocco (in the spring of 2003) also aimed at symbolic links between these regimes and the West. There's a wide perception that Moroccan intelligence agents have been torturing Al Qaeda agents, and are perceived by the people as being

subservient to the United States and working against Muslims. The war with Iraq and the Palestinian-Israeli stalemate has provided many potential recruits for Al Qaeda. Central Asia and North Africa will become a new battleground for Al Qaeda.[34]

Walking the Tightrope with the Radicals

This has put many current moderate Muslim governments in a real bind. They are in a delicate position when dealing with their own radical movements. If they crack down too hard, they risk alienating a growing part of their own populations. When it comes to this balancing act of placating the radicals, even Turkey is trying to carefully ride the fence with its own fundamentalist movement. But the *Islamists* are not in a rush. They are willing to plod on persistently.[35]

Is it possible an Islamic *jihad* will install the Beast at the head of a conquered state? Could it be Saudi Arabia with its holy sites? Could it be Pakistan with its nuclear weapons? Or will it be some other place? Perhaps he'll rise up in Iraq, the heart of old Babylon and the mouth of the kingdom of the Beast who is coming (Rev. 13:2). He will probably be one who has carried "a bow" in the *jihadi* movement for some time. A crown will be "given to him" and he will go forth "conquering" the Islamic world with the intention of then taking on the rest of the world "to conquer" (Rev. 6:2b). What is this individual going to be like? What will his program be? What will his doctrine be? Does the Biblical scenario fit into Islamic teaching and practice?

The Four Horsemen of Revelation and the Unleashing of Radical Islam (Revelation 6:1– 6:8)

And I saw when the Lamb broke one of the seven seals, and I heard one of the four living creatures saying as with a voice of thunder, 'Come.' And I looked, and behold, a white horse, and he who sat on it had a bow; and a crown was given to him; and he went out conquering, and to conquer.

And when He broke the second seal, I heard the second living creature saying, 'Come.' And another, a red horse, went out; and to him who sat on it, it was granted to take peace from the earth, and that men should slay one another; and a great sword was given to him.

And when He broke the third seal, I heard the third living creature saying, 'Come.' And I looked and behold, a black horse; and he who sat on it had a pair of scales in his hand. And I heard as it were a voice in the center of the four living creatures saying, 'A quart of wheat for a denarius, and three quarts of barley for a denarius; and do not harm the oil and the wine.'

And when He broke the fourth seal, I heard the voice of the fourth living creature saying, 'Come.' And I looked, and behold an ashen horse; and he who sat on it had the name Death; and Hades was following with him. And authority was given to them over a fourth

43

of the earth, to kill with sword and with famine and with pestilence and by the wild beasts of the earth. (Rev. 6:1–8)

John must have stood in the Spirit with his spiritual mouth agape at the unparalleled splendor he had witnessed. All of heaven had just finished a thunderous time of celebration and worship to the Lamb. Talk about an anointed worship service! Now the same Lamb came forward with a scroll in his hand (Rev. 5:7). A scroll written on both sides was typical of legal documents in Roman society, especially wills.[36] The scroll Jesus held was nothing less than the title deed of earth. It was the document of inheritance for the Lord Jesus, the rightful heir of planet earth.[37]

John witnessed the moment when Jesus finally received his full inheritance. The scroll contains the judgment that will ultimately usher in the kingdom on earth as it is in heaven. But before this scroll can be opened and its contents divulged, the seals around the scroll must be broken off, one at a time. The earth must be ripened for this judgment. The breaking of the seals begins the process.

The First Seal is Broken and the Anti-Christ Rides Forth (Rev. 6:1–2)

All of heaven watched in dramatic suspense as Jesus broke the first of the seven seals around the scroll. Suddenly one of four living creatures cried out, "Come." At this point, a rider on a white horse was allowed to come forth. Jesus also will ride on a white horse at his return (Rev. 19:11–19), but here Jesus is standing and holding the scroll. Who then is this rider? He seems to imitate Christ, but he cannot be Christ for Jesus is standing right there breaking the seals. He comes early and pre-empts the return of Christ. He is an impostor.[38] He is a fake. He is none other than the one John referred to as the anti-Christ (1John 2:18). In Revelation this same man, the anti-Christ is called the Beast. He will demand that all worship him (Rev. 13:8).

At this point of the drama, we probably won't yet be able to identify this individual as the actual anti-Christ. Not until he sets himself up in the "temple of God, displaying himself as being God"

(2Thess. 2:4) will any doubts as to his identity be dispelled. At this time, what is he doing as he starts to ride forth?

A Bow in the Hand

The first thing we notice about him is "a bow" in his hand (Rev. 6:2). This man is given to fighting and violence. His ultimate intention will be conquering. His cause will be a violent one, not at all unlike fundamentalist Islam's agenda. The Koran plainly states, "Make war on the unbelievers and hypocrites (false Muslims) and deal rigorously with them" (Surah 9:73). In all, at least sixty-nine general and detailed exhortations to violence are given to Muslims in the Koran. Unlike other religions, the faithful Muslim is called upon to engage in an ongoing fight for the conversion and domination of the entire world under Islam. Violence is not only acceptable in this war; *it is mandatory*. The Koran bluntly states, "Fighting is obligatory for you . . ." (Surah 2:216).

What is the goal of Islam? The Koran states that "It is He (Allah) who has sent His apostle with guidance and the Faith of Truth, so that He may exalt Islam above all religions . . ." (Surah 61:9). Through war, plundering, destroying and stealing of non-Muslims goods and their very lives, Allah intends to establish his religion as supreme in the world.

The Allah of Islam is like a thief attempting to steal the inheritance of the Son, the Lord Jesus Christ, and the only rightful heir to planet earth. As the seals are removed from the scroll in preparation of judgment, tremendous pressure will be placed upon the world to make a definitive choice between Jesus Christ and the anti-Christ. Nominal "Christians" will not be able to withstand the heat. They will get sorted out of the Church quite thoroughly. The world will be without excuse and ripened for judgment since the message of the Gospel will have already filled the earth (Matt. 24:14).

Many liberal Muslims say *jihad* (holy war) doesn't mean violence. However, in Muhammad's day there was absolutely no question it involved violence. The Koranic texts are numerous and descriptive. The witness of history erases all doubt about *jihad's* literal nature. The only Muslims Muhammad exempted from *jihad* are women, men caring for elderly parents and physically disabled Muslims. Liberal Muslims have tried to classify *jihad* as only a spiritual struggle of oneself with sin. But this exemption for physically disabled Muslims makes it clear that *jihad* is a physical and not just spiritual struggle. Ultimately, *jihad* is warfare on all fronts, cultural, political, economic and most especially, militarily. The Islamic fundamentalists wholeheartedly agree with this assessment, regardless of what liberal Muslims may say. The fact is the fundamentalists are right.

Just like a faithful fundamentalist Muslim, this rider on the white horse will start off as a warrior, but he will quickly distinguish himself and be set apart. The Scriptures state "a crown was given to him" (Rev. 6:2). Crowns are given to kings. The fact a crown is "given to him" probably indicates he has assistants help him secure leadership in a government. The fact he carries a bow may indicate he comes to power in response to a popular and violent uprising. Probably, he himself will help to inspire it.

Two-part Strategy of the Beast (Rev. 6:2b)

What will he do with this newfound power? The Scriptures say he will go forth "conquering and to conquer" (Rev. 6:2b). It is interesting that John doesn't merely state he will be conquering, but that he will go forth "conquering *and* to conquer." The Holy Spirit never wastes words. This may indicate a two-part strategy. First, he'll seize a particular region of the world. Then he will follow this with a total conquest of the remainder of the world.

Does radical Islam also have a two-part strategy? How does this potentially fit with Islam's struggle? Muslims are instructed not only to fight against all non-Muslims not subjugated to Islam; they are also given permission to slay Muslims who will not join them in the fight. It is no secret the leaders of fundamentalist Islam fully intend to unite the Islamic world under a revived fundamentalist Islamic regime. Using violence to become a leader of the Islamic kingdom is not only acceptable in Islam; it has been an accepted practice from its inception. Fundamentalists use violence against moderate Muslims who are "hypocritically" cooperating with the infidel West.

"The assorted purveyors of *jihad* are training more of their deadly energies on the Middle Eastern regimes that are cooperating with the US-led war on terrorism. Last week (in early May, 2004) Jordanian television aired what it said were confessions by suspects in a foiled operation to use improvised chemical bombs against three targets in the heart of Amman: an intelligence service headquarters, the prime minister's office, and the US Embassy. Authorities contend that up to 80,000 people might have perished if the attack had taken place, and they assigned the blame to the Jordanian-born terrorist Abu Mussab al-Zarqawi, a key al-Qaeda associate who is being hunted by US forces in Iraq."[63]

By the spring of 2004, resistance erupted full force in Najaf from radical cleric Muqtada Al-Sadr and his Mahdi Brigade when the United States decided that it wanted to arrest Al-Sadr for the murder of a pro-Western cleric in 2003.

As this book goes to press there was a release of pictures of American soldiers sexually and physically abusing Iraqi prisoners. Such disasters only cement the anger toward America and its allies. It seems to be growing by the day, pushing more and more Muslims toward sympathy for the radicals. Even if the US succeeds in establishing some semblance of stability in Iraq, anti-American and anti-Western anger in the Arab world runs deep. Radicals will not be satisfied with merely taking over the Muslim world; the West will continue to be a target for attack and eventual takeover as well. Could it be that the rider on the white horse will exploit these restless forces?

The Heavenly and Earthly Horses

To better understand what John saw, let's turn to a vision given to the prophet Zechariah:

> Now I lifted up my eyes again and looked, and behold, four chariots were coming forth from between the two mountains; and the mountains were bronze mountains. With the first chariot were red horses, with the second chariot black horses, with the third chariot white horses, and with the fourth chariot strong dappled horses.
>
> Then I spoke and said to the angel who was speaking with me, 'What are these, my lord?' And the angel answered me and said, 'These are the four spirits of heaven, going forth after standing before the Lord of all the earth, with one of which the black horses are going

forth to the north country; and the white ones go forth after them, while the dappled ones go forth to the south country. When the strong ones went out, they were eager to go to patrol the earth.

Then He cried out to me and spoke to me saying, 'See, those who are going to the land of the north have appeased My wrath in the land of the north.' (Zech. 6:1–8)

John sees three additional horses come forth after the first white horse (Rev. 6:3–8). But what did Zechariah see? It certainly seems that Zechariah's horses (Zech. 6:1–8) must somehow be connected to John's horses. But in Zechariah they appear in a different order than in Revelation. Why are the horses in Zechariah in a different order than those in Revelation? And why are the horses in Zechariah plural while in Revelation they are singular?

In short, Zechariah was looking down on earth (Zech. 6:1,5b). In contrast, John was looking at what was going on up in heaven (Rev. 4:1, 6:1). Zechariah speaks of them as "going forth *after* standing (up in heaven—parenthesis mine) before the Lord of all the *earth*" (Zech. 6:5b). Thus, from Zechariah we see that the order these horses appear on earth is different from their order of release in heaven.

Zechariah's four chariots pulled by the horses of various colors probably indicate earthly actors being pulled along by the spirits John saw get released in heaven. These actors will carry out their earthly assignment that was allowed to be unleashed in the heavens. Looking at these two visions together clarifies what they both describe.

There is not necessarily anything good about these spirits. Job tells us that Satan himself was able to have an audience with God (see Job 1:6–7, 2:2–3). However, neither they nor Satan can interfere with God's ultimate plans. Indeed, these spirits are only allowed to go when Jesus breaks the seal. In the heavens, in Revelation, each horse represents a spirit with a particular agenda. Thus, the horse in Revelation is singular. However, on earth that spirit operates in and through a number of key individuals. Thus, Zechariah sees a plural number of horses.

The white horse was the first horse released in Revelation. However, the chariot driver with the group of white horses doesn't show up on earth until two other groups of horses have already appeared.

The white horses are the third group to appear on earth. Why in this particular order? It probably means that the earthly identification of the white horse and its rider will not come until *after* the two other horses and their earthly effects have first been manifested on the earth. To help keep track of what each of the horses bring, turn to the last page in this chapter for the summary chart.

The First Horses to be Seen: Red Going Worldwide (Rev. 6:3–4)

The first chariot and horses that appear on the earth spring from the red horse. This horse is released when the second seal is broken. The Scriptures inform us that the rider who sat on the red horse was granted power to "take peace from the earth, and that men would slay one another; and a great sword was given to him" (Rev. 6:4). With his release, the earth experiences tranquility and peace slipping from its grasp. This horse brings all-out warfare.

When these red horses go forth, Zechariah is not told of any particular direction they are heading in. Why? Why don't they go in a particular way? Because this will not be just another world war. Unlike the Second World War, that left some portions of the earth virtually untouched, this conflict will be completely global in its reach. There will not be any sane, conscious people, unaware of the mortal conflict enveloping the earth. The Beast will have a cause and a plan to conquer the entire planet. It's a cause that will capture hearts and imaginations of many millions of people. Many of them will gladly give their lives and wealth in pursuit of his goals.

Is there such a cause that can galvanize such radical devotion? The most credible answer to that question is found in the elements of a cause that has been brewing on the planet a long time already. The Beast will electrify and unify these elements behind his cause. Could it be that Islamic fundamentalism is such a cause?

A fanatical, pervasive, all-out world war fits the nature of fundamental Islam. The call of the Koran is for Muslims to fight for the cause of Allah. They must fight until the religion of Islam reigns supreme over all. Warfare on the infidel is a demand of the Koran. In order to unite the whole world under Islam, war will have to be fought all over the world, including Muslim nations. The battle for the minds and hearts of Muslims is already underway. As one Saudi Arabian stated, "We are being carried in two directions at once . . ."[66] They are the opposing directions of modernism and fundamentalism.

Already many fundamentalists are making plans, laying the groundwork and taking action to separate Islam from modernism and the Western world. In the minds of many fundamentalists, this is even a war of defense, for it is only by defeating the West that they will save true Islam. The terrorist attacks we have seen thus far are just a pinprick on the surface of what they intend to do. The Islamic terrorists themselves have said as much.

On the eve of the second anniversary of 9/11, the Arab television network, Al-Jazeera released a video of Osama bin-Laden and his chief deputy Ayman al-Zawahri. Both men praised the 9/11 attackers calling them true believers who should be a model for all believers. Then Al-Zawahri ominously stated, "What you saw until now are only the first skirmishes. The true epic has not begun."[67] Arab journalist Fareed Zakaria summarizes the targets, "Radical Islam . . . has waged a civil war within Islam . . . but it has also taken the battle to the masters of modernity, the West, and in particular the United States."[68]

The Second Group of Horses: Black and Going North (Rev. 6:5–6)

The second chariot and horses that show up on earth are the black horses. These originate from the black horse released when the third seal is broken. John is shown that this black horse indicates a time of massive economic breakdown, undoubtedly a result of the outbreak of worldwide conflict. A voice in the center of the four living creatures declares a day's worth of food will become as expensive as an average day's wages. (Rev. 6:6). Some food items that were normally seen as everyday fare, as basic as oil and wine, will become very precious commodities. In Zechariah we learn "the black horses are going forth to the *north* country" (Zech. 6:6a).

Why are these horses seen as going forth to the north? Why don't they go in another direction? Why north? Today economists frequently talk about huge economic disparities in the world. They speak of unequal distribution of wealth between the northern and southern parts of the world. In general, the north is where most of the world's wealth is concentrated, and the south is an area of persistent poverty. Kofi Annan, the Secretary General of the United Nations also used this same phraseology when he said, "Weapons of mass destruction do not only threaten the Western or northern world."[69] Apparently, as this seal is broken, this economic disparity between the two areas will rapidly decrease due to growing poverty in the north.

The plan and cause of the Beast will lead to tremendous economic hardship for the wealthy nations of the world. The cause he represents will be glad to see such forces in operation. He will have a deep-seated hatred of what these wealthy nations stand for. Is there any cause on earth today that currently hates the wealthy north? Again, the elements of this cause have been in the pot a long time. The stew of hatred has been brewing for centuries and is merely awaiting the right leadership and inspiration to help it erupt in full force. Could it be these forces are found within Islam? It will take supernatural power to galvanize these restless forces, and the devil will be more than happy to provide it. He will do so once the restraining hand of God finally allows him (2Thess. 2:7).[70]

Both Colossians 3:5–6 and Ephesians 5:5–6 clearly indicate that one of the key reasons God will bring judgment upon the world is because of the idolatry of greed as well as immorality. God is angry at this gigantic idol of materialism and greed suffocating the spiritual life out of wealthy nations and the world. The day of his wrath shall come. The One speaking with Zechariah openly states, "See, those (the black horses and chariot) who are going forth to the land of the north have appeased My wrath in the land of the north" (Zech. 6:8).

Does Islam have the means to inflict serious economic damage on wealthy nations? What about our dependence on oil? As much as we talk about alternative fuels and drilling in Alaska, the fact is the United States and many wealthy nations of the world are extremely reliant upon crude oil under the control of Islamic nations. Many of the remaining reserves are also found there. Saudi Arabia's reserves

are largest in the world. Alone they are about 25% of all known
reserves.[71]

> With nearly two-thirds of proven conventional reserves, Middle
> Eastern lands will be the supply of last resort as oil production
> declines elsewhere . . . The US government's Energy Information
> Administration projects that in 20 years, the Persian Gulf will
> supply between one-half and two-thirds of the oil on the world
> market—the same percentage as before the 1973 embargo . . . In
> other words, the Middle East will have regained all its old power
> over oil [72]

But that's not all. If we include all Islamic nations, 76% of all
oil reserves are in the control of Islamic nations and another 8% are
in control of lands with large Muslim populations.[73] Many of us are
old enough to remember the huge spike in gas prices that hit the
US during the 1973 Arab-Israeli war. And this embargo only lasted
a few months. The Iranian revolution of 1979 also caused a spike
in prices as have other Middle East crisis. What if the Islamic world
was to become united under a fundamentalist regime? What would
happen?

The West and the United States would have the economic breath
knocked out of them if there was a complete embargo of oil from
Muslim nations. And the terrorists know it. A recent terrorist attack
in Saudi Arabia left twenty-two foreign oil workers in Saudi Arabia
dead. A Saudi spokesman explained that "the intent (of the attack)
was to cripple the world economy . . . ."[74] It clearly had an effect.
The first business day after the attacks, oil prices rose about $2.50
per barrel in one day. Such facts are sure to encourage the attackers,
three out of four whom escaped.[75]

We're not just talking about more expensive gas. "In the US about
two-thirds of the oil goes to make fuel for cars, trucks and planes. But
the synthetic fabrics in our wardrobe and the plastics in just about
everything we touch started out as oil too. We can also thank oil and
its cousin, natural gas, for the cheap and plentiful food grown at the
supermarket, grown with the help of hydrocarbon-based fertilizers
and pesticides."[76]

Not only would economic blackmail be a possibility, it is an obligation of holy war. As the Koran clearly says "The true believers are those . . . who fight with their *wealth* and their persons for the cause of God. Such are those whose faith is true" (Surah 49:15). The stage is ready to be set.

As Michael Youssef put it in his book *America, Oil and the Islamic Mind,*

> Some continue to think America should not strive for energy independence. The cost would be too high, they say, and it would result in social disruption since it would reduce energy consumption substantially. Their approach to the problem is for Americans to do what they do best and let the Arabs do what they do best. The United States is more efficient at producing wheat and computers, they reason, and thus it would retain a bargaining leverage with OPEC.
>
> That view, however, is too simplistic. It assumes a world in which everything is measured in dollars and mathematical formulas. If that were reality, such a plan would make sense. But again, it illustrates Western naiveté about the religious dimension. Muslim states are made up of people who believe that to die in opposing the infidel is to earn oneself instant paradise.[17]

If more than half of our oil supply (Muslim oil) was suddenly turned off like a water faucet and remained off indefinitely, the economic earthquake would be unquestionably staggering. Its impact will prepare the ground for the next horses to come.

The Third Set of Horses: White and Going... (Rev. 6:1–2)

The next horses seen on the earth are white horses. By the time they're seen, the rider on the white horse is probably ruling his own country and conquering most, if not all, of the nations in his region. He is probably now poised to conquer the entire world. Again, Revelation says he will go forth "conquering and to conquer," likely indicating a two-step plan. He has probably already finished step one of conquering his region because these horses in Zechariah are already moving in another direction.

Which direction are they seen moving in? Zechariah states, "The black horses are going forth to the north, and *the white ones go forth after them . . .*" (Zech. 6:6a). As long as he is concentrating on conquering his own region, the plan of completely conquering the earth may still be unknown to some. If his own region is in the middle of the world, the Middle East, then it makes sense for him to be moving north once his power is consolidated there. Where is most of Islam located? Clearly its heart is in the Middle East. Most of the wealthiest nations on earth lie north of there.

By the time the rider on the white horse is poised to conquer the entire world; the whole world will become aware of his existence. His diabolical plan will come into sharper focus as he leaves his own region and goes forth conquering the wealthy lands of the north. Would Islam be interested in eventually conquering and taking over the wealthy north?

Without question, the goal is not only the wealthy north, but also the entire world. Islam knows its chief enemy and restraint from world dominion is the rich north. Thus, it shall become a major target. The economic poverty, that will begin to overtake the once-wealthy north, will greatly weaken its ability to resist. There will also be incredible fear of the Beast. That fear will probably become paralyzing with the destruction of Babylon. But we're getting ahead of ourselves.

The Fourth Set of Horses: Dappled and Ashen (Rev. 6:7–8)

The last horses to show up on earth are the "dappled" and "ashen" horses. These go forth after the fourth seal in heaven has been broken, releasing the ashen horse. The one who sits on this ashen horse has the name of Death. Hades is following close behind him. The Greek word translated here as ashen is *chloros*. It literally means pale and can even mean pale green. In either case, its color seems to indicate the death it brings.

The Bible states "authority was given to *them* over a fourth of the earth to kill with sword and with famine and with pestilence and by the wild beasts of the earth" (Rev. 6:8). The first three horses have basically one task to accomplish through essentially one strategy.

However, this fourth one will bring death to the earth in a variety of ways. He will unleash violent anarchy, a variety of sicknesses and also attack by wild animals. It is probably for this reason Zechariah sees this pale, ashen horse as being a mottled and spotted one, indicating the multifaceted strategy it will follow to spread death and destruction.

Zechariah indicates these horses will go forth to the south country (Zech. 6:6b). Why the south? Two other sets of horses were going north and one was going everywhere. Why will this last group of horses go south?

The south represents the poorer nations of the world. These tend to be largely concentrated in the southern half of the planet. It includes parts of Latin America, Africa and Asia. Currently the wealthy north gives many billions of dollars in trade, aid money for medicine and direct shipments of medical supplies and food. This helps alleviate effects of famine and disease.

With economic collapse in the north, the aid helping to contain all-out disasters will dry up and come to an end. The stabilizing effects of this aid, as well as the political pressures of the wealthier north that help settle and contain conflicts will disappear. The result will be chaos growing and spiraling out of control. Disease and famine will begin to run unchecked in these poverty-stricken nations. There will be no one in a position to bring assistance. Desperate refugees will flee villages, towns and cities, wandering aimlessly in the wilderness. They will become prime targets for all sorts of wild animals. As we have read, scripture indicates one quarter of the world's population will die as a result of these problems.

There is no reason to believe these forces released with the broken seals won't continue to operate during the trumpet judgments until Christ returns. To review what the Bible seems to show us so far, look at the table on the next page.

But before we discuss the events of the next seals, we must ask ourselves some important questions. What must precede the coming of the four horsemen of Revelation? Is there anything that must happen before these seals can be broken and the Lord Jesus begins to pour out the judgment that will precede his return? What will be the trigger?

The Four Horsemen of Revelation

Horse Released in Heaven in this order:	Horses Seen on Earth in this order:	Actions Taken by the Horses manifest on earth in this order:
White Horse (Re 6:1-2)	**Red Horses going everywhere** (Ze 6:2a,5,7)	• Warfare throughout the earth
Red Horse (Re 6:3-4)	**Black Horses going north** (Ze 6:2b, 5-6)	• Extreme Economic Hardship spreading to wealthy nations of the earth
Black Horse (Re 6:5-6)	**White Horses going north** (Ze 6:3a,5-6)	• Going forth to conquer the once wealthy countries of the north
Ashen Horse (Re 6:7-8)	**Dappled - Ashen Horses going South** (Ze 6:3b,5-6)	• Going forth to spread death to the poorer south through: • The sword • Famine • Pestilence • Wild beasts

Chapter 3

. . . .

The Great Completion and the Transition to Christ's Return (Rev. 4:1–5:14)

I am originally from Dogukent, but I moved to Istanbul eight years ago, Mehmet began as he started to share his story. He was a rather tall man for a Turk. Other than that, his dark black hair with traces of gray, and deep brown eyes were typical for a Turkish man in his early 40's. His eyes seemed to drift into a distant gaze as he thought back to what was once a very different world.

"While in Dogukent I had no economic problems and was actually wealthy by the standards of the region. I was a very religious Muslim, regularly reading the Koran and praying the ritual prayers. I fasted religiously during the month of Ramadan and was strongly connected to a fundamentalist Islamic sect. I had become quite knowledgeable of Islamic theology."

Returning his gaze to his listeners, he continued, "Then I encountered extreme financial hardships and moved to our country's largest city with my family. My brother-in-law worked at a publishing house that joined a book fair. While there, he received an invitation for the *Jesus* film at the stand of a Christian Publishing House. He himself didn't go to the film but gave it to my wife. She gave it to me thinking that I liked films like this." A smile now pursed his lips.

"It attracted me even more when I learned the film was being shown in a church, so I decided to go. Jesus held an important place in Islam, but the Jesus portrayed in the film was a totally different Jesus than the Jesus I had read about in the Koran or in my studies."

"After the film I was invited to the Sunday worship meeting. My interest increased, and I began attending the Sunday meeting regularly even though I was still a Muslim." His voice now choked with emotion, and his lower lip quivered as he said, "When I joined the meetings I felt my heart beginning to burn because of the honesty, sincerity and beauty on the faces of these people."

"I began attending the church's house group meetings, and there God spoke to my heart, 'Don't try to solve all the apparent contradictions, you yourself are the contradiction. Now is the time for you to repent.' In the middle of the house group I repented of my sins and accepted Jesus weeping together with my new brothers and sisters in Christ." Once again tears welled up in his eyes as he remembered his life-changing encounter with Christ.

"I had been going regularly to a psychiatrist and had many psychological problems, but from that moment God began to heal me of all of my problems in this area. I was healed by the true Doctor of doctors that in turn solved many of the relationship problems with my family and friends. But when I told my wife that I had become a Christian she reacted in a violent manner. But in time she saw the huge change in my life and I eventually asked her, 'Do you want the old Mehmet or would you prefer the new one?" Mehmet smiled again and said, "Without pausing she said she wanted the new one. Today I praise the Lord with all my heart."[78]

Something wonderful is happening in the Muslim world. True stories like this are increasing in frequency, but not just in the Muslim world. The message of the Gospel is increasingly breaking into the lives of people from every religious, philosophical, linguistic, ethnic, and economic background. This is not a Western message, and you won't hear about it on CNN. But the Bible believing Church is growing throughout the earth and it's happening at a rate unprecedented in the history of the world. Even the once unthinkable prospect of fundamentalist Muslims converting to faith in Christ is becoming increasingly common. Could this exponential spread of the Gospel in the earth be related to the Second Coming of Christ? Is the advance of the Great Commission referred to in the pages of Revelation?

Let's backtrack for a minute to what happened just before Jesus took the scroll. After the messages to the churches recorded in chapters two and three of Revelation, the apostle John was suddenly transported into the future. He saw "*after these things* (the messages to the seven churches) a door standing open in heaven" (Rev. 4:1). He was beckoned to come up there. Why? Because John was told he would be shown "*what must take place after these things*" (Rev. 4:1).

Thus, most of the remainder of Revelation is a message of events that largely occur *after* the events, and prophetic words of the first three chapters. John is fast-forwarded to events near the end of the age. It will no longer be business as usual in God's dealings with the Church and the world. Something new and even more intense is about to happen.

The Court Sits for Judgment (Rev. 4:2–5:5)

What does John see? Heaven is stirring with excitement for what is about to come. First John sees God on the throne (Rev. 4:2–3). Twenty-four thrones are set up around the throne for 24 elders (Rev. 4:4). Daniel saw the same scene when he declared that "I kept looking until thrones were set up, And the Ancient of Days took His seat; His vesture was like white snow and the hair of His head like pure wool . . . Thousands upon thousands were attending Him, and myriads upon myriads were standing before Him; The court sat . . ." (Dan. 7:9:10).

A little later the angel explains to Daniel why the court sat. He stated, ". . . the court will sit for judgment . . ." (Dan. 7:26a). God is moving as lightning and sounds of thunder go forth from the throne (Rev. 4:5). The four living creatures around the throne continue in their endless worship (Rev. 4:9–10). The twenty-four elders "fall down before Him who sits on the throne" (Rev. 4:10) in a magnificent scene of heavenly worship.

Next John notices the scroll in the right hand of him who sits on the throne (Rev. 5:1).[79] Suddenly, tragedy appears to strike. God's program seems threatened with defeat. There is no one found worthy to open the scroll (Rev. 5:2–4). Events cannot move on. A thorough search is made, but no one is found. How can judgment proceed?

John begins to cry. Then, one of the elders tells John not to weep (Rev. 5:4). He comforts John that "the Lion that is from the tribe of Judah, the Root of David, has overcome so as to open the book (scroll) and its seven seals" (Rev. 5:5). That Lion was none other than Jesus Christ.

But why the delay? Why didn't Jesus immediately step forward since surely he was worthy all along? Why couldn't Jesus just step up and get the whole ball rolling sooner? Certainly the thorough search proved no one else was worthy. But there may have been another reason for the wait.

The Great Completion: Central to Understanding the Second Coming

What was essential and central to the early Churches' mission and purpose? It is that mission which holds the key to what the delay was all about. What was the Church delegated to do when Jesus ascended to heaven? When writing his final epistle to the Church, aware that he would soon be dead (2Pet. 1:14), Peter made a decision to remind the Church of something of great importance (2Pet. 3:1). They already knew this particular truth, but it was so critically important to Peter, he had to remind the Church one more time before leaving earth.

Peter exhorts, "that you should remember the words spoken beforehand by the holy prophets and the commandments of the Lord and Savior spoken by your apostles" (2Pet. 3:2). What prophetic words and commandments did he mention? Certainly all are important. But what required a reminder?

First, he warned them that ungodly people following their own lusts would mark the last days. Furthermore, he spoke of mockers making fun of the Second Coming of Christ claiming all things have been going on pretty much the same for as long as anyone has known. Peter chastises the mockers for deliberately choosing to ignore the fact the world had a beginning. And God had everything to do with that beginning. He goes on to say they reject the overwhelming evidence for a massive worldwide flood.⁸⁰ That's not exactly an ordinary event either. Contrary to what has become popular opinion, things haven't always gone on the same. Furthermore, he reminded them a "day with the Lord is like a thousand years and a thousand years like one day" (2Pet. 3:8b). In other words, the delay hadn't really been long at all, as far as God is concerned.

Then, Peter told us the primary reason why Jesus hadn't returned yet. And what was that? Why hasn't Jesus come back? He stated, "the Lord is not slow about His promise, as some count slowness, but is patient toward *you*, not wishing for any to perish, but for all to come to repentance" (2Pet. 3:9).

For years when I read that scripture, I always thought it described God's patience with the unsaved. "How nice of God to delay his coming so they won't perish," I thought. Then one day, I finally noticed Peter used an interesting object pronoun. He didn't say God is patient toward *them*. He said God is "patient toward *you*" not wanting sinners to perish. I asked myself, "Who are the *you* God is patient toward? Peter wasn't writing to unsaved sinners. He was writing to "those who . . . received a faith of the same kind as ours . . ." (2Pet. 1:1b–2a). Suddenly, I knew why Jesus hasn't returned yet. He is patiently waiting for *us* to get the gospel message out to all nations. The real hold-up is not Jesus, nor the sinners of the world; it's the Church dragging its feet in completing the Great Commission!

Sent Out into All the Earth (Rev. 5:6–10)

The same verses that give us the term *Great Commission* also place a link between the Great Commission and the end of the age. Jesus said, "All authority has been given to Me in heaven and on earth. Go therefore and make disciples of all the nations, baptizing them in the name of the Father and the Son and the Holy Spirit, teaching them to observe all that I commanded you and lo, I am with you always, *even to the end of the age*" (Matt. 28:18b–20).

Jesus said he would be with the Church always. In Acts 1:8, he proclaimed we would "receive power when the Holy Spirit has come upon you; and *you shall be My witnesses* both in Jerusalem, and in all Judea and Samaria, and *even to the remotest part of the earth.*" The power to witness comes from the Holy Spirit.

Returning to Revelation we notice John eventually saw between the throne and elders, a Lamb standing as if slain, about ready to take the scroll. But he also saw something else. This Lamb "standing as if slain" had "seven horns and seven eyes, which are the seven Spirits of God, *sent out into all the earth*" (Rev. 5:6). Here John sees the key behind the delay. Horns represent power. The horns, together with the eyes, are identified as the seven Spirits of God.

The seven Spirits of God are quite likely the presence of the Holy Spirit, the power to witness, residing in the Church. John saw that the seven Spirits of God had seven horns denoting that power to witness. The seven Spirits also had seven eyes. These help God's people see people of the world more as he does. As Paul stated, ". . . from now on we recognize no one according to the flesh . . ." (2Cor. 5:16a).

Notice that here, for the first time, it is mentioned these "seven Spirits of God" were "sent out into all the earth." Rejoice! John saw the seven Spirits of God finally go forth into all the earth. We're going to get it right. John saw into the future "what must take place *after* these things." The Church finally finishes going out into all the earth. John sees heaven reacting to the joyous conclusion of the Great Commission. The delay is finally over.

This is confirmed yet again by what happens next. When the Lamb finally does step forward and take the scroll, all of heaven breaks out into singing a *new* song. Notice this song is a *new* one for heaven. What is it that is sung in this new song?

"Worthy are You to take the book (scroll) and to break its seals; for You were slain, and *purchased for God with Your blood men from every tribe and tongue and people and nation*. You have made them to be a kingdom and priests to our God; and they will reign upon the earth" (Rev. 5:9–10). Before this time, they weren't able to sing that he had purchased men from *every* tribe and tongue and people and nation. Only now did the Great Commission finally become the Great Completion!

All heaven breaks out again in worship. Dominion belongs to the Lamb forever. Indeed, heaven knows it won't be long now. King Jesus is about ready to return to earth. He will complete the establishment of his rule over nations. When answering questions about the timing of his return, Jesus plainly stated to his disciples, "This gospel of the kingdom shall be preached in the *whole world* as a testimony to *all* the nations, and *then* the end will come" (Matt. 24:14).

The Gospel of the Kingdom Preached in All the World

Who will do the preaching? The Church will do the preaching, for Jesus summarized the prophets, saying, "Thus it is written, that the Christ should suffer and rise again from the dead the third day; and that repentance for forgiveness of sins should be *proclaimed in His name to all the nations*, beginning from Jerusalem. *You* are witnesses of these things. And behold, I am sending forth the promise of My Father upon *you*; but *you* are to stay in the city until *you* are clothed with power from on high" (Luke 24:46–49).

Paul confirms the necessity for the Church to preach the Gospel to the whole world when he stated, "How then shall they call upon Him in whom they have not believed? And how shall they believe in Him whom they have not heard? And how shall they hear without a preacher? And how shall they preach unless they are sent?" (Rom. 10:14–15a). Fortunately, we have the words of Jesus as assurance, it will happen just as the prophets said. Ultimately, the Church will not fail. Still, it is only *after* the Gospel of the kingdom is preached to *all* the nations that the end will come and not a minute before. Understanding this truth clarifies for us the timing of the future events of Revelation. They begin right after the Church completes the Great Commission.

Peter was reminding the Church of both the prophetic word and a command. What a privilege and how exciting to realize we, the Church of Jesus Christ, have a role to play in the return of our Bridegroom and fulfillment of Bible prophecy! Is there anything more fulfilling than living for that day?

Of course, only God knows the exact day, but we can have fun moving things along. What a joy to serve God! Peter urges us to be "looking for and hastening the coming of the day of God . . ." (2Pet. 3:12a). The early Church understood this. Remember this was only a reminder from Peter. No wonder the Gospel spread so rapidly in the first three centuries. For some of us, this may be the first time we heard of such a thing. Yet, to them it was just a reminder. The time has come for the completion of the Great Commission to be restored to its central place in the Church's agenda as it was for the early Church.

As one Chinese Church leader stated, "Christians in Africa, Europe, South America and Asia all have the same command from Jesus regardless of their social, political, racial or economic circumstances. They are to take the good news to the ends of the earth. All Christians who read God's commands will one day be responsible for what they did about it."[81]

God's Great Completion Agenda

The Apostle Paul's aspirations followed this agenda. Paul focused his efforts on taking the Gospel to those still unreached with the Gospel. He knew the Bible prophesied that the unreached would hear the Gospel. Thus, by working in step with Old Testament prophecies, he confidently knew he was in line with what was on God's heart.[82] He claimed his strategy involved fulfilling the prophecy in Isaiah 52:15 concerning the unreached so "they who had no news of him shall see. And they who have not heard shall understand" (Rom. 15:21). Since we are also told to follow Paul's example (1Cor. 11:1), we would do well to follow him and focus our foreign mission efforts on those least reached with the Gospel.

How incredibly exciting to think God has decided we all get to play a role in this Great Commission work! Are you looking for a deeper sense of purpose and direction in your Christian life? We already have a clear command, "Go therefore and make disciples of *all* the nations . . ." (Matt. 28:19a).

If the key in Revelation to the timing of Jesus taking the scroll is the completion of the Great Commission, then we have a very exciting question. Just how close are we to that Great Completion? And what remains to be done?

Chapter 4

Tracking the Great Completion (Rev. 5:6, 9–10)

I n our individualistic society it is easy to understand that God has a plan for our lives. Our evangelistic messages often center on this fact. However, we can easily overlook the fact that God has a plan for the entire world as well. In Genesis 2, God created man and woman, blessed them and delegated to them dominion over the whole world.

God's Unfolding Plan

Unfortunately, we know they hit a bump in the road on their way to dominion. That nasty adversary of God, Satan, came to fight. Following Adam and Eve's disobedience, the situation quickly deteriorated. Finally, the only righteous man left was Noah and his family. God had to give the world a bath and start over again. Once again, only a generation or two after the flood, mankind was rebelling. They were interfering with God's intention for them to fill the earth and subdue it. Humanism and idolatry reared their ugly head at the tower of Babel. God, in his wisdom, dispersed people into tribes and languages and nations. Ever since then, God has dealt with people not only as individuals, but also as nations.

It's tempting to get depressed at the rebellion against God in the world. But God apparently doesn't share our pessimism. God's redemptive hand was revealed not long after the judgment on the tower of Babel. Way back in Genesis 12, we see God speaking with Abraham. He first made mention of the Great Commission when he spoke to Abraham saying, ". . . in you *all the families of the earth* will be blessed" (Gen 12:3b). Paul explained God was actually preaching the Gospel here in advance (Gal 3:8).

Paul translated the Hebrew word used for *families* into the Greek word used for *nations*. The word *families* in Hebrew literally means clan or tribe, not a nation state. The point is clear, every tribe and tongue and nation shall be blessed with the Gospel and believers in Jesus. And God started talking about it to his friend Abraham long, long ago. God conveys an intimate concern for all nations, tribes, and families of the earth from their start. In fact, in the Old Testament alone, the nations are mentioned 299 times. Again and again, God makes clear a desire to reveal himself to all nations. It should not be surprising then to see the fulfillment of the Great Commission in the middle of a book describing God's revelation of himself to the whole world.

God is on the Move Today

The scope of this book doesn't permit us to go back over the many ways God has worked throughout history to spread his kingdom. To learn more about this, read the article "The Kingdom Strikes Back: Ten Epochs of Redemptive History" found in the book *Perspectives on the World Christian Movement.*[83] Instead of an overview, let's look at a few incidents in recent years that illustrate God at work in the nations winning a people for himself.

In the early 1980s, I can still remember Leonid Breshnev, then president of the Soviet Union, reportedly saying that by the year 2000, the "rotting corpse of Christianity" would cease to exist in the Soviet Union. However, on Christmas Day, 1991, Leonid Breshnev's corpse had long been rotting when the rotting corpse of Communism itself collapsed. The Soviet Union simply ceased to exist. It officially collapsed exactly on December 25, Christmas day. Does God have a sense of humor or what?

Communism came, in part, probably as judgment upon a spiritually "dead" church. Communism purified most of what was left of the Church and largely destroyed the influence of a spiritually "dead" church upon the people. Then God destroyed Communism. Its implosion left a huge spiritual vacuum in the hearts of the people. The people of the Soviet Union were wide-open to the Gospel. Millions of Russians have since been won to a saving faith in Christ.

New countries of largely nominally Muslim people groups completely, or almost completely, unreached with the Gospel were established. Countries such as Uzbekistan, Azerbaijan, Turkmenistan, Kazakhstan, Kyrgyzstan, and Tajikistan were opened up for the Gospel. Many Christians became aware of their existence for the first time. Some Christians entered places nearly impossible to enter under the Soviet Union. The result has been the beginnings of the Church among these peoples. God brought judgment upon Communism and, in the midst of judgment, working together with his people, advanced his kingdom in these nations. [84]

With the end of Communism came the breakup of the Republic of Yugoslavia. As war has engulfed one minority group after another, completely unreached people groups reached the news and hearts of Christians around the world. First in Bosnia, and then in Kosovo, Christians have come with practical help and the gospel of Jesus Christ. The result has been the establishment of a Bosnian church from essentially nothing to over 600 believers[85], as well as a church among Kosovar Albanians.

Of course, Communism has also collapsed in dozens of other nations. In every case, there have been tremendous advancements for the kingdom of God. In Albania, once the most outspoken atheistic government on earth, the Church is rapidly advancing. When Communism collapsed in 1990, the country was thrown into economic depression and near anarchy. Forbidden to believe in God, Albanians had essentially ceased to practice or even know Islam, Eastern Orthodoxy, or Catholicism.

As in all of Eastern Europe, the stranglehold of lifeless religion had been keeping the people in its grip. God raised up communist authorities to smash this stronghold. Then God smashed Communism. As in other communist nations, the people were left struggling for survival and a reason to exist. Into this vacuum came ministers of the Gospel. The result is that today, according to Albanian believers I recently talked with, there is hardly a village in Albania without a gospel preaching church. This is amazing when one realizes that barely more than ten years ago there were almost no known believers in Jesus in Albania.

Before Communism came to Mongolia, the Mongolian people were smothered under the stifling lie of Buddhism. Then Communism came, bringing judgment upon Buddhism and greatly weakening its control over the people. Once again, God crushed Communism. After Communism collapsed, the economy slid into massive depression. The government was desperate to educate its people. They needed to be able to communicate with the West and build new economic ties. In the early 1990s, they signed a contract with a Christian organization[86] to send at least 100 English teachers every year to teach English.

The organization informed the Mongolian government these teachers were Christians. They told them they would probably talk about the Bible from time to time. Desperate for economic development, the government unconditionally accepted. Again, as an English teacher I can vividly remember the excited folks with this group detailing this miracle in the literature they sent us. Many Christians came to Mongolia with the love of Jesus Christ. Today the Mongolian church is growing rapidly and has over 15,000 believers growing at a rate of 15.3% per year. Yet, barely more than ten years ago there were no known believers in Jesus Christ in this land of the people of Genghis Khan.[87]

The 1991 Persian Gulf War with Iraq led to some incredible breakthroughs for the Gospel in that region of the world, ultimately leading to the beginnings of the Church amidst a number of people groups. Unfortunately, for security reasons, it is not possible to write the details. But once again, God has opened up doors for the Gospel even in the midst of judgment. Because of the most recent Iraqi war, one Christian organization has been printing tens of thousands of Bibles in Iraq and widely distributing them.

We could go on to talk of even more recent examples, but space doesn't allow, and we mustn't needlessly endanger laborers out on the

front lines. Yet, in the midst of judgment and suffering, God is working with his people, setting people free, and advancing his kingdom
around the globe. Of course, Christians never offer their services to
the needy on condition of conversion. Such a mindset is contrary to
the mercy and kindness of God who blesses the righteous and the
unrighteous. It is this unconditional love of Christians toward people
of all faiths (unlike some of the local faiths) that is so attractive to
the locals. This unconditional love is winning many to Christ.

Of course, God doesn't use only hardships to advance his kingdom. The end of Psalm 2 states, "How blessed are all (nations) who
take refuge in him!" God uses blessing to advance his kingdom.
Many nations such as Switzerland, Holland, Great Britain, South
Korea[88] and the United States have been blessed with material blessings and relative freedom. Without a doubt, one key reason for the
blessings we have received is to be a blessing. Large numbers of our
people have shown respect and honor to Jesus Christ over the years.
People from these nations have also been in the forefront of taking
the Gospel to less-reached peoples. Certainly, we received blessings,
not only as a reward, but also to give us the means to further the
Gospel around the earth.

The rise of Great Britain as a world power coincided with its
renewed embracing of the Gospel. Interestingly, as the influence of
Christianity has decreased in Great Britain in recent years, so has
its influence in the world. Will America face a similar decline in the
future?

The Minimum Requirements of Mission Accomplished

With or without America, the Gospel advance will continue. But
just how far have we gotten in fulfilling the Great Commission? How
much farther do we have to go? Fortunately, today, with the aid of
modern technology, we have a much clearer picture of the precise
progress of the Great Commission than ever before. Biblically, we
know that not only must the Gospel be preached to all nations, but
also there will actually be believers from all nations. This does not
necessarily mean every individual will literally hear the Gospel, although it could.

Of course, when God speaks of nations, he doesn't mean the modern day nation-state. He is referring to all ethnolinguistic groups of people. These are people who are distinct both ethnically and/or linguistically. Similar groups of ethnolinguistic people may also sometimes be separated from each other by geographical and political boundaries creating more than one group. Jesus said where two or three gather in his name he is there in their midst, signifying the tiniest church is two or three believers (Matt. 18:20). Thus, for mission accomplished to happen, at the least, a tiny church must be established amongst every one of these groups on earth (Rev. 5:9–10).

We know for a fact, this has yet to be fulfilled, although we are closer to at least the minimum fulfillment as never before. Although there is reason for optimism, there also remains much to be done.

The Scope of the Remaining Task

There is disagreement about the precise way to count a distinct people group. However, it is generally agreed that the most stable and Biblical way to count a people group is by racial ethnicity and language. Such a distinction gives us a total of about 16,600 peoples. The total number of all unreached ethnolinguistic people groups, regardless of size, is a little over 6,500.[89]

Just what are unreached peoples? Unreached peoples are defined by most missiologists as people groups with less than 5% individuals who claim any form of Christianity. Also less than 2% are evangelical in faith.[90] In most cases, the number of believers is actually far less than this threshold. In hundreds of groups there are still no known Christians or missionaries living and working in their midst. Unreached people groups, taken together, make up approximately two billion people.

Unfortunately, only about 10,000 full-time missionaries out of a mission force of about 420,000 worldwide labor amongst the least reached.[91] Of the 420,000 missionaries in the world, about 384,400 missionaries are serving in countries where the majority of people call themselves Christians.[92] Only about 10,000 missionaries are serving among the 30% of the world least reached with the Gospel.[93] Stated another way that means only about 2.4% of all missionaries are working to reach the least-reached third of the world's population.

The overwhelming majority of all unreached groups are found in parts of Asia, Central Asia, North Africa and the Middle East. About 1.2 billion of the unreached are Muslim.[94] The ratio of evangelical workers to Muslims is only about 2 per million.[95] An overwhelming majority of Muslims have never had the opportunity to hear the Gospel even once.[96] Yet a significant dent was recently made in those numbers with the recent showing of *The Passion of the Christ* in many Muslim nations. Miraculously many governments allowed the film in theaters because they mistakenly believed it to be anti-Semitic. Since then, workers in the region and correspondence centers are reporting an unprecedented surge in interest in Christianity. Still, amazingly, no more than one-tenth of one cent of every dollar given to churches in North America goes to Christian outreach in the Muslim world.[97] Much work is hindered because of the lack of funds and workers.

Most of the remaining unreached peoples live as Hindus, Buddhists, atheists and adherents to Chinese religions. By the grace of God, the Church can and will change this picture.

Some have referred to that place in the world that contains most of the least-reached peoples of the world as the 10/40 window. The 10/40 window encompasses all nations between 10 and 40 degrees north latitude. This covers from North Africa and Southern Europe across through Asia. The latitudinal distinction is imperfect.[98] Yet it is helpful in letting us know the general vicinity on the planet where the least amount of missionaries and most amount of unreached peoples live. Ninety-five percent of the least-reached people in the world live in this area of the world.[99] It is here that most pioneering work needs to be concentrated. For a deeper understanding and discussion of what remains to be done in the world, the book *Perspectives on the World Christian Movement* is outstanding. More missions resources have been listed in the appendix of this book.

We can be assured, on the basis of the infallible Word of God that until these people are reached with the message of the Gospel and some of them believe, Jesus will continue to wait patiently to return. He waits patiently for a messenger of the Gospel to go to them. He wants them to have the same opportunity you and I had to either receive or reject the Gospel. We can be assured some will believe. The Bible makes this clear and so is experience in the field.

The day of monolithically closed-minded Muslims is past, if it ever really existed.

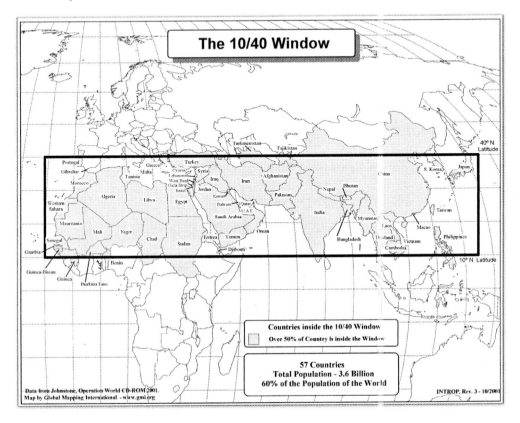

God is Working Among the Least Reached

In spite of the paucity of laborers, in one Middle Eastern country with Bible Correspondence Courses, the number of people (nearly all Muslim) who have written in to take these courses has nearly tripled over the past four years to 14,463 requests in 2002.[100] The number of new believers in this nation from a Muslim background, although still minuscule, has nevertheless increased five-fold in the past ten years. More Muslims have come to faith in Christ in the past twenty years than in the previous 1300 years combined.[101]

Stories of new toeholds and fresh breakthroughs are not isolated to one country. Even in the most repressive regimes of North Africa, the Church is slowly and quietly being born. In spite of intense opposition, the church in one North-African country has grown rapidly to some 50,000 members.[102] Other nations in North Africa are seeing similar breakthroughs, although the numbers are considerably smaller in some cases. As mentioned before, the birth of the Church in Central Asian countries of the former Soviet Union has also become a reality over the past ten years. In 1990 Kazakhstan had virtually no Muslim background believers, but by the year 2000 there were more than six thousand.[103]

In one book-table outreach in a city in the Muslim world, over 3,400 New Testaments were given out in one week. On another outreach, over 9,000 Bibles were distributed in one day and on this same outreach over 500 people came forward for prayer.[104]

As encouraging as such reports are, the harvest is great, but the number of long-term laborers remains pitifully low. For example, in the last mentioned example, most of those Bibles and prayers did not represent conversions or new disciples. Much of the harvest of new brothers and sisters in Christ in these countries is still in the future.

When the Lamb looks out over the multitude on that day in heaven that John witnessed, they will sing out in worship to him. The Lamb will see his children from among *every* tribe and tongue. He will see believers from the two million completely unreached Melayu Riau people of Indonesia. Today they are completely unreached with the Gospel. We know of no Melayu Riau people around his throne.[105] Yet one day, they will be there. The only question is who will have the privilege of helping to bring them the Gospel?

Will the Church rise to the challenge in our generation? In spite of becoming increasingly aware of the remaining unreached people groups for the past twenty-five or so years, the Western church has still largely failed to adequately target them. Will the Church succeed? Ralph Winter, the founder of the US Center for World Missions answered that very question in the following way:

The task is not as difficult as it may seem for several surprising reasons. In the first place, the task is not an American one, nor even a Western one. It will involve Christians from every continent of the world.

More significant is the fact that when a beachhead is established within a culture, the normal evangelistic process that God expects every Christian to be involved in replaces the mission strategy, because the mission task of 'breaking in' is finished.

Furthermore, 'closed countries' are less and less of a problem, because the modern world is becoming more and more interdependent. There are literally no countries today that admit no foreigners. Many of the countries considered 'completely closed'—like Saudi Arabia—are in actual fact avidly recruiting thousands of skilled people from other nations . . .

We have potentially a world-wide network of churches that can be aroused to their central mission. Best of all, nothing can obscure the fact that this could and should be the final era (in missions). No serious believer today dare overlook the fact that God has not asked us to reach every nation, tribe and tongue without intending it to be done. No generation has less excuse than ours if we do not do as He asks.[106]

The non-Western Church is beginning to embrace the call to the unreached peoples of the world. In eastern China the Church has grown astronomically in recent years. Today there are approximately 80 to 100 million born-again Christians in China.[107] The net growth rate of the Chinese home churches is between 12.5% and 17.5% per year with about 30,000 Chinese coming to faith in Christ each day. That's about one million new Chinese Christians each year.[108]

Fortunately, our Chinese brethren are not content to keep the Gospel only to themselves. The Chinese Church now has a powerful mission's vision to complete the Great Commission. As one of the leaders of the Chinese missions movement has stated,

We believe God has given us a solemn responsibility to take the fire from his altar and complete the Great Commission by establishing his kingdom in all the remaining countries and people groups in Asia, the Middle East and Islamic North Africa. When this happens, we believe the Lord Jesus Christ will return for his bride . . . .[109]

The Chinese missions movement is called the "Back to Jerusalem" movement. It got its name to describe their goal of taking the Gospel from the energized rapidly growing churches of eastern China across the regions of the world least reached with the Gospel. Namely those areas that stretch from western China through Central Asia all the way to Jerusalem. The leaders of this movement explain that years of persecution to the point of death have especially equipped the Chinese Church to play a major role in this final thrust of world evangelism. They have already learned to live with intense persecution and already have counted the cost and are willing to die for the Lord. They are inviting us in the West to share the privilege of joining them.

As one of the leaders of this movement stated, "Perhaps we will see you along the Silk Road (the old trade routes of Central Asia) as you join with us in evangelizing all the nations of the world for Jesus! Oh how these unreached nations . . . need the gospel of Jesus Christ!"[110]

Already there are hundreds of Chinese Christians laboring in this part of the world, and there are thousands more being trained to follow close behind.[111] Their goal is to send out about 100,000 laborers, a 10% tithe of the approximately one million full-time Chinese church leaders. Although they are quick to emphasize that their goal is not to merely send 100,000 laborers out from China. Their goal is "nothing less than the completion of the Great Commission so that the Lord Jesus Christ will return for his bride." They emphasize that "if it takes more than 100,000 workers then there will be more workers . . . ."[112]

Who of us from the West will join them? Of course, only God knows, with any certainty, exactly when the Great Completion will happen. Following the completion will be more intense labor pains that will culminate in his return. There will come a time of judgment, purging and deliverance such as the world has never seen.

At the Great Commission's completion, Jesus will finally take the scroll and all of heaven will break out in joyous worship. Then the world stage will be set for the final transition to the return of Jesus Christ. What will start to happen at the beginning of this transition to judgment? We have already seen in the second chapter what will begin to unfold on the earth following the Great Completion.

In heaven following joyous celebration in worship, John saw the Lamb breaking one of the seven seals (Rev. 6:1). The scroll contains judgment. But before this scroll can be opened and its contents divulged, the seals around the scroll must be broken off, one at a time. The breaking of these seals comes before the opening of the scroll with all its judgments. Judgment cannot fall until the earth is fully ripe. As the seals are broken, the earth is ripened. The stage is set.

When the first four seals are released in heaven, the four horsemen go forth and have a direct effect on the earth preparing it for judgment. The next two seals are probably intended to prepare heaven for what is to come. The last seal allows the scroll to be opened. It is with the breaking of the seventh seal that direct judgments of God are finally released upon earth. These judgments will come in response to what has already been happening on terra firma. What does John see after the fourth horseman of the fourth seal?

Chapter 5

The Great Tribulation: The Jihad Against the Bride (Rev. 6:9 – 8:2)

W hen the fifth seal is broken, John describes seeing "underneath the altar the souls of those who had been slain because of the word of God, and because of the testimony that they had maintained; and they cried out with a loud voice, saying, "How long, O Lord, holy and true, will You refrain from judging and avenging our blood on those who dwell on the earth?" (Rev. 6:9–10).

The Fifth Seal: Martyrs (Rev. 6:9–11)

Here we see a picture of those who have been martyred. They probably include all martyrs throughout the history of mankind up to this time. They are becoming restless under the altar. Perhaps they are able to witness what is happening on earth (Heb. 12:1). The question asked here by them may or may not be literally stated, but it certainly captures what is going on in their hearts and minds. All they see is ever-growing numbers of martyrs. Could this be the result of a worldwide *jihad* (holy war)?

As the Koran states, "Muhammad is Allah's apostle. Those who follow him are ruthless to the unbelievers . . ." (Surah 48:29). The followers of the Beast shall be ruthless indeed. It seems that once again justice is left undone on the earth as persecutors pursue the saints and overcome them with relative impunity (Rev. 13:7).

Beheading will be the preferred form of execution (Rev. 20:4). The Koran states, "When you meet the unbelievers in the battlefield, strike off their heads . . ." (Surah 47:4). It is interesting to note that the only nations on earth that continue to use beheading as a form of capital punishment are Muslim. This is because the Koran refers to beheading and Islamic Law (*Sharia* Law) also encourages its use.

Whatever their reason for questioning God, the martyrs are comforted. They are greatly encouraged as they are given white robes and told to be patient just a little longer. Why only a little longer? Because there must first be the full number of brethren to be killed as they were, before the wrath of God is poured out (Rev. 6:10). Thus, there will be yet one more round of martyrs. Except this time, it will be only a little longer until it's finally over. By handing them their white wedding robes, these saints of old now have tangible proof in their hands the time is now extremely short. The time has come to get dressed for the wedding!

The Sixth Seal: The End Result of Judgment Revealed (Rev. 6:12–17)

Now the sixth seal is broken. Here the martyrs and all of heaven are given a future glimpse of a now rapidly approaching time when the final wrath of God shall be poured out. They see the sun become as black as sackcloth. The moon becomes like blood. The sky splits like a scroll. Every island and mountain is removed. Every unsaved person on the planet cringes in fear. They look to hide from him who sits on the throne and from the wrath of the Lamb (Rev. 6:12–17). Although every individual cringing on the earth will almost certainly not literally cry out for rocks to fall on them, the statement recorded here fully captures their attitude of abject, complete fear. This fear will grip the unsaved world at Christ's return as it dawns on them that they have chosen the wrong side.

We discover elsewhere in Revelation that most events recorded in this sixth seal are directly linked with events immediately prior to and during the Lord's return. Later in Revelation we see again a darkening canopy covering the earth (Rev. 16:10) just as the sixth seal describes. Also, just before his return there is the greatest earthquake ever, that flattens the mountains and causes all the islands to disappear (Rev. 16:18,20).

Why are we suddenly transported to the final act coinciding with the Lord's return? The fact this sixth seal takes us right up to the end probably signifies that conditions released by the opening of the seals will continue until the very end. The first five seals preceded the trumpet judgments in their time of release. Yet the events of the sixth seal come after all of the trumpet judgments, except for the seventh final trumpet, which the sixth seal seems to match in most particulars (Rev. 11:15–19).

There is perhaps another reason why the sixth seal is opened with its contents revealing the end. It speaks clearly of Jesus' commitment to pour out complete judgment upon the earth and to completely reclaim the earth from the wicked. It also emphasizes the temporary nature of the success of the kingdom of the Beast and his agenda that John will soon witness.

The opening of the sixth seal lets the martyrs know Jesus is right at the door. When he returns in Revelation 19:14, we see him coming with "armies which are in heaven, clothed in fine linen, white and clean . . . following Him on white horses." The white robes are "fine linen, white and clean." The ones wearing them are the martyred saints themselves, together with all brethren. They are all members of the Lord's army, coming with him to cleanse and receive planet earth as a wedding present from their Bridegroom, the Lord Jesus Christ. Jesus will not be greedy with his inheritance. Just as the bride and bridegroom share all things in common, so too Jesus will share his inheritance with his bride. As Jesus stated, "Blessed are the gentle, for they shall inherit the earth" (Matt. 5:5). As the apostle Paul said, ". . . Do you not know that the saints will judge the world?" (1 Cor. 6:2a).

All the seals laid the necessary groundwork for the final period of judgment. But they also introduced us to key players during the three and one half years of the Beast's rule. With the first horse and the white horses and chariots, we see the anti-Christ himself, his entourage and his plan of world rule. With the second horse, we see total warfare and bloodshed unleashed by this Beast. With the third horse we see forces of economic disaster trampling upon the wealthy nations. Fabulously rich Babylon best represents these nations. With the fourth horse we see the death and destruction that will prevail. With the fifth seal we see the Church and the intense suffering and martyrdom they will face during the Great Tribulation. And then with the sixth seal we see the foretelling of the Lord Jesus himself pouring out his judgment. He reassures us he will rescue his bride and fully reclaim the planet for himself and his bride.

The 144,000 (Revelation 7:1–8)

It is after all of this happens, with all of heaven poised and waiting in anticipation for the wrath of God to commence, we suddenly see angels at the four corners of the heavens instructed to wait. Why the pause now?

In Revelation 7:1–8, John discovers that there is still something left undone. 144,000 of God's bondservants must be sealed on their foreheads. There are 12,000 representatives from each of Israel's tribes.[113] This seal is another word for a signet. This can be a stamp placed upon something when it is purchased to indicate ownership like a purchase stamp. Chapter 14 tells us they have indeed been purchased from the earth (Rev. 14:3b).

It is not clear whether or not these saints will be aware of the fact they have been sealed. They may be unaware of this until they are in heaven in chapter 14. Just who these 144,000 are has been a subject of much discussion down through the years. If we carefully divorce what the Scriptures actually say from our speculations, we realize there is little detail about what they will actually do. We are free to speculate, provided we realize that is what we are doing.

Yet in chapter 14 we do discover the following facts about them:

- They get to sing a new song before the Lamb that only they can learn.
- They are in heaven when singing this song.
- They have not been defiled with women, keeping themselves

chaste.
- They follow the Lamb wherever he goes.
- And they are like first fruits to God from among men.

These 144,000 are also marked as not having a lie in their mouths. They are blameless. This doesn't mean sinless, just blameless. Of course, Jesus has washed away their sins. Yet it seems they are exceptional brethren. They will be in such "sync" with the Holy Spirit that they will go wherever the Lord Jesus wants them to go. They will have long since abandoned selfish desires for building their own little kingdoms. The life agenda and delight of their souls will be to obey what Jesus tells them. Nothing else will do. No other agendas need apply. Any statements beyond this about what they will do while walking on earth would be speculation. It may be that this is the full extent of what will set them apart and nothing more.[114]

The sealing of these 144,000 bondservants precedes another magnificent event. John sees a gigantic multitude "which no one could count, from every nation and all tribes and peoples and tongues, standing before the throne and before the Lamb, clothed in white robes (just like the martyrs who went before them), and palm branches were in their hands; and they cry out with a loud voice, saying, 'Salvation to our God who sits on the throne, and to the Lamb" (Rev. 7:9–10).

The Great Tribulation is Already in Progress (Rev. 7:9– 8:2)

When John asks who these individuals are and where they came from, he gets an answer that is overwhelming in its implications. One of the elders says "these are *the ones who come out of the great tribulation*, and they have washed their robes and made them white in the blood of the Lamb" (Rev. 7:14). Here we see that the Great Tribulation, the holocaust of Christians, has been going on in earnest for some time. It likely hits full stride after the rider on the white horse begins to rule (Rev. 6:2) and probably sometime just before the opening of the fifth seal.[115]

The reach of this tribulation will be vast. The kingdom of priests from every tribe, tongue and nation now also has a multitude of martyred representatives from every tribe and tongue and nation in heaven itself! Why are they in heaven now? They died. For that is what happens to those who directly refuse to worship the Beast (Rev. 13:15). John is seeing those who refused to bow the knee even unto death. They are all martyrs from the Great Tribulation. Can one even imagine the widespread reach and ferocity of this final tribulation? Surely, it will be nothing like the world has ever seen (Matt. 24:21).

Unlike the earlier martyrs, there is no delay in them getting their white robes, for when John sees them, they already are clothed in them. Their immediate clothing indicates the time for the wedding is very near. Very soon they will be returning with the Lamb to earth to rule and reign with Christ (Rev. 20:4).

Just as the early disciples had palm branches in their hands while Jesus entered Jerusalem on Palm Sunday, they too have palm branches in their hands. And just as the early disciples laid down branches on Jesus' path in his final entry to Jerusalem, perhaps they will as well. Perhaps together, with repentant Israel, they will lay their palm branches down to welcome the King of Israel back to Jerusalem from his battle of cleansing the earth. Once again his disciples shall cry out, "Blessed is He who comes in the name of the Lord," and all of Israel that is left on the earth will join them. The curse that has been upon Israel since her first rejection of Messiah will finally be shattered (Matt. 23:37–39, Zech. 14:11).

For now, we see the martyrs in heaven being taken care of by God. They will be comforted after what must have been some of the most harrowing and trying of circumstances. Still they have come home victorious. They are "before the throne of God; and they serve Him day and night in His temple; and . . ." He "will spread His tabernacle over them . . . the Lamb in the center of the throne will be their shepherd, and will guide them to springs of the water of life; and God will wipe every tear from their eyes" (Rev. 7:15,17).

What is to come after this unprecedented tribulation has produced martyrs from every tribe and tongue and nation? Eventually, the full number of brethren to be killed, as the earlier martyrs were will be reached. In response God will unleash judgment on a scale the world has never seen. He will refrain no longer. He will now answer the cry of the martyrs to bring justice on the earth (Rev. 6:10). And when Jesus comes again, he will have martyrs and saints representative from every tribe and tongue and nation to serve him in ruling all the nations (Rev. 20:4).

The next thing John sees is the Lamb reach out and break the final seventh seal that is around the scroll. A truly holy and sober moment has arrived. All of heaven pauses to catch its breath. Then quietly and slowly, the seven angels[116] are given the seven trumpets to herald the judgments of God (Rev. 8:2). How will God respond to this wholesale slaughter of his Church? What will God do about the outrageous blasphemy of this ultimate false Christ and his right hand man, the false prophet? What will he do with the instigators and foot soldiers of this wholesale slaughter of Christians? As the prophet Habakkuk cried out over 2,500 years ago, "Why are you silent when the wicked swallow up those more righteous than they? . . . Will they therefore empty their net and continually slay nations without sparing?" (Hab. 1:13b,17).

Chapter 6

God Responds to the Jihad Against his Bride (Rev. 8:1–11:19)

How long will the Church have to endure the great tribulation before God begins to respond? The exact timing of God's response is unclear and will be unknown to the Church. It could be that many of these judgments in response to the slaughter won't come until the final year or so of the Beast's three-and-one-half-year reign of horror. As John essentially stated twice about that difficult time, great patience will be necessary, "Here is the perseverance and the faith of the saints" (Rev. 13:10, 14:12). Our faith will be tried and tested. Finally, after an undisclosed period of time, John saw heaven fall silent, probably because heaven knows God has had enough (Rev. 8:1). What follows the silence will be unprecedented. The breaking of the seventh seal now allows the scroll to finally be unrolled. Those who have murdered God's people are fair game. They have been attacking the very bride of Jesus, his lover and his friend, the Church of the Living God. Boy is he ever angry!

The die has been cast and as Joel saw, ". . . multitudes, multitudes in the valley of decision! For the day of the Lord is near in the valley of decision" (Joel 3:14). Everyone will have made a decision. The whole world will have had an opportunity to make a decision to follow Jesus Christ, for this gospel of the kingdom will have already been preached to all nations. The only alternative to Jesus will be to bow down and worship the Beast. This decision will help sort out the pretenders from the genuine disciples who have already taken up their cross and denied themselves to be Jesus' disciple.

The Church will be purged of the tares. The tares will be separated out from the true Church. They will be exposed to the judgment of God for they will be unwilling to suffer in the Great Tribulation for the sake of Christ. Certainly there will still be time for them to repent, as long as the Lord has yet to return, but the prophetic record for many doing that is not very good.

In actuality, there will be a great apostasy (2Thess. 2:3) and many will turn from Christ in an attempt to save their lives. Ironically, the salvation of the apostate will prove temporary, whereas the salvation of the martyr will prove eternal. As Jesus said, "He who wishes to save his life will lose it, but whoever loses his life for My sake and the gospel's will save it" (Mark 8:35).

The oldest existent commentary we have on the book of Revelation was written by an early church father named Iraneus (A.D. 120–202). Iraneus was himself discipled by the martyr Polycarp (A.D. 65–155) bishop of Smyrna. Polycarp was personally discipled by the Apostle John, the author of Revelation. When talking about the Great Tribulation, Iraneus writes,

". . . Throughout all time, man . . . is made after the image of God: the *chaff*, indeed that *is* the *apostasy*, being cast away; but the wheat, that is, those who bring forth fruit to God in faith, being gathered into the barn."[117]

Thus, in Iraneus's view the apostasy that Paul talked about represents the chaff in the Church. This is consistent with 2Thessalonians 2:3–4a that tells us the Lord's coming will not happen "unless *the apostasy* comes first, *and* the man of lawlessness is revealed, the son of destruction who opposes and exalts himself above every so-called god or object of worship." The revelation of the man of lawlessness (a description of the Beast) happens at the same time the apostasy happens. The word *and* indicates these occur at the same time. Essentially, the Great Tribulation will be necessary to expose the apostate and clean out the Church.

The Prayers of the Saints and the Judgment of God

What will finally trigger the beginning of judgment? An angel holding a golden censer comes to the altar and is given incense to put in his censer. He takes the prayers of the saints and adds it to this incense-filled censer. Its smoke and its prayers go up before God. God responds to the cries and prayers of his people. The angel fills his censer with fire and hurls it to earth. There is lightning and an earthquake. Thus, begins the opening salvo of God's response on behalf of his suffering Church. It begins in direct answer to the prayers of the saints (Rev. 8:3–5).

In his parable on prayer involving the widow and the unjust judge (Luke 18:1–8), we see Jesus' exhortation for his people to pray and never give up. He immediately gives this exhortation following a passage of scripture where he talks about his Second Coming (Luke 17:22–37). Incredibly, the one praying is a widow, and she is praying for justice. How many widows will be crying out to God for justice during the Great Tribulation, wondering if they will ever see justice? Jesus ends this parable by saying ". . . will not God bring about justice for His elect who cry to Him day and night, and will He delay long over them? I tell you that He will bring about justice for them quickly" (Luke 18:7,8a). Then Jesus ends this parable with the most haunting question of all, "However, when the Son of Man comes, will He find faith on the earth?" (Luke 18:8b).

The question is a challenge for the suffering Church to keep their trust in God even during the most trying time that will ever come. Fortunately, we know the answer to the question. There will be those who will pray and God will faithfully answer. With this earthquake, his first strike in answer to the prayers of the suffering Church has been pitched. Much more is about to follow.

God Protects his People

An important principle to understand at this point is that God will largely protect his people on earth during this time of judgment from the direct impact of his judgments (Rev. 7:3, 9:4, 16:2). God's judgment shall not directly fall on most Christians. Even as God protected the Israelites from the plagues he sent on Pharaoh and

Egypt, so too God will protect his people. "For God has not destined us for wrath, but for obtaining salvation through our Lord Jesus Christ" (1Thess. 5:9). The Church will not be direct objects of God's wrath falling down on earth. Those of us in the Church will know the fearful judgments that are falling portend hell for the lost. They will be labor pains for us, reminding us of a new world to come. We can have hope since we know this is but a temporary transition to a much more glorious day that will soon follow. Thus, our affections will not be tied down to this current earth. As Peter stated, "since all these things are to be destroyed in this way, what sort of people ought you to be in holy conduct and godliness, looking for and hastening the coming of the day of God . . . According to His promise we are looking for new heavens and a new earth, in which righteousness dwells" (2Pet. 3:11–12a, 13).

We mustn't forget that, at first, before their deliverance, the Israelites suffered more at the hand of Pharaoh, even as God began to bring judgment on Pharaoh. The Bible tells us that Pharaoh made their labor much harder and had them beaten to the point that they were threatened with death (Ex. 5:1–23). In other words, the suffering of Israel, as bad as it had been for many, many years, got much worse just prior to her deliverance. In the same way, the Church will be suffering its stiffest persecution ever, just prior to her rescue. God will be responding to the cries of his people, just as he did to Israel in Egypt. He will not let up in his wrath until justice is done. However, once God's wrath did begin to fall on Egypt, the people of Israel were repeatedly spared (Ex. 8:21–23, 9:4, 9:25–26, 10:21–23, 11:4–7) and protected from his direct judgments.

In another example, Ezekiel saw the slaughter about ready to come upon Jerusalem during its judgment at the hands of the Babylonians. He heard the Lord say, "Go through the midst of the city, even through the midst of Jerusalem, and *put a mark on the foreheads of the men who sigh and groan over all the abominations which are being committed in its midst.'* But to the others He said in my hearing, 'Go through the city after him and strike; do not let your eye have pity and do not spare. Utterly slay old men, young men, maidens, little children, and women, *but do not touch any man on whom is the mark*

. . .'" (Ezek. 9:4–6a). Once again, we see God protecting his people in the midst of judgment.

After all, if God

> did not spare the ancient world, but preserved Noah, a preacher of righteousness with seven others, when He brought the flood upon the world of the ungodly . . .

and

> . . . if He condemned the cities of Sodom and Gomorrah to destruction by reducing them to ashes, having made them an example to those who would live ungodly lives thereafter; and if He rescued righteous Lot, oppressed by the sensual conduct of unprincipled men . . . then the Lord knows how to rescue the ungodly from temptation, and to keep the unrighteous under punishment until the day of judgment (2Pet. 2:5–7,9).

Again, God preserved Noah *in the midst* of the flood.

In each of the examples given in the Scriptures, the judgment on Egypt, the sacking of Jerusalem by the Babylonians, the flooding of the ancient world of Noah's day, and the destruction of Sodom and Gomorrah, God never removed his people from the earth. Instead, he divinely and miraculously protected them from these earthly judgments by protecting their lives.[118] For the most part, the only lives lost by Christians during the time of judgment will be at the hands of persecutors.

The First Trumpet Sounds: What is the hail and fire mixed with blood? (Rev. 8:7)

Back in heaven, the first trumpet sounds. Hail and fire mixed with blood rains down on the earth. Just what is this hail and fire? Nowhere here does John seem to be referring to something spiritually symbolic in nature. When he does that, the text generally makes it clear. Here there is no indication he is doing this. Thus, it's probably improper to overly allegorize the text and try to identify the hail and fire as some spiritual attack on the Church, or a representation of some army or something like this. On the contrary, John is trying his best with first-century eyes and understanding to describe as accurately as he can what he is seeing. Given this, we can make an educated guess as to what he saw in twenty-first-century terms and understanding.

The hail and fire mixed with blood may very well describe, in first-century terms, a massive meteor shower of tiny rocks and fragments of iron oxide bombarding the atmosphere. If this shower hits the atmosphere on the daylight side of the earth, it might not be seen as falling stars, at first. Seeding clouds helps produce precipitation by giving particles for condensation. A massive influx of particles ranging in size from dust and stones to small rocks and boulders and the heat of massive numbers of meteors bombarding against the cold air in the upper atmosphere may produce perfect conditions for massive and rapid condensation, hail and rain. Huge quantities of iron oxide dust may very well produce a red precipitation that looks like blood. Scientists who have examined meteors that have made it to earth without burning up (meteorites) have confirmed they often are made up almost entirely of iron.[119] Iron, of course, turns red in water.

Some meteorites could fall to earth still burning hot from their atmospheric entry. They may ignite trees, burn up grass, and start numerous brush fires, causing massive fires in general. How many homes, buildings and businesses will be burned up is not mentioned in the text. However, conditions for fire will be ripe. The two prophets will have shut up the sky so that there will be no rain during the 1260 days of their prophesying (Rev. 11:6). Things will be tinder dry. With one-third of the earth and its trees and all the green grass burned up, infrastructure damage will undoubtedly be massive. As massive brush fires in the western US and other parts of the world have shown, it takes only a spark to start a massive fire.

Although God could certainly literally supernaturally mix blood with hail and fire, an absolute literal fulfillment is not necessary for the text here. At the very least, it will appear to look like blood. The message God will communicate to the world will be clear. He is pouring out his wrath to avenge the blood of his saints, the martyred Church.

The Second Trumpet Sounds: What is the great mountain burning with fire? (Rev. 8:8–9)

We don't know the exact length of time between the first and second trumpet. It may be anywhere from several hours to several weeks, but many months seem unlikely. The second angel sounds and "something like a great mountain burning with fire was thrown into the sea, and a third of the sea became blood, and a third of the creatures which were in the sea and had life, died, and a third of the ships were destroyed" (Rev. 8:8–9). John himself makes it clear that he has difficulty describing exactly what he sees. He says only that it is "*something like* a great mountain burning with fire." It is something *like* a great mountain because real mountains ordinarily don't behave that way. Again, the fact many animals and ships (not governments or armies or something else) are plainly identified as being destroyed by this impact clearly communicates results of a real physical disaster. One would expect this result if a literally gigantic, mountain-like object, hit the sea.

What probably is this in twenty-first-century terms? John's description seems to be a very vivid account of exactly what would happen should a large meteorite hit an ocean. Scientists are already concerned about the possible impact of just such an asteroid. "Its name is 1950DA. It's the size of a small mountain, and it's headed for earth. According to one grim scenario, 1950DA will hit its target—most likely water, since there is more water than land on our planet—and plunge to the seabed in a fraction of a second. When the asteroid meets the ocean floor, it will explode, excavating a crater 11 miles wide. A column of water and debris will shoot a few miles into the sky—to the height of a low-flying jetliner. Then skyscraper-high walls of water will head for shore, eventually breaking in the shadows and flooding the coast."[120]

Some movies in recent years, such as *Deep Impact* in 1998, popularized just such a notion. The impact of such a wave would obliterate surrounding shorelines. It would destroy ships in its path. Many fish would be killed not only from direct impact, but many more would die from the massive shock wave and force traveling through the water. Many more would be hurled up on nearby shores riding the tidal wave. Scientists don't only believe huge meteorites can theoretically hit earth. They firmly believe it has already happened in the earth's past.[121] In reality, every time we see a "falling star" we are seeing a meteor entering the upper atmosphere.

Scientists believe the impact of a large meteorite would be so devastating that many believe it was such a catastrophic impact that led to the extinction of dinosaurs. Whatever one thinks of the age of the earth and the accuracy of such a theory, the important fact is that scientists theorize it would be devastating. Listen to their description of a large asteroid impact when talking about this theory of dinosaur extinction. "One theory credits an eleven-kilometer-wide asteroid with roasting dinosaurs alive . . . The enormous impact sent debris flying back into space—some of it halfway to the moon. When the asteroid bits reentered the atmosphere, the heat that was generated flash-baked plant and animal life."[122]

One science article goes on to say, "make no mistake, there are plenty of space rocks out there; one missed earth by only 75,000 miles in June 2002—and wasn't spotted until after it had whizzed by."[123] Fortunately, 1950DA is not expected to come within striking distance of earth for another 877 years. However, scientists believe that there are at least 400 potential global killers out there and over a million other hard-to-spot smaller asteroids capable of massive regional destruction. It is not currently possible to come close to detecting all of them. Besides, finding them is not the only problem. "As Jay Melosh, a planetary scientist at the University of Arizona points out, 'The question is, If we find one with our name on it, can we do anything?'"[124]

Some scientists are beginning to try to think of ways to prevent one from colliding with earth. There are a few ideas, but they require spotting the asteroids many years in advance to even have a chance of diverting its path. "'The key,' says Donald Yeomans, who heads the NEO (Near Earth Objects) Program Office at JPL (NASA's Jet Propulsion Laboratory), 'is you've got to find them early. If they're on an approach trajectory and you've (only) got a few months, there's not much you can do.'"[125]

If the first trumpet describes a massive meteor shower entering the atmosphere, the second may portend a massive meteorite with a greater impact than that of many nuclear weapons.

Jesus said "there will be signs in the sun and moon and stars, and on the earth dismay among nations, *in perplexity at the roaring of the sea and the waves, men fainting from fear and the expectation of the things which are coming upon the world, for the powers of the heavens will be shaken*" (Luke 21:25–26).

Could the roaring of the sea and the waves be from the impact of a giant meteorite? Could some of "the things" coming upon the world refer to a massive meteorite shower? Could it be world scientists and others, through astronomical observations, will see a massive meteor approaching, only to realize our helplessness to stop it? The world will be absolutely perplexed. Hollywood movies notwithstanding, we won't be able to thwart this massive collision. Mankind's dependence upon their own ingenuity and their pride in their own intelligence will be utterly confounded.

The Third Trumpet Sounds: What is the great star that falls from heaven? (Rev. 8:10–11)

With the third trumpet John sees something fall out of the heavens, much like a falling star. The Second Trumpet hit the earth so directly it looked like a giant burning ball or mountain slamming into earth. Perhaps John refers to this one as a star because it will be a comet hitting the atmosphere at an angle. It may be a comet gradually pulled in by the earth's atmosphere. This would produce a light show of incredible proportions. John describes it as a massive "burning . . . torch," a perfect description of a comet.

If so, as it is breaking up, its dust, particles and frozen poisonous liquids will rain down on the springs of water and rivers (i.e. the fresh water). A third of the waters will be polluted. Comets are made up of common space elements such as hydrogen, carbon, nitrogen and oxygen. However, they also contain large quantities of frozen methane, ammonia and water.[126] The first two of these are highly poisonous. Whether it breaks up and melts completely and is entirely sucked into the earth, or whether it is only partly sucked in to the atmosphere is not important. Either way, the effect will be the same. These materials, found in large quantities in fresh water, might explain the deaths from drinking poisonous waters.

Comets have been known to range in size from larger than the planet Jupiter to only a few cubic miles in size.[127] Whatever its actual size, the effect of poisoning one-third of fresh water will earn the star the name Wormwood (Rev. 8:10). Again, the text is very direct. People die from drinking bad water (Rev. 8:11). These deaths result from some object that looks like a burning torch. This closely follows the probable meteor showers of the first two trumpets. Not surprisingly, scientists have found that "a close relationship exists between the orbits of comets and the orbits of meteor showers."[128] It seems meteors and comets tend to move within the same orbits.

Comets have long been associated by people around the world as a sign of calamity and important cosmic events. This will undoubtedly be the case here as well.

The Fourth Trumpet Sounds: How are a third of the sun, moon and stars darkened? (Rev. 8:12–13)

The fourth trumpet sounds and we see a third of the sun, moon and stars darkened for a third of the day and night (Rev. 8:12). Just like the earlier three trumpets, this also impacts about a third of the sun, moon and stars. This consistency with the three earlier trumpets reinforces the likelihood these earlier trumpets are related to one another and the fourth trumpet.

If that is the case, the phenomena of a third of the sun, moon and stars being darkened may result from the break-up of the previous comet as it is penetrating the atmosphere. In its wake it would leave a blanket of dust and debris. Those areas where the comet passes through and breaks up would probably have a particularly high concentration of dust in the atmosphere. Also, dust from the previous huge meteorite and meteor showers could add to this effect. Taken together, these could greatly diminish the amount of light reaching the earth from the sun, moon and stars.

Of course, volcanoes have produced similar effects in the past. However, meteor showers and a comet can explain all of these trumpets and tie them together. These seem most consistent with the actual description given by John. If these trumpets are indeed meteor showers and they are connected with each other, then the timing of these first four trumpets could be within a day or two. Certainly, it would be hard to imagine them lasting more than several months in duration. However, time markers are not specifically mentioned here.

The Fifth Trumpet: What is the first woe of the bottomless pit? (Rev. 9:1–12)

A star falls from heaven. He is given the key to open the bottomless pit, releasing locusts. These creatures will torture but not kill men with their sting for five months. It is not entirely clear whether or not this star is a physical object divinely directed. Perhaps this "star" actually refers to an angel. In verse 11 we do discover these locusts have an angel who is king over them (Rev. 9:11). He's identified as the angel of the abyss with the Greek name of Apollyon, which means destroyer. Could it be this "star" that falls from heaven is the same as this angel with this special assignment? It's certainly possible. Most Bible translators identify this fifth star with the pronoun *he* which seems to suggest a living being.

On the other hand, it is also possible this "star" is divinely directed on a personal assignment from God. Such a personalized assignment may "enliven" the "star" necessitating use of a personal pronoun. [129]

In either case, the result of the opened pit is horrifying. Locusts! Who or what are these locusts? What are they actually doing? These beings sound horrible in appearance. They are "*like* horses prepared for battle; and on their heads *appeared* to be crowns like gold, and their faces were *like* the faces of men" (Rev. 9:7). They also had "breastplates *like* breastplates of iron; and the sound of their wings was *like* the sound of chariots, of many horses rushing into battle" (Rev. 9:7,9). It is tempting to assume they describe something military in nature. Some have suggested attack helicopters launching chemical weapons with pilots wearing chemical gas masks.

But then how are these locusts not given power to kill people? Why are they also prevented from attacking "the men who have the seal of God on their foreheads" (Rev. 9:4). How would human armies be able to separate out and distinguish Christians from non-Christians? If they are human armies connected with the Beast, why are they completely unable to harm Christians when the Bible makes it clear the Beast will do so with a vengeance? Locusts, with such restricting characteristics, seem to indicate a supernatural force, with strict limits placed on it by God.

Some feel these forces are not only supernatural, but also perhaps even demonic in nature. Would demonic forces be restricted in whom they could attack? In Job, Satan is restricted by God in very specific ways in the damage he was allowed to do (Job 1:6–2:7).

Again, it should be of great comfort to Christians that these creatures, being part of God's divine wrath are not directed or allowed to harm Christians. Certainly, God's servants, sealed on their foreheads, would include any of the 144,000 still on earth. But it would almost certainly include all Christians as well. Paul wrote to the Ephesians "having also believed, you were sealed in Him with the Holy Spirit of promise" (Eph. 1:13b). The Spirit of God has sealed every genuine believer.

Who knows? For Christians on the earth, these creatures may actually be welcome for they will not harm any Christian. Might they actually provide them with some protection? After all, no unbeliever will want to be near them. Perhaps they even help keep all Christians from getting wiped out.

Whatever they are, John announces that when the duration of five months is up, the first woe of these locusts is finally past. Two woes, that encompass the last two trumpets, are still coming. What woe is next? Judgment of fearfully epic proportions is yet on the way.

The Sixth Trumpet: What is the second woe of the army from the east? (Rev. 9:13–21)

Next John sees the four angels previously bound by the river Euphrates released (Rev. 9:14–15). What are these four angels doing? And who are these armies of horsemen numbering two hundred million (Rev. 9:16) that John sees?

Many have suggested these are descriptions of literal armies of men. Either India or China, by itself, has plenty enough men to have armies of that size. When the sixth bowl of wrath is poured out in Revelation 16:12, the river Euphrates is dried up. With the sixth bowl, the way is prepared for the kings of the east. In order for troops from India or China, or any points east of central Iraq to come to Israel, they have to pass over this river.[130] Some suggest that the description of the horses, their riders and their firepower approximate a first-century description of a tank (Rev. 9:17–19).

Unlike the locusts, these armies may directly involve the Beast. However, this trumpet may simply involve a huge war breaking out that involves China and India. These two countries combined have a population of almost two-and-a-half billion people, about forty percent of the world's population. Both countries also have tactical nuclear weapons that can be released from military vehicles. Perhaps this is what John saw.

A few have suggested these armies are supernatural. The fact that four angels have been "prepared for the hour and day and month and year" (Rev. 9:15a) for the express purpose "that they would kill a third of mankind" (Rev. 9:15b), seems to speak of a clearly supernatural element. On the other hand, the angels being released may merely be supernatural forces behind armies of men.

Either way, this army kills about a third of the world's population (Rev. 9:15). Still, the world will refuse to repent (Rev. 9:20–21). What do they refuse to repent of? They refuse to repent of idolatry not only toward statues and objects, but also greed (Col. 3:5b). They also refuse to repent of murders. This certainly must include the slaughter of millions of aborted babies and euthanized adults. In the United States alone, well over 43 million babies have been aborted since legalization in 1973. They also refuse to repent of sorceries. This includes illicit drugs, as well as casting spells on people. And they refuse to repent of immorality. That would certainly include immoral TV programs, pornographic literature, web sites, DVD's, videos and movies. The world also refuses to repent of its thefts. It stubbornly refuses to turn to the living God in spite of all these overwhelming judgments.

The Mighty Angel and the Little Scroll (Rev. 10:1– 11:13)

Around this time, John notices another strong angel coming down from heaven.[131] The seven thunders respond with their voices once this mighty angel places his right foot on the sea and his left on the land. But we won't know what is said in advance, for what they say is sealed up and unknown to us, at least until it happens.

What we do find out is that there will be delay no longer. The Lord Jesus is on the verge of returning. "In the days of the voice of the seventh angel, when he is about to sound, then the mystery of God is finished, as He preached to His servants the prophets" (Rev. 10:7). What mystery of God will be finished just prior to the angel sounding the last trumpet call? Does the New Testament identify a mystery to be finished immediately before the sounding of the final trumpet of God? The Scriptures speak of fourteen different mysteries, thirteen of which are explained and referred to in this footnote.[132] But which one is being referred to here?

Ephesians 1:9–10 says that "He made known to us the *mystery* of His will, according to His kind intention which He purposed in Him with a view to an administration suitable to the fullness of the times, that is the summing up of all things in Christ, things in the heavens and things on the earth" (Eph. 1:9–10). When the time is suitable, what is true about Christ now in the heavenlies will be fully manifested on earth as well. The Scriptures state, Christ is "far above all rule and authority and power and dominion, and every name that is named, not only in this age, but in the one to come. And He put all things in subjection under His feet, and gave Him as head over all things to the church, which is His body, the fullness of Him who fills all in all" (Eph. 1:21–23). Thus, the mystery to be fulfilled is the summing up of all things in Christ as he takes his place of complete authority in governing earth.

The last trumpet call, among other things, will be an announcement of the kingdom of this world becoming the kingdom of the Lord Jesus Christ (Rev. 11:15). But, let's not blow the seventh trumpet yet. Before this happens, John has to take a little scroll from the hand of the mighty angel. He eats the scroll. It is sweet to the taste but bitter in the stomach. It is sweet to see God's judgment. Judgment will finally fully usher in his kingdom on the earth. Yet it is bitter, because this final process is very unpleasant for all.

After eating the little scroll, John is informed he "must prophesy *again* concerning many peoples and nations and tongues and kings" (Rev. 10:11). The statement he must prophesy "again" clarifies that John will again see things covering some of the same ground and time period he has already seen. Zechariah also saw the first scroll opened by the Lord Jesus. That scroll was quite large, in part because it gave a macro view of the judgment. This scroll that John now eats is little, probably because this scroll will dissect the curse of the larger scroll into finer detail. John will now get a zoom-lens view of various aspects of this worldwide judgment.

It is here, in the smaller details, we learn of the ministry of the two witnesses who prophesy. It is here that we learn details of the Beast, the False Prophet and the Beast's kingdom. Here we see the whore of Babylon and the judgment that befalls her. We get a closer view of the suffering saints and anyone else who refuses to worship the Beast. And we learn the details of Christ's physical return and the aftermath.

After John is commissioned to prophesy further about the nations, he is given a measuring rod like a staff. He is instructed to do a most peculiar thing. A voice tells him to "Get up and measure the temple of God and the altar, and those who worship in it" (Rev. 11:1b). He is further told "leave out the court which is outside the temple and do not measure it, for it has been given to the nations; and they will tread under foot the holy city for forty-two months" (Rev. 11:2).

Immediately following instructions to take these measurements, he is told about two witnesses prophesying for 1260 days (Rev. 11:3). This trampling of the temple area will correspond with the abomination of desolation and an attack on Israel (Matt. 24:15–16). More on this in later chapters. Coinciding with this trampling is the granting of authority to two witnesses clothed in sackcloth to prophesy for 1260 days. Who are these witnesses? What will their ministry involve? What will be going on in the world as these witnesses battle with the Beast and his forces? Unfortunately, the scope of this book does not allow us to get into great detail about their ministry. To summarize, their ministry runs virtually parallel with the rule of the Beast and his kingdom. Many believe that their ministry will include the prophesying of the trumpet judgments and bowl judgments.

The Last Trumpet (Rev. 11:14–19)

When the ministry of the two witnesses is finally completed, the rule of the Beast will also come to an end, for the Lord Jesus himself will return almost immediately after. The second woe, coinciding with the sixth trumpet blast is declared to be after the end of the two witnesses' ministry.

Concerning the timing of the third woe and, thus, the seventh and last trumpet, John says, "The second woe is past; behold, the *third woe is coming quickly*" (Rev. 11:14). When the seventh angel sounds his trumpet, loud voices in heaven say, "The kingdom of the *world* has become *the kingdom of our Lord and of His Christ*; and He will reign forever and ever" (Rev. 11:15b).

This last trumpet and what ensues are talked about not only in verses 17–20, but also Rev. 14:14–20, 16:15–21, 19:7–20:2. For purposes of continuity and ease of storytelling we will postpone a detailed look at what happens at the last trumpet until later in this book. So what does John see next after this last trumpet? It is here that he is given a description of the Beast, the False Prophet, Babylon and the Kingdom of the Beast. Are credible seeds of these things in the earth right now? What are those seeds? Specifically, could Islam produce the Beast and the False Prophet and their agendas? Can we find in Islam an explanation without loopholes, missing links or contradictions against scripture? We will examine these questions in the remaining chapters.

Chapter 7

· ·

Great Signs in the Heavens (Rev. 12:1–17)

A fter seeing the end come in fairly general terms, John now observes things from another vantage point. He is shown other great signs in the heavens in order to receive new insight in greater detail.

The Woman

The first sign John is shown is "a woman clothed with the sun, and the moon under her feet, and on her head a crown of twelve stars . . ." (Rev. 12:1). This woman is quite likely a picture of she who will ultimately rule the world. The sun and moon under her feet are vaguely similar to what Joseph saw in his dream, foretelling his rule of Egypt under Pharaoh (Gen. 37:9, 41:38–44). At that time Egypt ruled as the dominant power in the known world. The woman's crown of twelve stars probably represents the twelve tribes of Israel.[133]

Whatever these stars may be, we see this woman with child cry out, "being in labor and in pain to give birth" (Rev. 12:2). This found its literal fulfillment in Mary the mother of Jesus. But since this woman also appears to represent Israel and perhaps the Church, it may also show the struggle of Israel to bring forth the Messiah. In a similar way it may show the struggle of the Church to bring him back the second time by completing the Great Commission. As those instruments God is working through to establish his kingdom upon the earth, both have suffered greatly laboring down through the ages while being targets of the enemies of God.[134]

The Red Dragon, Satan (Rev. 12:3–4, 7–17)

Suddenly, the greatest archenemy of God abruptly barges into John's vision. He appears as "a great red dragon" having seven heads and ten horns, and on his head were seven diadems (Rev. 12:3). This red dragon has the same number of heads and horns as the kingdom of the Beast described in Chapter 17 (Rev. 17:3). The Beast on the earth also is scarlet in color (Rev. 17:3). Clearly the Beast and his kingdom are outward expressions of the kingdom of Satan himself. This dragon is plainly identified as ". . . the devil and Satan . . ." (Rev. 12:9).

It may be that the seven diadems on each head represent Satan's presence in his earthly emissaries, the rulers of these kingdoms. They are perhaps a satanic imitation of the seven lampstands around the throne.[135] We see Satan sweeping away a third of the "stars" down to the earth, probably to help him with his mission there. Some scholars believe this is a reference to angels that have fallen and joined him in his rebellion. After all, the seven stars of Revelation 1:20 are identified as angels.[136] The beginning of this stretch of text is clearly described as a sign (Rev. 12:1a). Thus, we can expect symbolic language and pictures to be in use here. Yet they clearly represent something concrete.

The "dragon stood before the woman who was about to give birth, so that when she gave birth he might devour her child" (Rev. 12:4). Although Satan opposed Israel and deceived many Israelites leading many into rebellion, he knew that God would eventually find a way to bring forth the Messiah. Still he didn't acquiesce. He chose to fight dirty. The story of Herod shows his desperate attempt to "devour her child" (Matt. 2:1–23). Tragically, Herod slaughtered Bethlehem's infant boys under 2 years old. That was an earthly manifestation of the devil's vicious effort to kill the Messiah before he could undertake his ministry. Of course, he failed. God warned both the wise men and Joseph in dreams.

The Woman (Israel) Flees

Next John informs us "The woman fled into the wilderness where she had a place prepared for her by God, so that she would be nourished for one thousand two hundred and sixty days" (Rev. 12:6). What did this statement describe? When did the woman flee into the wilderness for 1260 days?

Less than a generation after the child of the woman "was caught up to God and to his throne" (Rev.12:5b), war broke out between the Roman Empire and the Jews. It lasted from A.D. 66–73. Eventually the siege of Jerusalem began. It fulfilled Jesus' prophesy that judgment would fall upon her for not recognizing the time of God's coming to her (Luke. 19:42–44, 21:20–23). Of course, in A.D. 70 the city of Jerusalem fell. Nearly all of the temple and the city were demolished just as Jesus said they would be. Sadly hundreds of thousands of Jews were slaughtered in the process. However, believing Jews in Jerusalem were sheltered and protected from this judgment. They were aware of the coming judgment and gave heed to Jesus' warning to leave the city. They fled prior to the attack on Jerusalem and found a place in the wilderness. They safely remained sheltered until the Roman war with the Jews finally ended with the conclusion of the siege of Masada in A.D. 73.[137] Thus, they remained in safety for the remaining three-and-a-half years (or 1260 days) of the Roman-Jewish War, just as John described.

The Cosmic Struggle of the Ages

Following this, John sees what begins to happen in the heavens after the child of the woman who is to "rule all the nations with a rod of iron . . ." is ". . . caught up to God and to His throne" (Rev. 12:5). In verses 7 and 8, we now see a great cosmic struggle between Michael and his angels and the dragon and his angels. Satan now turns his efforts toward doing everything he can to prevent the spread of the Gospel on earth.

Above all else, the devil does not want God to have a people from every tribe and tongue and nation on the earth. If that should happen, it would be a sure signal that his doom is around the corner. Thus, the devil does whatever he can to prevent the spread of the Gospel. He battles with Michael for control of governments.[138] He inspires evil men to perform ethnic cleansing and genocide against people groups often before the Church has been birthed in them, as in the case of Bosnians and Kosovar Albanians (fortunately he lost in both those situations). Satan battles for people who will carry out his wishes to combat and destroy the Church if possible, or if that can't be done, then to at least box in the Gospel and prevent its worldwide spread (2Cor. 4:3–4). For years this has been the devil's battle plan. History makes sense if we understand that.

The Devil Loses the Battle of the Great Commission (Rev. 12:9–12)

Ultimately, we see in verses 9–12 that his struggle to prevent the spread of the Gospel fails. By verse 9 God has a people from every tribe and tongue and people. Satan no longer has a leg to stand on. There no longer exists a people group over which he can have a stranglehold (Luke 10:17–20). He loses his grip and is thrown to the earth together with his angels. Heaven rejoices at the sight of the devil gone.

Heaven cries out, "Now the salvation, and the power, and the kingdom of our God and the authority of His Christ have come, for the accuser of our brethren has been thrown down, he who accuses them before our God day and night" (Rev. 12:10). This victory was won in large measure by the victory of Christ through the cross and his resurrection.

Even so, the full consequences of this certain victory will not be fully manifested in the heavens until the Church, by God's grace, does its part in completing the Great Commission. The next verse tells us how the Church will do it. It says "they overcame him (Satan) because of the blood of the Lamb *and* the word of *their testimony,* and *they did not love their life even when faced with death"* (Rev. 12:11).

Many have assumed this is a statement of how believers in Christ will overcome the Beast during the Great Tribulation. Certainly, they will undoubtedly overcome him in this way during that time. In Revelation 15:2 we see in heaven "those who had been victorious *over the beast* and his image and the number of his name." How did they get to heaven? They were obviously martyred, since this is what happens to those who refuse the mark, and so "they did not love their life even when faced with death" (Rev. 12:11b).

Yet, that is not the context of the verse in Revelation 12:11. For it is only *after* the Church overcomes in the way described in verse 11 that the devil is thrown to the earth (Rev. 12:9,12). And it is *after* he is tossed out of the heavens to the earth that Satan makes all-out war on the Church (Rev. 12:17b). It is only then that the Great Tribulation begins.

Thus, this declaration of overcoming is a direct reference to *the way* the Church will ultimately triumph in being disciples and completing the Great Commission. It's *the way* they will live lives that defeat the enemy of their soul. All throughout the history of the Church, pioneering breakthroughs among unreached people groups have happened time and again because of the labors and prayers of saints willing to go to "risky" areas to proclaim the gospel of Jesus Christ. History is filled with stories of those who not only took the risk, but also willingly paid with their lives.

As one Chinese church leader stated about the task facing the Church as it labors to complete the Great Commission, "Satan will not surrender without a bloody fight! But when the devil fights against God's children he is fighting against God himself, and our Lord's weakness is much stronger than the devil's strength. Nevertheless, we expect much blood will be spilled."[139]

Who will be the courageous saints of our generation to take the baton from those who have gone before them? Who will take that final lap around the track? Will our generation be the one to run the race and go to the remaining unreached peoples of the world? They are almost entirely found in places where there is at least a theoretical risk of persecution and, yes, possibly death. Who will be the ones who will "not love their life even when faced with death" and go?[140]

In the final analysis, there will be sufficient numbers from a generation who will rise to the task. Why not let it be ours?

So we see here yet another aspect of what will result when a
people is won from every tribe and tongue and people and nation.
A loud voice in heaven says, ". . . Rejoice, O heavens and you who
dwell in them. Woe to the earth and the sea, because the devil has
come down to you, having great wrath, knowing that he has only a
short time" (Rev. 12:12).

The Devil Attacks Israel Following the Great Completion

The temporary result of the Great Commission's completion
on the earth's inhabitants will not be pleasant. The devil will come
down to earth with great wrath. He plans to keep fighting. After being
thrown down he "persecuted the woman who gave birth to the male
child" (Rev. 12:13). The woman is clearly a reference to Israel.

Satan will know that he can no longer prevent God from having
a people from every tribe and tongue and people and nation. This
will have already happened by then. But he also knows Messiah
will return to the Mount of Olives and establish Jerusalem as the
center of his earthly kingdom during the millennium.[141] Jesus will
also completely spiritually revive the nation of Israel.[142] Desperate to
prevent this from happening, the devil decides the time has come to
completely establish his own kingdom on earth. After all, he has no
other place to go. And he has no time left to move. His time is short.
He must move now.

The devil will attempt to attack Israel and wipe it out so as to
prevent the word of God from being fulfilled. Satan's goal of eliminating Israel is shared by many Muslims. What do Muslims think
about a solution to the Israeli-Palestinian problem? Solid majorities
throughout the Muslim world "doubt that a way can be found for the
state of Israel to exist so that the rights and needs of the Palestinian
people are met."[143] Eighty percent of Palestinians held this view, 85
% of Jordanians and 90% of Moroccans shared this opinion. Only
in western nations, least connected with and most ignorant of the

problem, did a majority of the populations believe a lasting peace could be found.[144]

Whatever reasons Muslims may give, the devil probably hopes to destroy Israel before she can be spiritually revived. Thus, Jerusalem is attacked at the beginning of the Great Tribulation. At this same time, the Beast will be clearly manifested as the abomination that causes desolation. He is found standing in the holy place of the Temple Mount (Matt. 24:15). Yet, he will be unsuccessful in his attack on Israel, for the woman will once again find a refuge in the wilderness. It will be a place where God will protect her (Rev. 12:13–16).

However, "the two wings of the great eagle were given to the woman, so that she could fly into the wilderness to her place, where she was nourished for a time and times and half a time, from the presence of the serpent" (Rev. 12:14). The time, and times and half a time are quite likely a reference to exactly three and one half years. Many theologians believe a "time" is likely to be equivalent to a year and "times" to two years. Interestingly 3 1/2 years is also 42 months or 1260 days according to the Jewish calendar of 360 days. That is the same amount of time that the Beast will reign over the earth (Rev. 13:5).

This persecution and attempt to get the woman Israel is frustrated because the two wings of the great eagle are given to the woman (Rev. 12:14). It may be that this is a reference to airplanes airlifting Jews to a place of refuge. As the Beast attempts to wipe out the Jews, one place remains out of his grasp. This place is likely to be in the wilderness of the state of Israel. He has by now taken control of all governmental authority in the world. He will certainly go after Jews wherever he finds them. Probably aware their fate is tied up in the survival of Israel, most Jews will make their way to the hills of Judea. The Beast will not attempt to use nuclear weapons on Israel; however, for he himself wants to rule from Israel and perhaps he fears a nuclear counterattack. Likewise Israel would only use them as a final resort due to the danger of radioactive fallout. They will likely prove unnecessary.

Zechariah saw this day when Jerusalem would be attacked, but the attack stymied. "I will gather all the nations (who are now under the authority of the Beast) against Jerusalem to battle, and the city will be captured, the houses plundered, the women ravished and *half of the city exiled, but the rest of the people will not be cut off* from the city. Then the Lord will go forth and fight against those nations, as when He fights on a day of battle" (Zech. 14:2–3).

The Temple Mount Overrun: The initial sign of Christ's soon return

Notice we get an additional detail here. When the trampling of the holy city mentioned in Revelation 11:2 happens, Zechariah informs us it will actually involve only half of the city. Palestinians and their allies will probably already possess the Palestinian dominated half of the city, now under the Palestinian Authority's administrative control and populated by Palestinians. Thus, it is the Jewish half that will now be overrun. The Jews will have to flee to the mountains and be exiled from their half of Jerusalem (Matt. 24:15–17).

The Temple Mount will be lost and the abomination that causes desolation will be found standing there. Something disastrous will happen to the Western Wall that we will talk about later. This "abomination that causes desolation" is the sign that Jesus gave to believing Jews and Christians in a future day to abandon Jerusalem and the Judean cities and head for the hills. For Jesus said, ". . . when you see the abomination of desolation which was spoken of through Daniel the prophet, standing in the holy place (let the reader understand), then those who are in Judea must flee to the mountains" (Matt. 24:15–16). Indeed *this* will be the sign for all of us that the Messiah's return is near.

On the Temple Mount the Beast will declare his supremacy over Judaism and Christianity and all other religions. As Paul stated, He "opposes and exalts himself above every so-called god or object or worship, so that he takes his seat in the temple of God, displaying himself as being God" (2Thess. 2:3–4). It is there that the official beginning of his world rule commences. Could it be that Islam plays a central role in this? It is no secret that the Palestinians want to have Jerusalem as their capital. It is well known that Jerusalem is a holy city to Muslims. It is also acceptable practice in Islam to "ravish" women during war as Zechariah says they will be (Zech. 14:2).[145]

There is also no question that the goal of Islam is to make itself the supreme and indeed the only religion in the world.

The devil tries to "pour water like a river out of his mouth after the woman so that she might be swept away by the flood" (Rev. 12:15). As the last pocket of remaining state led resistance to his rule, he desires to overwhelm the little country of Israel. He will try with an overwhelming flood of forces, but he will fail, for God himself will come to Israel's aid. Satan's efforts will falter, for the earth will swallow up his flood of fighters. The literal earth swallowing the flood probably means the Jews first gather in the mountains of Israel. Then God will unleash powerful geological forces to defend them from their enemies. Perhaps this may involve an earthquake with a massive upthrust of earth (Zech. 14:4–5, Rev. 12:16). Perhaps it will involve mountains literally collapsing on enemy armies. God split the Red Sea once before, now it seems it will be the earth itself.

Satan Attacks the Church (Rev. 12:17)

Stymied in his efforts to wipe out Israel, Satan will now adjust his strategy. "The dragon was enraged with the woman, and went off to make war with the rest of her children, who keep the commandments of God and hold to the testimony of Jesus" (Rev. 12:17). Who does the dragon go to make war with? It is with those who "hold to the testimony of Jesus." These are none other than the saints, the people of God, the Church of the Lord Jesus Christ. In other words, Satan embarks on all out warfare against all followers of Jesus Christ in a desperate attempt to clear the earth of them. In his desperation he probably hopes to somehow prevent God's kingdom from being fully manifested on earth. Perhaps, he reasons, if he can at least wipe them off the planet, then only heaven will get to have them. Maybe he can hurt them in the process and somehow force a few back to his side, if that were possible (Matt. 24:24).

How does Satan carry out this diabolical program? What will his program to destroy all Christians involve?

Chapter 8

The First Six Heads of the Beast Kingdom (Rev. 13:1–4, 17:3–17)

Johnn sees the Beast "coming up out of the sea" (Rev. 13:1) to implement the dragon's program to exterminate Christians. The sea is probably representative of masses of people.[146] This initial description of the Beast is actually a description of the kingdom of the Beast, not the individual who is also called the Beast. The Beast of Revelation is *both* a kingdom and an individual who heads that kingdom. Thus, we see here that this kingdom is a movement of masses of people. It is a reconstituted kingdom having ten horns and seven heads. On the horns are ten diadems and each head has a blasphemous name on it (Rev. 13:1).

Revelation 17 gives us a greater description of the kingdom of the Beast. It is here these ten horns are described as "ten kings who have not yet received a kingdom, but they receive authority as kings with the beast . . . they have one purpose, and they give their power and authority to the beast" (Rev. 17:12a, 13). Even as the Roman Empire had ten evil emperors who persecuted the Church,[147] this final anti-Christian kingdom will likely have ten regional rulers under the authority of the Beast (i.e. the anti-Christ). Each will be executing his plan and his wishes. This ". . . scarlet beast, full of blasphemous names, having seven heads and ten horns" (Rev. 17:3a) is declared to be a mystery. The whore of Babylon is also a mystery. The angel promises John in verse 7 he will explain these mysteries. He begins with the scarlet beast first.

Who are the Seven Heads of the Beast?

> The beast that you saw was, and is not, and is about to come up out of the abyss and go to destruction. And those who dwell on the earth, whose name has not been written in the book of life from the foundation of the world, will wonder when they see the beast, that he was and is not and will come. Here is the mind which has wisdom. The seven heads are seven mountains on which the woman sits, and they are seven kings; five have fallen, one is, the other has not yet come; and when he comes, he must remain a little while. The beast which was and is not, is himself also an eighth and is one of the seven, and he goes to destruction. (Rev. 17:8–11)

Who then are these seven heads? Specifically, we find out here these "seven heads are seven mountains on which the woman sits, and they are seven kings . . ." Thus, the seven heads represent seven kingdoms led by kings. "Five have fallen, one is, the other has not yet come; and when he comes, he must remain a little while." These heads have blasphemous names, all found on the dragon as well (Rev. 13:1). The blasphemous names likely indicate that these kingdoms spearhead Satan's demonic assault on God's kingdom. They are probably connected with alternate worldwide deities the devil set up in these kingdoms with the intent of replacing God. Through these false deities he received worship to himself and took it away from God. False deities would certainly be blasphemous. Those deities were intertwined with these seven kingdoms as each kingdom's head deity. Five had already fallen by the time John saw this vision. This leads us to the obvious question. Who were those five kingdoms with their false deities?

In order to answer that question, we must ask ourselves, who is most likely to receive the frontal assault of Satan's attacks? Where would the devil be most likely to concentrate his efforts at defeating God's purposes? Prior to the Church, it is reasonable to assume that Israel would bear the brunt of Satan's attacks. That being the case, can we think of five kingdoms that tried to destroy Israel and that also attempted to set up a false deity to reign supreme over all other gods? Given their involvement with Israel, we could also reasonably expect each of these five kingdoms to be found in the pages of the Scriptures. The fact is, we can find a clear historical trail of exactly five kingdoms with all these key characteristics:

- world dominance
- dominance of and hostility toward Israel
- a false deity as their head of government.

Which five kingdoms had all of these characteristics?

First Kingdom: Egypt

The first kingdom was the Diospolite Dynasty kingdom of Egypt. It was during this dynasty that Satan used Pharaoh to try to extinguish the seed of the Messiah by having all the baby boys killed (Ex. 1:7–22). Also, from about the middle of the eighteenth dynasty and after, Pharaoh's subjects worshipped him as divine.[148] The year this happened was about 1450 B.C.[149] Bible scholars are in some disagreement as to the timing of The Exodus. Some say it happened about 1445–1440 B.C., others say it occurred around 1400 B.C. and still others say it happened about 1290 B.C.[150]

Whichever date is true we can be assured that the divinity and worship of Pharaoh was an established practice in Egypt during all of those time periods as well as *prior* to them. Thus, it's not hard to see why Pharaoh, considering himself supremely divine, did not want to submit to the Lord. When Moses demanded Pharaoh let the Jews go, Pharaoh disdainfully replied, "Who is the Lord that I should obey his voice . . . ?" (Ex. 5:2a).

Second Kingdom: Assyria

The second kingdom was likely the Assyrian Empire. It dispersed the northern kingdom of Israel and its ten tribes. Then it threatened to destroy Jerusalem itself. Sennacherib, ruler of Assyria, also boasted of no god being able to rescue Judah, since he himself was greater than all other gods including the God of Israel (2Chron. 32:10–15).

Third Kingdom: Babylon

We know who the next three fallen kingdoms will be, as well as the sixth kingdom that "is," from detailed prophetic descriptions in Daniel 2, 7 and 8. The third kingdom, (the first in Daniel's visions and interpretation of dreams) was identified as Babylon by Daniel when he interpreted Nebuchadnezzar's dream in Daniel 2:36–38. Babylon ransacked Judah and Jerusalem, destroying the first temple. Furthermore, Nebuchadnezzar was puffed up in pride and exalted himself above God. He also attempted to receive worship unto himself by setting up a golden statue of himself requiring worship from all people on pain of death (Dan. 3:4–7). Thus, the third kingdom was the Babylonian Empire.

Fourth Kingdom: Medes and Persians

Daniel identified another kingdom coming. He stated this one would come and take the place of Nebuchadnezzar's Babylonian kingdom (Dan. 2:39). We know from history that the next kingdom to arise and overthrow Babylon was the kingdom of the Medes and Persians. Thus, the Medes and Persians represent the fourth head of Revelation. It was the Persian king Darius who was tricked into signing a decree that for thirty days the only god anyone could pray to would be him. Thus, Darius was also considered a god, and at least for thirty days, was supposed to be *the supreme* God (Dan. 6:6–15). We also learn in the book of Esther, that it was under the Persian king Artaxerxes that the evil Haman attempted to have all the Jews annihilated (Esther 3:13).

Fifth Kingdom: Greece

Then Daniel saw another kingdom replacing this kingdom. It would be particularly large in its size (Dan. 2:39b). History informs us the fifth kingdom to come along was the Greek kingdom established by Alexander the Great. Just as Daniel saw, it proved to be larger than all the previous kingdoms. Alexander also eventually considered himself to be divine and ordered his subjects to worship him.[151]

After his death his kingdom fractured into four parts, just as Daniel foretold (see Dan. 8:21–22). From within the Greek Empire sprang up the Seleucid Dynasty, a huge remnant of the Greek kingdom. It retained the Hellenistic flavor and vision of Alexander's kingdom. This dynasty eventually spawned Antiochus IV who attacked Jerusalem and desecrated the temple in 169 and 167 B.C.[152] Ultimately, he had a coin printed with the words *Theos epiphanes*, which means *god manifest*.[153] Thus, he also considered himself to be god. We have now identified the first five kingdoms.

Sixth kingdom: Rome

The sixth kingdom, the Roman Empire, came along and replaced the Greek offshoot kingdom of the Seleucid Dynasty. This kingdom was in power when John received his revelation. It was thus, the "one is" kingdom. Perhaps this is why John sees the current manifestation of the seven-headed beast as having "seven mountains on which the woman sits." Rome is famously known as the city of seven hills. However, the seven continents of the world, in one sense, are also essentially seven gigantic mountains. Thus, the woman sitting on these seven mountains may simply symbolize world domination. Perhaps both truths were represented in John's vision.

Just like the previous kingdoms, the Romans also instituted worship of the emperor as a god. In all, ten Roman emperors carried out active persecution of the Church. When Daniel saw ten horns on the fourth beast, it was these emperors he saw (Dan. 7:24b). During the Roman Empire, violent persecution of the Church was not continuous, but irregular. During persecutions, officials often insisted Christians demonstrate loyalty by worshipping the emperor. Ten periods of intense persecution of the Church came due to policies and encouragement from the ten evil emperors that Daniel saw. Those emperors are listed in the chart on the next page:

THE TEN PERSECUTING ROMAN EMPERORS

Roman Emperor:	Time of Reign:
Nero	54-68 AD
Domitian	81-96 AD
Trajan	98 – 117 AD
Marcus Aurelius	161 – 180 AD
Septimus Severus	193 – 211 AD
Decius	249 – 251 AD
Valerian	253 – 260 AD
Gallienus	260 – 268 AD
Diocletian	284 – 305 AD
Galerius	305 – 311 AD

154

By A.D. 395 the empire administratively split once again into two halves, with one half ruled out of Constantinople from which sprung up the Byzantine Empire. The other half of the empire was ruled out of Rome. In A.D. 380, less than seventy years after Constantine issued his edict of tolerance bringing the persecutions to an end, the Empire adopted Christianity as the state religion.

After A.D. 476, with the sacking of Rome by the Barbarians, the authority and organization of the Church in governmental affairs increasingly filled the vacuum left by the government. By the late 500s the dividing line between church and state was blurring in the remnants of the Roman Empire. This union eventually evolved into a government of Papal States by the late 700s. Thus, some of the remnants of the Roman Empire gradually became intertwined with the Church of Rome. One could possibly say the Roman Empire has never entirely disappeared. The Vatican continues to exist to this day as an independent state. It has been greatly weakened, but it still exerts influence over Roman Catholics, and to an ever-lessening extent, some governments. It even temporarily regained control of Jerusalem, lost in A.D. 683 to the Muslims, during the crusades.

Nevertheless, the Roman church has had a number of fine followers of Jesus who have genuinely believed and spread the Gospel. Even so, by the late Middle Ages the policies and doctrines of the Church government of Rome often clashed with the Word of God. It increasingly began to present "another gospel," a "gospel" of good works to earn salvation.

Additionally, in the late Middle Ages, attempts at writing the Bible in the tongue of the lay person were violently resisted. Still, thanks to the Church of Rome, much of the West was saved from becoming Muslim. The doctrine of the divinity of Christ, and many ancient Bibles themselves were preserved in monasteries throughout Europe. Even so, it is hard to ignore the bloody opposition of the Church of Rome against attempts to reform it and return it to a more Biblical theology. Was the Roman head, the sixth head of the Beast eventually transferred to the Papal States, of which the Vatican remains? It is hard to say definitively. In any case, the Roman head will not play the central role in the Beast of Revelation 17, as we shall see.

This brings us to the seventh kingdom. John said, ". . . when he comes, he must remain a little while" (Rev. 17:10). We often think of "a little while" as a short period of time. But maybe this phrase has different significance from heaven's perspective. If "a day is as a thousand years and a thousand years is as a day" to the Lord, then none of the first six kingdoms, except perhaps Rome, lasted even a day in his sight. Perhaps it is possible "a little while" may actually signify a time frame *longer* than normal by our standards. Perhaps this seventh kingdom actually lasts longer than the other beasts of Revelation. So, what was this seventh kingdom?

Barely more than 100 years after the sacking of Rome, a new empire began to spring up. It exerted its influence throughout the Middle East and eventually North Africa, Western and Central Asia and even parts of Southern Europe. It began inconspicuously enough.

Chapter 9

Muhammad, Islam & The Seventh & Eighth Kingdoms (Rev. 13:1–4, 17:3–17)

Born around a.d. 570, a few months after his father's death, Muhammad became an orphan at the age of six when his mother died. His grandfather took responsibility for him. When his grandfather died a few years later, his uncle raised him. His uncle was a caravan merchant named Abu-Talib, from whom Muhammad learned the business of buying, selling and transporting goods. They were from the Hashimite clan of the Quraysh tribe, a relatively poor branch of a ruling tribe of Arabs.

Muhammad was an honest and dependable merchant. He eventually won the heart of a wealthy merchant widow named Khadijah. She was forty when they married and he was only about twenty-six. Yet, she bore him six children. He married no other woman during her lifetime. Their marriage was said to have been strong. He was unusual in his culture, as most wealthy men took more than one wife. He didn't do this until after Khadijah's death when he was fifty years old.

Most Arabs believed in a polytheistic animism. Still, there were also Christians, Jews and Hanifs (monotheistic Arabs) in their community. Freed up with his instant wealth, Muhammad began to withdraw to caves for extended times of meditation. It was here on one night that he received his first revelation.

The most accepted Muslim account relates the following:

> When it was the night on which God honoured him with this mission and showed mercy on His servants thereby, Gabriel brought him the command of God. 'He came to me,' said the Apostle of God, 'while I was asleep, with a coverlet of brocade whereon was some writing, and said, 'Read!' I said, 'What shall I read?'—And *this I said only to deliver myself from him*, lest he should do the same to me again. He said: 'Read in the name of thy Lord who created, who created man of blood coagulated. Read! Thy Lord is the most beneficient, Who taught by the pen, Taught that which they knew not unto men' (96:1–5). So I read it, and he departed from me. And I awoke from my sleep, and it was as though these words were written on my heart.[155]

The Doubtful Prophet

Muhammad was in some doubt himself as to the origin of this statement. He was actually afraid that he had been possessed by a jinn (demon). When he related this to his wife, Khadija, she reassured him that Allah would not harm him and that he was not possessed. After this first encounter, he went three years before a further revelation. His wife tried to comfort him and repeatedly reassured him that he would become the prophet of the Arab nation. Tortured by uncertainty and confusion he retreated again to a cave. During this time he became despondent and suicidal.

He doubted he had heard a message from God and finally decided to throw himself off a cliff and kill himself. According to some accounts, he was on his way to die when Gabriel suddenly appeared on the horizon and assured him that he was indeed the Apostle of Allah (the Muslim name for God). The Koran may allude to this when it says, "No, your compatriot (Muhammad) is not mad. He saw him (Gabriel) on the clear horizon. He does not grudge the secrets of the unseen; nor is this (the Koran) the utterance of an accursed devil" (Surah 81:22–26).

His wives believed that he was a prophet of Allah, in part, because he would often enter into epileptic frenzies while receiving a revelation. Unlike any of the prophets of Israel, Muhammad went through a prolonged period where he thought that he might be going mad or possessed by a demon. Such things never occurred to any of the Hebrew prophets. They never expressed uncertainty as to who was speaking to them.

Early Rejection

Things were difficult at first, with only a few believing his messages and his prophetic calling. After his wife, Khadijah, died and his uncle as well, Muhammad lost his two most important supporters. Times got tougher. As Muhammad denounced the polytheism of his fellow Arabs he was persecuted and ridiculed as a crazy madman or demon possessed. Eventually they tried to have him killed. He eluded capture and went to Medina with his small band of followers. There he found a community with a large number of Jews and a greater acceptance of monotheism. His band of followers gradually grew and he increasingly united the Arab tribes in the area. However, the Jews noticed contradictions between the Koran and the Torah and quickly rejected him as a prophet. This greatly offended him.

Having lost his ability to make a living when he fled Mecca, Muhammad began raiding other tribes that wouldn't submit to Islam. He took the spoils and divided them among the faithful. Not all Muslims wanted to join this warrior-prophet on his forays. It was not long before the Koran was adding incentives to the fighting faithful and ridicule for those who didn't fight.

Eventual Success for a New Empire

The tide began to turn for Muhammad as he began to have success in uniting warring clans under his leadership. In A.D. 630, Muhammad invaded Mecca and succeeded in taking it with hardly a fight. His chief antagonist converted as he entered the city. This helped insure a swift and peaceful takeover. By the time he died in A.D. 632, the prophet had succeeded in virtually uniting the Arabian Peninsula under his rule.

This rapidly spreading empire moved across North Africa and also began to move north, conquering Jerusalem in the early 680s. This new Empire was virulently anti-Christian (whether Catholic, Eastern Orthodox, or otherwise) anti-Jewish and anti-pagan in its thrust. It was devoted to spreading the religion of Allah. In A.D. 685, the Muslim ruler, Abd el Malik had the Temple Mount cleared down to the foundation rock to prepare it for construction. It was there that the Dome of the Rock was constructed over the sight of the temple. Its purpose was to show the supremacy of Islam over Judaism and Christianity. As Albert Hourani, noted Arab historian stated,

> The building of the Dome in this place has been convincingly in-
> terpreted as a symbolic act placing Islam in the lineage of Abraham
> and dissociating it from Judaism and Christianity. The inscriptions
> around the interior, the earliest known physical embodiment of
> texts from the Koran, proclaim the greatness of God, 'the Mighty,
> the Wise,' declare that 'God and His angels bless the Prophet,' and
> call upon Christians to recognize Jesus as an apostle of God, His
> word and spirit, but not His son![156]

The seventh kingdom that John saw coming in the future had arrived.

Except for trading Jerusalem with the remnants of the Roman Empire during The Crusades, one form or another of the Islamic Empire ruled Jerusalem until the British took control around 1917. The Islamic Empire actively worked to oppress and oppose the Jews

The 7 Heads of the Beast	
Kingdom:	**Year:**
Egypt (Diospolite Dynasty)	1567 – 10thCentury BC
Assyrian Empire (Old Babylonian Empire)	1100 – 625 BC
Babylonian Empire	625 – 536 BC
Medes – Persian Empire	536 – 330 BC
Greek Empire • **Seleucid Dynasty**	330 – 164 BC
Roman Empire • **The Eastern Roman Empire / known as the Byzantine Empire (capital Constantinople).** • **Western Roman Empire, direct affiliation w/ Roman Catholicism**	63 BC – 476 AD 476 – 1452 380 AD – Today?
Islamic Empire	630 - 1922

and Christianity; strictly forbidding any proselytizing of Muslims on pain of death, and threatening Muslims who converted with the same. It also placed extra taxes on all whom refused to convert to Islam. Many restrictions were placed on Christians:

- Christians had no right to build new places of worship.
- Christians had no right to remodel a church.
- Muslims could confiscate churches in towns taken by storm.
- Muslims had the inherent right to destroy any church, as they saw fit, in a conquered land.[157]

The Islamic Empire ended much how it began, with a bloody onslaught of Christians. It was during World War I, under the waning remnants of the Islamic Empire that the Armenian genocide happened. Possibly as many as two million Christian Armenians residing in the Ottoman Empire were slaughtered by the Ottoman authorities. Tens of thousands of these Armenians were evangelical believers in Jesus. As one group of believers was being taken off to death they were heard singing,

"We are going to be with Jesus. We do not fear death. Let them kill us. We are going to be with Jesus."

"They take away our clothes and leave us naked. They beat us so much, we cannot sleep at night. We had to sleep in a dark room, but we praise the Lord. They cut off our heads with an axe. We are going to be with Jesus."[158]

Zionism and Adolph Hitler

There was a new movement loose in Palestine by this time, known as Zionism. It was an attempt to find the Jews a permanent homeland, preferably the ancient home of their fathers in what was then called Palestine. Even before the final defeat of the Ottoman Empire at the end of World War I, the "Christian" Empire of Great Britain promised a permanent Jewish homeland to the Jews in Palestine with the Balfour Declaration in 1917. After World War I, Great Britain officially assumed control of Palestine and Jerusalem and ultimately helped create conditions that eventually led to the existence of the state of

Israel. Jerusalem had finally fallen into hands somewhat favorable to the Jews, but the dream of a nation for Jews would not be realized until after a time of great trouble which Jeremiah the prophet may have referred to as "the time of Jacob's distress" (Jer. 30:7).

The Jews had to endure the rise of the Third Reich of Adolph Hitler's Germany. It is no secret that Hitler was against not only the Jews, but also the confessing church. He had a law passed declaring that all crosses on German churches must be replaced with swastikas.[159] The devil decided to try again to wipe out Israel and neutralize the Church, thereby nullifying God's promises to Abraham, Isaac and Jacob.

It is possible Jeremiah saw these days when he prophesied that

. . . The Lord spoke concerning Israel and concerning Judah: 'For thus says the Lord, 'I have heard a sound of terror, of dread, and there is no peace. Ask now, and see if a male can give birth. Why do I see every man with his hands on his loins, as a woman in childbirth? And why have all faces turned pale? Alas! For that day is great, there is none like it; and it is the time of Jacob's distress, but he will be saved from it. It shall come about on that day,' declares the Lord of Hosts, 'that I will break his yoke from off their neck and will tear off their bonds; and strangers will no longer make them their slaves' (Jer. 30:4–8).

Jeremiah goes on to declare that Israel will go on to serve the Lord in peace. The latter half of that prophecy will not be fulfilled until the return of Christ. Nevertheless, the first part of this prophecy seems to match a description of the horror of Jewish men, trying to cover their nakedness while being led off to the showers of concentration slave camps and nearly certain death. Fortunately, Adolph Hitler was defeated before he could eliminate the Jews and, in May 1948, Israel became a nation. As Jeremiah stated, the Jews were once and for all delivered from their slavery to other nations (Jer. 30:8).

With the conquest of Hitler and the creation of the state of Israel, and none of the kingdoms of Revelation 17 (except perhaps a weakened Rome) remaining, we may have very well entered a prophetic transition period. It has been since the end of World War II that the spread of the Gospel in the earth has been nothing short of astronomic. As stated before, there have been remarkable breakthroughs for the Gospel in Latin America, as well as parts of China, South Korea and elsewhere.

Since 1960, the number of born-again Christians in the world has quadrupled. In 1960, nearly two-thirds of all believers were found in the Western world. Today the figures have flip-flopped. While the evangelical church in the West has doubled since 1960, more than two-thirds of all believers are now found in the non-Western world.[160] It seems the Church is getting within striking distance of the Great Completion of the Great Commission. With the collapse of Communism, most virulent opponents to the Gospel were seemingly disarmed. Yet, Satan is not ready to give up. He has saved his last effort to be his greatest.

What is the Identity of the Eighth Kingdom, the Kingdom of the Final Beast?

One thing John is told is that the Beast he is looking at is a beast that "was, and is not, and is about to come up out of the abyss . . . ." More specifically, John is told "the beast which was and is not, is himself also an eighth and is one of the seven . . ." (Rev. 17:11). Here we learn a most interesting thing. This last and final beast is actually a distinct eighth beast. Yet, it originates from one of the previous seven. John also finds out that "he was and *is not* and will come" (Rev. 17:8b).

Thus, we can know with certainty the Beast actually has roots in a beast or beasts that came *before* the Roman Empire. How is that so? And can we know which of the seven it will originate from? The Roman Empire was current with John, but John tells us the future Beast "was and *is not.*" Therefore, since it "is not," it cannot originate from the Roman Empire that was current with John.

Additionally, the "*will come*" John mentions *may* indicate that he will also originate from the last and seventh kingdom, that came *after* the Roman Empire. The Beast that "will come," the seventh beast itself has roots in the former beasts since it "was, and is not." Notice that its deepest roots are found in all beasts *except* Rome.[161] Again since the eighth beast "is not," it cannot be founded on the beast that was current with John. The fact that he "was" *and* "he is about to come up out of the abyss" once again seems to link him to the beast that comes *after* the contemporary Roman beast of John's time.

Fortunately, John sees the beast that has seven heads and ten horns. He can thus give us a detailed description that helps us more clearly identify this future beast. Specifically, he says "the beast which I saw was like a *leopard*, and his feet were like those of a *bear*, and his mouth like the mouth of a *lion*" (Rev. 13:2a). Here we see that the beast partly resembles three of the four beasts that Daniel saw. In fact, it greatly resembles parts of the three beasts (kingdoms), immediately *preceding* the Roman Empire. Just like John said, it "was." For further clarification on the makeup of this beast, let's look at Daniel. Daniel also gave us a prophetic glimpse of the Beast's kingdom. As we go through each of these ancient kingdoms, observe what each of them have in common today.

Mouth of a Lion

In Daniel chapter 7 we get a detailed description of these three kingdoms.[162] The first beast is also described as being a lion (Dan. 7:4).[163] This beast is Babylon. It had its power base in what is modern day Iraq and included a sliver of southern Turkey, Syria, Israel, Lebanon, Jordan, Kuwait, the Palestinian Authority and a portion of eastern Egypt and northern Saudi Arabia. The Beast of Revelation has "the mouth of a lion." Today Islam dominates all of ancient Babylon, except for Israel. The heart of this ancient kingdom was in modern-day Iraq. Perhaps the lion's mouth of the Beast indicates the head and/or mouthpiece of the Beast's kingdom. Is it possible this shows the Beast himself originating from this area? At the least, this region (see map of the Babylonian Empire on the next page), or a leader from it, will have a leading role in this kingdom.

Feet of a Bear

The second beast Daniel saw was "resembling a bear" (Dan. 7:5). This kingdom is identified as being the kingdom of the Medes and Persians. It had three capitals: Ectabana (summer capital), Susa

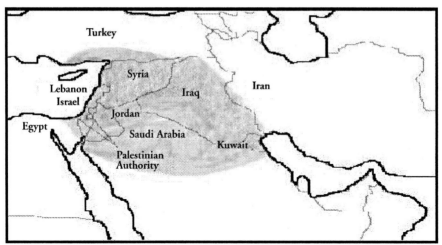

Babylonian Empire

(winter capital), and Persepolis (ceremonial capital). All three of
these centers of power are located in modern day Iran.

Its power stretched across Western and Central Asia to the Indus
River through the modern day countries of Azerbaijan, Turkmenistan, Uzbekistan, Kyrgyzstan, Tajikistan, Afghanistan, Pakistan and
portions of western China and northwestern India. In the west it
included much of modern day Turkey, most of Syria. In the south it
stretched through Lebanon, western Jordan, Kuwait, the Palestinian
Authority, Israel, Egypt, and eastern Libya. Islam dominates all these
regions except Armenia and Israel. Even the slivers of non-Muslim
eastern Greece and southern Georgia contain significant Muslim
minorities.

John sees the beast of Revelation as having "the feet of a bear"
(Rev. 13:2). Could it be feet represent the foundation of the Beast's
kingdom or perhaps the active enforcer of the policies of the Beast?
The heart of this kingdom was located in what is today Iran. Perhaps
in the early stages of the development of the Beast's kingdom this
area will form its base. It was in Iran in 1979 the first modern Revolutionary Islamic State was born with a vision to export revolution
elsewhere. On the other hand, the feet may simply speak of a willingness to trample over all adversaries of the Beast's kingdom. That
is essentially the role of the false prophet who will force everyone

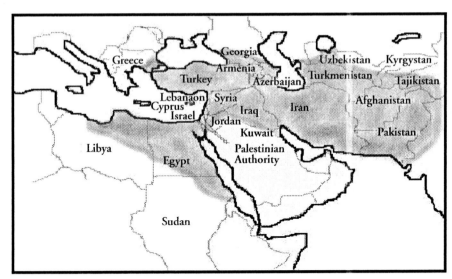

Medo-Persian Empire

to worship the Beast. Could it be the false prophet will spring from this region?

The Body of a Leopard

The third beast that Daniel saw was "like a leopard" (Dan. 7:6). This has been unanimously identified as the Greek Empire of Alexander the Great. The Beast of Revelation is "like a leopard" (Rev. 13:2). Since the leopard is not given a body part, it can be assumed the Beast's entire body (apart from heads and feet) resembles a leopard. The Greek Empire of Alexander was extremely large. It stretched the farthest from east to west of the three ancient empires. Perhaps its long reach symbolizes its ability to encompass all populations of the Islamic world. This will be its wide base of support. These will be the foot soldiers.

The Greek Empire began in what are today northern Greece and southern Macedonia. It spread to include large sections of the Balkans where historically most of Europe's Muslim population has lived. It continued its movement east and then south to engulf most of Turkey, all of Cyprus, most of Syria, Lebanon, Israel, the Palestinian Authority and a piece of Jordan, as well as large portions of Egypt, and Libya.

Alexander also continued his march east and engulfed Iraq, Iran, and most of Central Asia, and northeastern India. Also his forces probably moved deeper into Western China than the Medes and Persians did. Muslim minority groups dominate western China. Once again, today Islam dominates all these regions, except for Israel, Armenia and half of Cyprus (although the northern half of Cyprus is Muslim). Today, the only majority Muslim state in India, Kashmir, was at one time under the control of Alexander's Greek Empire.

Daniel also identified this beast as sprouting "four heads" that prophetically spoke of its splintering at Alexander's death into four parts (Dan. 7:6, 8:21–22). The part that ruled Israel was the Seleucid Kingdom. It maintained the Hellenistic culture and vision of Alexander's Empire. The Seleucids ruled most of Turkey, Syria and

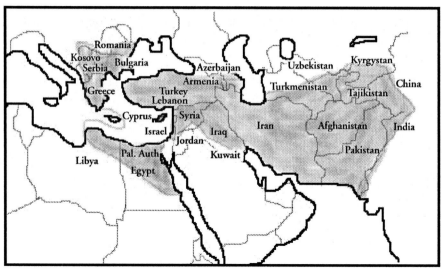

Alexander's Greek Empire

Egypt, as well as what is today Lebanon, Jordan and Israel. Again, except for Israel, they are all Islamic nations today.

Think about what the descendants of all those ancient empires have in common today. If the Beast of Revelation arises in our lifetime, then nearly its entire body and the very heart and soul of his kingdom is actually made up of nations dominated by Islam. But before we get ahead of ourselves, let's continue with Daniel's helpful vision.

After those three beasts, Daniel saw a most dreadful fourth beast. It was extremely strong. It had iron teeth and was going fourth and devouring the previous three beasts. This beast was, of course, prophetic of the Roman Empire. It ruled in John's day, and it was identified as having ten horns. As mentioned earlier, these horns identify the ten Roman Emperors (Dan. 7:24a) who actively persecuted the Church.

Daniel's fourth beast is the sixth head of the Beast of Revelation. It was during the reign of this fourth beast "the God of heaven will set up a kingdom which will never be destroyed . . ." (Dan. 2:44a). That kingdom would ultimately "crush and put an end to all these kingdoms, but it itself will endure" (Dan. 2:44b). This, of course, identifies Jesus establishing his Church.

All of the kingdoms, not just the Roman one, will ultimately be crushed by God's kingdom. However, it is what happened after those ten horns appeared that concerns us now.

Chapter 10

The Beast's Islamic Empire (Rev. 13:1–4, 17:3–17)

D aniel says, "while I was contemplating the horns, behold, another horn, a little one, came up among them, and three of the first horns were pulled out by the roots before it; and behold, this horn possessed eyes like the eyes of a man and a mouth uttering great boasts" (Dan. 7:8). Just who is this little horn and what does it represent? This horn has the eyes of the man indicating it is closely identified with an individual person who will utter great boasts. We shall see that this little horn is likely a direct reference the rise of the false prophet Muhammad and his kingdom. To date, perhaps no other man of authority has ever made as many outrageous, blasphemous and false claims as the prophet Muhammad did. We shall examine this in detail when we examine the characters of the Beast and the False Prophet and compare them to the spirit and prophet of Islam.

Moving along for now, we see that after the rise of the little horn, Daniel, "kept looking" and looked into the future of what would happen after little horn arose. Eventually thrones are set up that reflect what John saw in Revelation 4–5. Judgment is poured out on this little horn. Daniel described it this way, "I kept looking because of the sound of the boastful words which the horn was speaking; I kept looking until the *beast* was slain, and its body was destroyed and given to the burning fire" (Dan. 7:11).

Notice that suddenly Daniel changes terms and this little horn gets named "the beast." This is no coincidence. This seamless change from speaking of the little horn and then speaking of the Beast may mean they are the same, or more likely, may indicate the inseparable link between these two characters. Furthermore, it's clear that not only do the horns represent rulers, but they can also represent beasts. Most importantly, the last beast Daniel mentions is unique from the others in description. When its body was destroyed it was "given to the burning fire." This is exactly the description of what happens to the Beast of Revelation when he is destroyed (Rev. 19:20). Thus, this little horn quite likely brings forth the same kingdom as the Beast's kingdom of Revelation.

As Daniel sought further explanation, he was given some key information. We are reminded again this little horn "had eyes and a mouth uttering great boasts and which was larger in appearance than its associates" (Dan. 7:20b). The fact it is larger than the other ones (the horns of the ten Roman Emperors) may be informing us this horn is larger in its influence than they were. He is larger than the previous horns in terms of political authority and the territory his kingdom would eventually rule. Perhaps he is also larger in the harm his kingdom will perpetrate on God's people compared with these other horns. The persecutions that broke out under the previous ten Roman Emperors were rarely systematic in approach and generally unevenly carried out. They were often a convenient way to blame problems in the Empire on Christians and divert attention from real issues. This last horn is far greater and more horrible.

Daniel "kept looking, and that horn was waging war with the saints and overpowering them until the Ancient of Days came and judgment was passed in favor of the saints of the Highest One, and the time arrived when the saints took possession of the kingdom" (Dan. 7:22). On at least sixty-nine occasions in the Koran, Muslims are told to fight for the cause of God.[164] This includes numerous, specific declarations to fight against all those who do not accept the Koran as God's revelation. Muslims are told to keep up this fight until the only religion left in the world is Islam. "Fight against such of those to whom the Scriptures were given (i.e. Jews and Christians) as believe neither in Allah nor the Last Day, who do not forbid what Allah and His apostle have forbidden, and do not embrace the true Faith, *until they pay tribute out of hand and are utterly subdued* . . . It is He who has sent forth His apostle with guidance and the true Faith *to make it triumphant over all religions*, however much the idolaters dislike it" (Surah 9:29–30,33).

An Extension of Life is given to Three Earlier Beasts

Not only does this horn make waging war on the saints an essential part of his rule; he also *keeps on* waging war against them *until* Jesus Christ (the Ancient of Days) returns to set up his kingdom on earth. After these ten Roman Emperors (horns) arise, Daniel emphasizes that "another will arise after them, and he will be different from the previous ones and will subdue three kings" (Dan. 7:24b). What three kings will he subdue?

The answer is found in a fascinating addendum about the first three beasts. Daniel makes an intriguing statement about them. He says, "As for the rest of the beasts (the three prior to Rome and the little horn), their dominion was taken away, *but an extension of life was granted to them* for an appointed period of time" (Dan. 7:12).

What a curious thing! How would these three beasts be given an extension of life after Rome collapsed? Daniel told us earlier that the three prior beasts lost the remainder of their dominion when the fourth beast came forth trampling and devouring them. Rome completely and thoroughly decimated the previous three beasts. Yet, here we learn that after the rise of the little horn, an *extension of life* is given to the earlier beasts. Somehow the previous three kingdoms would be revived after the rise of the little horn. Eventually Daniel sees this extension of life as temporary because "one like a Son of Man" comes and sets up his kingdom on earth that "all the peoples, nations and men of every language might serve Him" (Dan. 7:14b). This, of course, refers to the return of the Lord Jesus Christ and the establishment of his kingdom on the earth. He will then destroy these revived kingdoms.

But how did this extension of life happen? This extension of the previous three dominions of the three earlier beasts or horns[165] and the subduing of three kings by the little horn may refer to the same thing. After the coming of the little horn from his obscure beginnings in the Arabian Peninsula, Muhammad successfully conquered the entire peninsula before his death. After his death, his disciples continued to spread out conquering to the west through Egypt, Libya and eventually all the way to Spain. However, at the same time, they also went to the north and the east. Muhammad's Islamic kingdom eventually conquered the territories of the earlier beasts in both geographical and ethnic terms. They included the territories of Babylon, the territories of the Medes and Persians and the territories of the Greek Empire. For a time, large sections of the European Roman Empire were even conquered. Territories such as Spain (portions for almost 800 years), and Sicily (300 years) were occupied for a long time by Muslims.

The Extension of Babylon with the Umayyads (A.D. 661–750)

The first major Islamic Dynasty was known as the Umayyads and had its headquarters in Damascus. Although the capital was Damascus, "the main strength of the Muslim community lay further east. The cities of Iraq were growing in size, as immigrants came in from Iran as well as the Arabian Peninsula."[166] Thus, the concentration of power was increasingly in modern-day Iraq with its capital in Syria. Both were in the heart of ancient Babylon.

The language and culture of Arabia began to overwhelm the ancient Assyrian/Babylonian cultures. Perhaps this extension of life was granted to Babylon, as the people and center of ancient Babylon became the center of the new Islamic Empire. Also "three of the first horns (of which ancient Babylon was likely one) were pulled out by the roots before it (the little horn) . . ." (Dan. 7:8). The descendants of this ancient Babylonian kingdom were *subdued* under Islam (Dan. 7:24b). While there was an extension of life given to the Babylonian Empire in the form of the new Islamic Empire, the cultures of these Babylonian peoples were being radically pulled out by their roots. Arabic took over as the dominant tongue of these ancient people.

This is characteristic of Islam's impact on native cultures wherever it is firmly established.

The Extension of Medo-Persia with the Abbasids (749–1258)

A second major dynasty lay further east.[167] A new city known as Baghdad was built on the point where the Tigris and Euphrates River met. "Within a generation a new ruling elite of high officials had been created. Some were drawn from Iranian families with a tradition of service to government and newly converted to Islam."[168] The physical capital was in modern-day Iraq. However, the ethnic center of this Empire had a heavy Persian element.

Once again, the language and culture of Arabia began to be infused into this part of the empire. Once again, an extension of life was given to the descendants of the Medes and Persian Empire, but in the process its ancient culture was being pulled up by its roots.[169] Still Persian (known as Farsi) did manage to hold out as the common language of Iranians. Nevertheless, Arabic became the language of government and religion. It filled Farsi with many thousands of new words. And Arabic Islamic culture was adopted wholesale.

The Extension of the Greek Empire with the Ottomans (1281–1922)

The last dynasty was the Ottoman Empire. This consisted of the Turkish people, a Central Asian people who had gradually migrated west to the Anatolian Plateau (modern Turkey). It also drew into its ruling class many Greeks, European Circassians, and Georgians from the Byzantine Empire. Many of them converted to Islam.[170] Thus, it had a strong Greek and Byzantine ethnic makeup in the government. The Ottoman Empire was at its height in the 1500s, under the reign of Suleyman the Magnificent (reigning 1521–1566). Amazingly, just as the ancient Greek Empire, while at its height, was split in four parts after Alexander's demise, so too, the Islamic Empire found itself in four parts at its peek of greatness. One part included the Safavid Empire to the east of the Ottomans. They ruled in Iran and Central Asia. Another part was the Mughal Empire further east in

India. There were also the Hafsids who ruled in Tunisia and Eastern Algeria. In 1574, this latter Empire was finally absorbed into the Ottoman Empire.

In spite of this split in Islam, the heart of the Islamic world was now centered in Istanbul, home of the Ottoman sultans, caliphs (something like a Muslim Pope) of the faith. The Ottomans saw themselves as the primary protectors and propagators of Islam; much as the Seleucid Dynasty (the offshoot of Alexander's Greek Empire) was the chief propagator of Greek culture and language following the split up of Alexander the Great's Greek Empire.

Just as Alexander the Great's Empire was the largest of the ancient empires, so too the Ottoman Empire was the last and greatest of the Islamic empires. It was also the last to take over control of both Israel and the holy cities of Mecca and Medina. Similarly, the offshoot of the Greek Empire, the Seleucid Dynasty was the last of the ancient pre-Roman empires to rule Israel. The Ottoman Empire included North Africa, as well as the Middle East and Asia Minor. It also ruled large sections of southeastern Europe and the portions of the Caucasus regions of modern day Russia that include the Muslim regions of Dagestan and Chechnya.

So we see that the descendants of the Greek Empire found their extension of life in the Ottoman Empire. However, just as the previous peoples of the other ancient empires experienced, their culture and way of life was rooted out and radically altered by conversion to Islam. Many residents of Asia Minor were subjected to hundreds of years of Islamic law.

The Nature of an Islamic Beast Empire

The fact that these previous three kings would be "pulled out by the roots," probably signifies the all-encompassing cultural change that Islam would impose wherever it went. As Hourani noted, "By the end of the tenth century there had come into existence an Islamic world, united by a common religious culture expressed in the Arabic language, and by human links which trade, migration and pilgrimage had forged."[171] Furthermore, "By the fifteenth century the flood of Arabic Islam had covered the whole region."[172]

This culture touched every aspect of an individual's life and part in society. "All human actions in direct relationship to God or other human beings could be examined in the light of the Koran and the Sunna (the practices of Muhammad), as interpreted by those qualified to exercise *ijtihad* (interpretation of Islam by the leaders of the Umma or Muslim community)."[173] No part of life was off limits to Islam. There was literally a proper way to peel an orange, have sex, and relieve oneself, among many other things. The proper way to act was "classified in terms of five norms: they could be regarded as obligatory (either for the community as a whole, or for every single member of it), recommended, morally neutral, reprehensible, or forbidden."[174]

The pervasiveness of this cultural transformation cannot be understated when discussing the world of Islam. Here is Hourani's description of Islam during the Ottoman Empire.

> Whether they lived within the Ottoman Empire or outside its frontiers, those who professed faith in Islam and lived through the medium of the Arabic language had something in common that was deeper than political allegiance or shared interest. Among them, and between them and those who spoke Turkish or Persian or the other languages of the Muslim world, there was the common sense of belonging to an enduring and unshaken world created by the final revelation of God through the Prophet Muhammad, and expressing itself in different forms of thought and social activity: the Koran, the Traditions of the Prophet (Hadith), the system of law or ideal social behavior (*Sharia*), . . . the schools, the travels of scholars in search of learning, the circulation of books, the fast of Ramadan, observed at the same time and in the same way by Muslims everywhere, and the pilgrimage that brought many thousands from all over the Muslim world to Mecca at the same moment of the year. All these activities preserved the sense of belonging to a world that contained all that was necessary for welfare in this life and salvation in the next.[175]

Making War a Holy Obligation

The prophet Daniel further emphasizes the spirit and nature of this Beast king and his kingdom. It matches perfectly with the nature of Islam. He states, "I kept looking, and that horn was *waging war with the saints* and overpowering them . . . (Dan. 7:21). "He will speak out against the Most High and wear down the saints of the Highest One . . ." (Dan. 7:25a)

Fundamentally, Koranic Islam's *modus operandi* is to make all-out warfare on the world outside of Islam (Dar al-harb) in order to establish Islam in the whole world. The entire world is divided into these two regions for the devout Muslim: the region of peace known as Dar al-Islam (under true Islamic rule) and the region of war, Dar al-harb (any area not under true Islamic rule). The realm where Islam is imposing itself on non-Islamic societies is the realm of *jihad,* or holy war. This is why *jihad* must continue nonstop until the entire world is under Islamic rule.

The Koran clearly teaches this in many places. One of many such verses states, "Fight against such of those to whom the Scriptures were given (i.e. Jews and Christians) as believe neither in Allah nor the Last Day, who do not forbid what Allah and His apostle have forbidden, and do not embrace the true faith (Islam), *until they pay tribute out of hand or are utterly subdued*" (Surah 9:29). Thus, for the devout Muslim, *jihad* must continue since all "those to whom the Scriptures were given" have still not been subdued under Islam.

Muslims who refuse to fight are mocked, considered second class and sometimes not even considered true Muslims according to the Koran. They are certainly considered worthy of punishment.

> Believers, why is it that when it is said to you: 'March in the cause of Allah,' you linger slothfully in the land? . . . If you do not fight, He will punish you sternly and replace you by other men. (Surah 9:38,39)

> Do you pretend that he who gives a drink to the pilgrims and pays a visit to the Sacred Mosque is as worthy as the man who believes in Allah and the Last Day, *and fights* for Allah's cause? These are not held equal by Allah . . . . Those that have embraced the Faith, and left their homes, *and fought* for Allah's cause with their wealth and with their persons, are held in higher esteem by Allah. (Surah 9:20–23)

Other verses indicate that Muslims who don't fight are half-hearted and will be condemned as unbelievers.

> ... they (those that won't fight) have denied Allah and His apostle. They pray half-heartedly and begrudge their contributions ... they swear by Allah that they are believers like you (Muslims who will fight). Yet they are not. They are afraid of you (Muslims who will fight). (Surah 9:54,56)

> Those that believe in Allah and the Last Day will not beg you to exempt them from fighting with their wealth and with their persons. Allah best knows the righteous. Only those seek exemption who disbelieve in Allah and the Last Day, and whose hearts are filled with doubt. (Surah 9:44)

Any unfortunate souls under Islamic rule who later wished to recant and turn from Islam found themselves in a difficult spot. For Allah told Muhammad,

> Prophet, make war on the unbelievers *and the hypocrites* and deal rigorously with them. Hell shall be their home: an evil fate. They swear by Allah that they said nothing. Yet they uttered the word of unbelief and renounced Islam after embracing it . . . Allah will sternly punish them, both in this world and in the world to come. They shall have none on this earth to protect or help them. (Surah 9:73,75)

The only choice was a deeply heart felt (or well-acted) immediate repentance or death.

Does such a threat against infidels who have rejected Islam still remain today? In his writing, *The Punishment of an Apostate According to Islamic Law*, Islamic teacher Abul Ala Mawdudi states the views of many when he writes:

> To everyone acquainted with Islamic Law *it is no secret that according to Islam the punishment for a Muslim who turns to kufr (infidelity, blasphemy) is execution.* Doubt about this matter *first arose* among Muslims during the final portion of the nineteenth century as a result of speculation. Otherwise, *for the full twelve centuries prior*

*to that time the total Muslim community remained unanimous about it
. . . All these collectively will assure you that from the time of the
Prophet to the present day one injunction only has been continuously and uninterruptedly operative and that no room whatever
remains to suggest that perhaps the punishment of the apostate is not
execution.*[176]

Fighting for the cause of Allah is the one sure thing that could
insure a believer of paradise.

Those that fled their homes or were expelled from them, and those
that suffered persecution for my sake and fought and were slain:
I shall forgive them their sins and admit them to gardens watered
by running streams, as a reward from Allah; Allah holds the richest
recompense. (Surah 3:195)

Muslims were encouraged by the Koran to ignore their own
consciences and inclination to dislike fighting. Fighting the *jihad* is
considered a holy obligation. "*Fighting is obligatory for you*, as much
as you dislike it. But you may hate a thing although it is good for
you, and love a thing although it is bad for you. Allah knows, but
you do not" (Surah 2:216).

The Example of Muhammad

Muslims consider Muhammad only a man. But he is also considered the greatest prophet of Allah and someone whose example is to
be followed and revered. The Koran exhorts believers to follow his
example when it says, "There is a good example in Allah's apostle
for those of you who look to Allah and the Last Day and remember
Allah always" (Surah 33:21).

So what kind of an example did Muhammad give? Did he only
use violence as a last resort? After one battle, a Persian poet named
Uqbah ibn Abu Muayt was captured. He insisted his tales were more
pleasant and entertaining to listen to than the Koran. He was promptly
ordered executed. When ordered to be executed, he is said to have
pleaded with Muhammad saying,

O Muhammad, if you kill me, who will take care for my children?' The prophet replied, 'Hell's fire.' Other prisoners were more fortunate than this poet. Many were set free without condition if they had large families. Some were released on condition they teach others how to read and write. It seemed the actions of the warrior were erratic, depending upon his mood and his perception of the prisoner's vice.[177]

Once, a woman poet was seized and murdered by a military leader among the Muslims, Umayr ibn Awf. She was a satirist who made fun of the prophet in some of her poems. While in the middle of nursing one of her seven children, she was brutally slaughtered by ibn Awf. While killing her, he was gleefully rejoicing. He then went off and told Muhammad his actions. The prophet praised him! Incredibly, this action is actually justified by many Islamic scholars, since shortly after this, her whole tribe converted to Islam![178]

In a major campaign against the Meccans in 627, the Meccans were driven off from Medina. A tribe of Jews who were protected by the Meccans was left unprotected. Muhammad seized the opportunity and rounded up the eight hundred men from the tribe and spent the entire day and evening beheading all of them simply because they were Jews. In this way, he eliminated all the Jews left in Medina.[179]

Even so, Muhammad was not as cruel as many other Arab tribal rulers and could at times be merciful. But he wholeheartedly approved of brutal methods to extend Islam. He often showed no distinction between killing men or women or children in the cause of spreading Islam. Here is the man who is to be the Muslim's prime example. Is it any wonder Islam has a problem with producing terrorists? As one *jihadist* in Iraq said, "For us *jihad* is tourism . . . it is something that we do with pleasure."[180]

Making Alterations in Times and in Law

Daniel says the Beast ". . . will intend to make alterations in times and in law" (Dan. 7:25). This is exactly what Islam does under *Sharia* law. Where *Sharia* (Islamic) law is established, not only are local laws altered, calendars are all changed to correspond with the time of Muhammad's flight from his enemies in Medina. The Islamic calendar gives the year 1 for A.D. 622. Thus, the year 2004 is actually the year 1382 for the citizen in Saudi Arabia or Iran.

The day of rest in these countries is also Friday, instead of Saturday or Sunday. The truly Islamic legal system, or *Sharia* law, is based entirely on the Koran, the Islamic Hadith (reported lifestyle and sayings of Muhammad) and the interpretation (*ijtihad*) of these from respected leaders of the *Umma* (the Muslim community of believers). Thus, the legal system of Islam is radically different from any other legal system in the world. Laws are not made by the consent of the governed as in democratically elected representative forms of government. Nor are laws to be made by the whims of a non-Islamic dictator or king.

Devout fundamentalist Muslims consider both these alternative forms of government evil and satanic. They are contrary to Allah's revealed will for governmental law as seen in the Koran, the Hadith and the *ijtihad*. This is why democracy, as we know it, cannot flourish in truly Islamic societies. Even in societies where a moderate form of *Sharia* is enforced and elections are held (as in Iran), the representatives can only make suggestions and proposals for law. Every proposed law must be run past the recognized leaders of the Islamic community. This Islamic council decides whether or not it is compatible with Islamic law. Much like the Supreme Court of the United States, the Islamic leaders have final authority in deciding whether or not something violates Allah's "constitution." They tend to be strict in their interpretation. They are not relativistic revisionists like many on the United States Supreme Court.

Daniel immediately follows his description of the kingdom of the little horn by saying the saints

> . . . will be given into his hand for a time, times, and half a time. But the court will sit for judgment, and his dominion will be taken away, annihilated and destroyed forever. Then the sovereignty, the dominion under the whole heaven will be given to the people of the saints of the Highest One; His Kingdom will be an everlasting kingdom, and all the dominions will serve and obey Him. (Dan. 7:25b–27)

Ultimately, this kingdom of Muhammad will temporarily triumph. The "time, times and half a time" correspond to three and one half years, the same time as mentioned in Revelation for the Beast's reign.[181] This Beast will have authority and physical victory over God's people. Eventually, the Lord Jesus Christ will return and destroy little horn's lion-leopard-bear seven-headed kingdom and fully establish his own kingdom on earth as it is in heaven.

The Other Three Heads of the Beast

The final kingdom will have its power base in a revival of the Islamic Kingdoms, that themselves were revivals of the Babylonian, Persian and Greek Empires. These were revived and radically altered as the central Islamic Empires from 661–1922. Yet this Beast is seven-headed, not four-headed. What about the other three heads of the Beast? How will they play a role in this final mega-beast kingdom? The first head was Egyptian, representing Pharaoh and the kingdom of Egypt. Egypt is currently dominated by Muslims and is very oppressive toward its Christian minority. The second head is representative of the Assyrian Empire. The Assyrian Empire had its power base out of Nineveh. That is in modern day northern Iraq, and also included parts of modern day Iran, Syria, southeastern Turkey, Lebanon, Jordan, Israel and Egypt. Here again we see these areas, with the exception of Israel, are predominantly Muslim. They will all share the Beast's agenda.

Of course, the third head represents Babylon, the fourth, Medo-Persia and the fifth, Greece. This leaves us with the last beast we have yet to talk about in context of the final beast. This is the sixth beast, or the sixth head, the one current at the time of John. It was the Roman Empire. We often think of the Roman Empire as European. Yet it also encompassed large swaths of what are today Muslim lands.[182]

The European part of the Roman Empire never conquered by Islam includes countries almost exclusively in Western Europe. Interestingly, this is where most of the Islamic population in Europe is concentrated and growing rapidly. Europe, especially the West, has been targeted by Muslim evangelists and radicals for conversion. The strategy is working, and Islam is growing rapidly there. Not only is "Christian" Western Europe not keeping pace in growth, it is literally shrinking. Although immigration from Muslim countries has been slowed somewhat since 9/11, Muslim families continue to

have far greater numbers of children than "Christian" families and
the overall trend is crystal clear. The history of the world is also full
of examples of minorities seizing control of governments. Look at
these population trends in these countries of Europe from the old
Roman Empire.

Country	% Muslim	% Muslim pop. Growth Rate	% "Christian" pop. Growth Rate
France	12% (1 out of 8)	+ 2.5%	- 0.1%
United Kingdom	2%	+ 1.2%	- 0.6%
Spain	1.2%	+ 3.7%	- 2.7%
Italy	2.4%	+ 2.7%	- 0.4%
Germany	3.7%	+ 5.1%	- 1.0%
Austria	2.23%	+ 3.8%	- 0.2%
Portugal	0.5%	+ 4.6%	- 0.1%

It is clear the old Roman Empire is actually an empire that has
and is being influenced by Islam. The populations of Europe that
have been most pro-Arab and anti-Israeli in that conflict tend to be
the countries of "old Europe," as Donald Rumsfeld is fond of calling them. These were part of the old Roman Empire. Whatever one
thought of the second Iraqi War, it is fascinating to realize that, with
the exception of Britain that was essentially split, all these populations of old Europe strongly opposed the United States.

What will the old Roman Empire's role be in this final Beast
kingdom? Some believe this final head of the revived Roman head
will actually be an alliance between the Roman Catholic Church and
Islam.[183] Although under intense pressure, such a move could not be
ruled out, it seems unlikely. Even so, while living in a Muslim nation,
I was appalled to learn that leaders of the tiny Eastern Orthodox and
Roman Catholic communities had made public declarations stating
Muhammad was a legitimate prophet of God. Of course, they still
claimed to be followers of Christ as well.

It's intriguing that Muhammad states in the Koran that true Christian believers acknowledge he is an apostle of God, and the Koran
is God's revelation. "Those to whom We gave the Scriptures (Jews
and Christians) believe in it (the Koran), and so do some of your
own people. Only the unbelievers deny Our revelations" (including
the Koran) (Surah 29:47). Apparently, these church leaders would
fit Muhammad's definition of true believers.

Might a future Pope confer and sanction legitimacy on Islam by officially recognizing Muhammad as a legitimate prophet of Allah? Might this even be a part of "the apostasy" that Paul said must come first before the return of Christ? Paul seemed to indicate the apostasy and revealing of the "man of lawlessness" essentially take place at the same time (2Thess. 2:3). Whether a future Pope confers legitimacy on Muhammad or not, many so-called "Christians" will bow down to the Beast out of fear and desire for self-preservation. Either way, this will certainly involve a great apostasy.

If Roman Catholicism did give its backing to an Islamic Beast, it is likely that its support would be rather tepid and largely administrative. It would probably do it out of a desire for self-preservation rather than conviction. Might this also explain why the body and makeup of the seven-headed beast is not Roman in appearance? The only place Rome is found in this beast is as part of one of its seven heads. Such a small connection may indicate weak, lukewarm, merely administrative support. Might this suggest only the government leaders and perhaps not the majority of the population will be behind it? Regardless, most will undoubtedly outwardly submit to it.

Still, the main body of heartfelt support for the Beast will predominantly be from Islamic nations.

Violent Revolutionaries don't need Votes and Rarely Hold Elections

Could radical Islam really gain such widespread control of governments? Accustomed to democratically elected governments, we tend to think a majority must lend support for a revolutionary movement to gain control. This is not only untrue, it is rarely true. Nevertheless, it *is* required for one side of a conflict to be more passionate and committed than the other side. Many historians believe the American Revolutionary War was fought and won by about one-third of the American colonists. Almost the same amount were actively aiding and sometimes fighting for the British[184] and about one-third were trying to stay out of the conflict and get on with their lives. The Patriots proved victorious. This, in spite of the fact they lacked military superiority and proper training. What they had was a depth of passion and commitment and sense of moral clarity and rightness that the other side generally lacked.

In the case of communist Russia, columnist George Will has noted, "The Russian Revolution was started by a few thousand determined radicals in a country of 150 million."[185] That's not exactly a majority. In the spring of 2004, US officials estimated that Iraqi rebel cleric Muqtada Al-Sadr had approximately 5,000–6,000 fighters working for him.[186] Although Al-Sadr may not succeed, as Fareed Zakaria noted,

> . . . someone else (besides Al-Sadr) could emerge. After the fall of the Shah of Iran in 1979, Islamic fundamentalists did not take power . . . leading figures at the time of transition were . . . Western style liberals like Prime Minister Abolhasan Bani Sadr. But within a year Bani Sadr had been impeached, his successor assassinated, and the clerics were firmly in power. In revolutionary situations, the Lenninists (radicals) usually win.[187]

As Morgan Norval, the Executive Director of the Selous Foundation, a Washington D.C. based think-tank that studies unconventional warfare noted, "Force against faith is fundamentally useless . . . The Islamic fundamentalist has a faith in some ways more zealous than the early Christians. Yet we in the West seem to be losing ours . . ."[188]

He goes on to state that

> the militant Islamic fundamentalist's actions are centered around his world view and he sincerely believes himself to be fighting to save the *umma*, or the universal Islamic community . . . The fundamentalists are convinced beyond any doubt they are locked in a life-or-death struggle with the forces of evil and unbelief that threaten Islam from every quarter.[189]

In this sense they can and do argue that they are fighting for the defense of Islam.

To look at examples of an evil minority gaining power, one must only consider Adolph Hitler. It's true his party won more seats than any others did in Germany's last parliamentary elections before World War II. Still he never got a majority. He persuaded, bribed, smooth talked, lied to and intimidated some from other parties to give him absolute control.

Outside of the tiny country of San Marino, communists have never gained power in any nation through the peaceful means of the ballot box. In the places where they have tried the ballot, such as Nicaragua, Western Europe and North America, they have always lost. They fared far better using force. Communists succeeded for years in many countries because their minority of combatants proved far more committed to their cause then any competing power groups. They had a moral legitimacy in the eyes of their revolutionary foot soldiers. In many nations the silent majority eventually quietly acquiesced. The few that continued to resist were rarely heard from again. Eventually the communists and their sympathizers ruled about half of the world.

It was only when equally committed minorities who believed in representative democracy were willing to risk their lives that many of these regimes finally weakened and fell. Does the West of today have the same sense of moral clarity and absolute conviction as radical Islam? Will the West and liberal Muslims be able to stop the revival of a fundamentalist Islamic Empire?

. . . .

Chapter 11

The Apostle of Islam: The Beast (Rev. 13:4–18)

This resurrected Beast kingdom is also personalized as an individual (see Rev. 13:3,12,14). Perhaps the individual who eventually comes out to rule the Beast kingdom will be one who was presumed killed and dead earlier in the conflict. This Beast, the anti-Christ, will arise from among the sea of this mass movement and will be one who carries "a bow" (Rev. 6:2). This probably indicates one who has been fighting in the movement.

How does this scenario fit with Islamic end-times theology? Interestingly, fundamental Islam also believes in the coming return of Jesus.

Most also associate the last days with the coming of the Mahdi. Who is the Mahdi? Some Muslims, mostly Sunnis, are not sure yet who he will be. Many Shiites believe he is a twelfth-century imam who disappeared and is believed to be hiding on the earth. It is believed he will one day appear to establish worldwide Islam. It is not difficult to see how these two Islamic end-time characters, the Islamic Jesus and the Mahdi, leave the Islamic world well-prepared for what is mentioned in the Bible. The important thing to realize is that these beliefs are common in the world of Islam. We will examine the Bible's teaching on the character, doctrine and plan of this Beast and False Prophet. Then let's compare this to the character, doctrine and plan of Muhammad, Islam, the Mahdi, and this future Jesus that Islam says will come. Let's see if these reasonably match up with the Bible's description of the Beast and the False Prophet. Can they fit into this Islamic picture without straining common sense and good Bible hermeneutics in the process?

Worshiping the Dragon and the Beast

The Scriptures say that the world "worshiped the dragon because he gave his authority to the beast; and they worshiped the beast . . ." (Rev. 13:4a). It is important to realize that *both* the dragon and the beast are worshipped. The dragon is, of course, the god who is behind the Beast. He could certainly be the Allah of Islam.

What is the anti-Christ or Beast like? We find out this Beast, ". . . opposes and exalts himself above every so-called god or object of worship, so that he takes his seat in the temple of God, displaying himself as being God" (2Thess. 2:4). At first glance, this makes it hard to understand how Muslims could worship an Islamic Jesus, an anti-Christ, since they believe in Allah having no partners in the flesh. Muslims do not believe that Allah can incarnate himself in human flesh, as Christians believed happened with Jesus. But is worshipping a man truly an unthinkable occurrence in Islam? Or is the Islamic world actually well prepared to worship the Beast? Could it be that strictly monotheistic Islam would bow to a man?

Amazingly, in the Koran, on several occasions, it is reported that the angels were ordered to bow down to Adam, a mere man. Supposedly, only Satan refused to bow down to Adam. It is stated here as follows:

> Your Lord said to the angels: 'I am creating man from dry clay, from black molded loam. When I have fashioned him, kneel down and prostrate yourselves before him.' The angels, one and all, prostrated themselves, except Satan. He refused to prostrate himself with the others.

> 'Satan,' said Allah, 'why do you not prostrate yourself?' He replied: 'I will not bow to a mortal whom You created of dry clay, of black

molded loam.' 'Begone,' said Allah, 'you are accursed . . .' (Surah 15:29–33)

Thus, the Koran makes it clear that in its estimation, bowing down to a man is *not* necessarily worship since one is also told to only worship Allah. Furthermore, the message is clear that only the evil one, Satan, refused to bow down to the man Adam.

Additionally, followers of Islam and those being introduced to the apostle of Allah and his revelations are *ordered* to fall down to their knees in awe and adoration at the reading of the Koran (Surah 32:15). Look at what the Koran says Muslims are told to do toward the prophet Muhammad, who they say was a man.

We have sent you (Muhammad) forth as a witness and as a bearer of good news and warnings, so that you (Meccans) may have faith in Allah and His apostle and that you may assist Him, honor Him, and *praise Him* morning and evening.

Those that swear fealty (allegiance) to you (Muhammad), swear fealty to Allah himself. The Hand of Allah is above their hands. He that breaks his oath breaks it at his own peril, but he that keeps his pledge to Allah shall be richly rewarded by Him. (Surah 48:8–10)

Meccans are told to both honor and praise Muhammad morning and evening and have faith in him. This verse in the Koran was written after newly conquering Mecca. The desire was to insure the loyalty of these new converts to Islam. The Meccans are exhorted to put their faith in Muhammad and praise him, at least twice daily. Furthermore, swearing allegiance to Muhammad is equated with swearing allegiance to Allah. *They are considered one and the same!* As the Koran states in another place, "Obey Allah and obey the Apostle (Muhammad)" (Surah 64:12). Although a Muslim would not technically consider this worship of the apostle of Allah, or the Koran, true Christians and the Word of God say otherwise.

In the Gospels we see that Satan tries to get Jesus to "bow down before him" (Luke 4:7). Jesus answers the devil's demand by saying, "You shall worship the Lord your God and serve Him only" (Luke 4:8). When the Gentiles bow down to Peter, he instructs them to get up for he is only a man (Acts 10:26). When John fell down to worship at the feet of the angel who was speaking to him, the angel replied "Do not do that, I am a fellow servant of yours and of your brethren the prophets and of those who heed the words of this book. Worship God" (Rev. 22:9).

Yet the Koran says the following: "None believes in Our revelations save those who, when reminded of them, prostrate themselves in adoration . . ." (Surah 32:15). And Allah commands angels, "kneel down and prostrate yourselves before him (Adam)" (Surah 15:31).

Clearly Islam has paved the way for the Beast of Revelation.

The Islamic Jesus "Returns" to Subdue Jews and Christians

Again, let's remember that all devout Muslims believe not only the Mahdi, but also Jesus will return at the end of the age. They believe Jesus will come to establish the Islamic kingdom that will rule the entire world. Furthermore, they generally believe that Jesus didn't die. Also, they believe the Koran that states, "People of the Book (Jews and Christians) . . . must believe in Him (Jesus) before His death" (Surah 4:159).

As Caner put it, "According to Islam, since Jesus—a human as was Adam—has not died, his ministry cannot be complete. Tradition explains that he will appear to all just before the final judgment. He then will battle the anti-Christ, defeat him, confess Islam, kill all pigs, *break all crosses, and establish a thousand years of righteousness.*"[190] This means that he will destroy every church of its Christian symbols, of which the cross is paramount. He will probably convert them into mosques. This has been a common practice in the history of Islamic conquest.

At the Dome of the Rock, located at the Temple Mount, the oldest written physical embodiments of the Koran left on earth are found on its walls. The text states,

People of the Book (Christians), do not transgress the bounds of your religion. Speak nothing but the truth about Allah. The Messiah, Jesus the son of Mary, was no more than Allah's apostle and His Word that he cast to Mary: a spirit from Him. So believe in Allah and His apostles and do not say: 'Three.' Forbear, and it shall be better for you. Allah is but one God. Allah forbid that He should have a son! . . . The Messiah does not disdain to be a servant of Allah. (Surah 4:171,172)

This is nothing short of amazing when compared with the description of the Beast in the Scriptures. According to Islamic teaching, it is not difficult at all to see how the false Christ of Islam, denying to be Allah's son, nevertheless, demands praise and recognition as the true Messiah, the word and spirit of Allah and his servant. He would likely also demand bowing down to the Allah of Islam as he reads the Koranic text and declares himself the Christ, the apostle of God. Indeed, as seen already, bowing down to him and pledging allegiance to him could easily be equated with allegiance to Allah himself. This is consistent with the Koran that teaches unswerving obedience to Allah's apostle and declares that all the apostles (including the Islamic Jesus) operate in Allah's authority. "Whatever the Apostle gives you, accept it; and whatever he forbids you, forbear it. Have fear of Allah; Allah is stern in retribution" (Surah 59:7). "Obey Allah and obey the Apostle" (Surah 64:12).

It further states that "those that oppose Allah and His apostle shall be brought low. Allah has decreed: 'I will surely triumph, Myself and My apostles.' Powerful is Allah, and mighty. You shall find no believers in Allah and the Last Day on friendly terms with those who oppose Allah and His apostle, even though they be their fathers, their sons, their brothers, or their nearest kindred" (Surah 59:20–22). For the Christian and certainly for God, by claiming to be Jesus Christ, this Islamic Jesus is automatically equating himself with being God. For the Muslim, this will appear to be an exciting fulfillment of Islamic end-times prophecy. What a convincing show it will be! But that is not all. The Bible makes it clear there will be more signs than that.

The Islamic Jesus and his "Indisputable" Signs

The Koran frequently predicts and affirms that when God sends apostles, like Jesus, they always come with indisputable signs. The sign at Muhammad's first coming was said to be the Koran itself, because of its supposedly incomparable nature and beauty. Jesus is specifically said to have come with signs. The Koran states: "Jesus came with evident signs, he said: 'I have come to give you wisdom, and to make plain to you some of the things you differ about. Fear Allah and follow me. Allah is my Lord and your Lord: therefore serve Him. That is a straight path" (Surah 43:63–64).

The Bible declares that, ". . . the lawless one will be revealed . . . the one whose coming is in accord with the activity of Satan, *with all power and signs and false wonders*" (2Thess. 2:8a, 9). The False Prophet will perform false signs and wonders in the presence of the Beast, the false Jesus, in order to deceive people. "He performs great signs, so that he even makes fire come down out of heaven to the earth in the presence of men. And he deceives those who dwell on the earth because of the signs which it was given him to perform in the presence of the beast . . ." (Rev. 13:13–14a).

The Koran explains that when any of Allah's apostles, including Jesus, performed signs, the unbelievers rejected those signs saying, "This is but plain sorcery" (Surah 5:110). It also says, ". . . whenever an apostle came to those that flourished before them they cried: 'Sorcerer!' or 'Madman!' Have they handed down this cry from one generation to the next? Surely they are transgressors all" (Surah 51:51). True Christians will probably say something quite similar and not acknowledge this Jesus as the true Jesus and thus, incur his wrath.

The pressure will be intense and the signs convincing to many. "For false Christs and false prophets will arise and show great signs and wonders, so as to mislead, if possible, even the elect" (Matt. 24:24). At this time if anyone says, "Here he is," Jesus exhorts us, "don't believe them." By ordering Christians and the world to bow down and acknowledge the Koran and the apostle of Allah and the denial of God begetting a son, the Beast and the False Prophet will be demanding worship of a false Jesus. In their eyes, it is only "the unbelievers (who) set up other gods as equals with their Lord" (Surah 6:1). In a Muslim mind, setting up Jesus as an equal to Allah happens when Christians say he is Allah's son. True Christians will also be equated as unbelievers because they will refuse to bow down to the false Jesus of Islam.

The false Jesus' message was and is, "Fear Allah *and* follow me. Allah is my Lord and your Lord: therefore serve Him" (Surah 43:63). This dual nature of worship of both the Beast and the Dragon together is exactly what Revelation says will happen. ". . . They worshiped the dragon because he gave his authority to the beast; *and* they worshiped the beast, saying, 'Who is like the beast, and who is able to wage war with him?'" (Rev. 13:4).

Interestingly, Muhammad repeatedly and confidently affirms that both the scriptures of the prophets and the Gospel predicted his coming. Search as they might, Muslims have not been able to find any such scriptures (partly for this reason they assert the Bible has been changed) that speak of him. Could it be that in his perverse way the devil knows that Islam is the source of the False Prophet and the Beast of Revelation and can't help boasting in advance? Let's look a bit more at the character, teaching and nature of Islam and its prophet Muhammad to see what this Islamic Jesus would teach and impose on the world.

Characteristics of this Man of Lawlessness

The Scriptures inform us the Beast is the "man of lawlessness" (2Thess. 2:3,8) or the "lawless one." When we look at the example of the founder of Islam, Muhammad, we see a man who did not consider himself bound even by the Koran itself. Indeed, in a real sense, he was the law. At that time, Islamic law was essentially the Koran and the example of Muhammad. Also Muhammad was given exceptions from following the Koran that taught that men should have no more than four wives. Muhammad had "special dispensation" to have at least 11 wives and several concubines. "He killed critics for speaking their minds, ordered the severe beating of a woman to retrieve information from her . . ." and ". . . was a ruthless general and raided caravans merely for financial gain to expand his movement."[191]

Furthermore, he had his adopted son divorce his wife so that he could marry her instead. He also had a six-year-old girl, Aishah, betrothed to him. He consummated the marriage when she was only nine years old! It is inconceivable that a moral person could do such a thing. Even in the culture of the day, such a young consummation of marriage with a pre-pubescent child was unheard of.

Also, paradise is supposed to be a place of sexual bliss for the Muslim.

> When one of his followers posed the question: 'Oh Messenger of God, do we have sexual intercourse in paradise?' He replied in extravagant words indicating the intensity and total preoccupation with sexual expression . . . Then he added: 'There is no bachelor in paradise.' When another asked him how one man could have the strength to (be intimate with) seventy girls in one day he responded: 'He would be given the strength of one hundred men!'[192]

As the Koran states, "therein are bashful virgins whom neither men nor jinee will have touched before . . . . virgins as fair as corals and rubies . . . in each there shall be virgins chaste and fair . . . dark-eyed virgins sheltered in their tents" (Surah 55:54,55,68,69). In the Holy Scriptures, as opposed to unholy, Peter declares that sexual lust and immorality is a trademark of false prophets (2Pet. 2:10). In fact, Peter says they promise sexual rewards to win converts (2Pet. 2:18).

Jerusalem: Mystically Sodom and Egypt

It is interesting to note that Jerusalem, immediately prior to the return of Christ, is *mystically* identified as Sodom and Egypt (Rev. 13:8). Since the actual word "mystically" is used by the Biblical text, we know that Jerusalem under the Beast will be a symbolic Sodom and Egypt. Certainly sexual immorality is most closely associated with Sodom. Egypt is most closely associated as a sign of bondage and slavery. As we saw earlier, the Beast will overrun Jerusalem driving out the Jews (Zech. 14:2). He will take Jerusalem as his own possession and announce his supremacy on the Temple Mount (Matt. 24:15). He will proclaim himself to be Jesus, the Word and Spirit of Allah and the earthly head of Islam from the Temple Mount (2Thess. 2:4).

Only half of the residents of Jerusalem will be driven out, for the Muslim Palestinians will be allowed to stay and the "Christian" Palestinians given the opportunity to convert. Thus, the only occupants of Jerusalem during the reign of the Beast will be Muslims and subdued

"Christian" converts to Islam. Given its perverse, earthy promise of never-ending sexual bliss in paradise with countless maidens, and the actual oppressive bondage it brings to all who submit to its authority, it is not hard to see how the Jerusalem of Islam could be mystically identified as Sodom and Egypt.

The Mahdi

As mentioned earlier, a very widespread belief in Islam is the idea of the coming of the Mahdi. The Mahdi is "the man guided by God and sent by him to restore the rule of justice which would come before the end of the world."[193] Previously, in the history of Islam, some men have been thought, for a time, to be this man. In the past, the coming of such individuals has led to violence in support of these so-called Mahdi.[194]

There is another common belief in Islam that makes Muslims especially vulnerable to the Beast and the False Prophet. It is the idea that one should have "a master of the spiritual life (a *Shaykh*). According to a saying that became familiar (to devout Muslims), 'he who has no *shaykh*, the devil is his *shaykh*.' The disciple should follow his master implicitly; he should be as passive as a corpse beneath the hands of the washer of the dead."[195]

Furthermore, in Islamic society, gaining power by violence is perfectly legitimate. Hourani notes that "it was generally accepted that power was acquired by the sword . . . . How he (a Muslim ruler) obtained his power was less important than how he used it. The just exercise of power was a kind of religious service."[196]

Clearly, the susceptibility of Muslims to a charismatic spiritual ruler has been well developed over the centuries. Once again Hourani informs us that Muslims came to believe that

> in every age and time, God chooses one member of the human race and, having endowed him with goodly and kingly virtues, entrusts him with the interests of the world and the well-being of His servants . . . To do what he is chosen by God to do, the ruler must stand outside the different orders of society. He is not chosen by them . . . nor is he responsible to them, but only to his own conscience and . . . to God.[197]

Islam has been finely tuned to accept a ruler who combines both absolute physical political authority with absolute spiritual leadership. The close aid and assistance of other spiritually and intellectually qualified assistants is also acceptable. "The best of states is that which is ruled by one who is both a philosopher and a prophet, in contact through both his intellect and his imagination with the Active Intelligence which emanates from God . . . . The state can be virtuous if it is ruled by a combination of those who collectively possess the necessary characteristics . . . ."[198]

A God of Fortresses/Ignoring the Gods of his Fathers

What other characteristics does the Bible give us about this individual? Daniel described him in this way,

> He will show no regard for the gods of his fathers or for the desire of women, nor will he show regard for any other god; for he will magnify himself above them all.

> But instead he will honor a god of fortresses, a god whom his fathers did not know; he will honor him with gold, silver, costly stones and treasures. He will take action against the strongest of fortresses with the help of a foreign god; he will give great honor to those who acknowledge him and will cause them to rule over the many, and will parcel out land for a price. (Dan. 11:37–39)

As we have already seen, "a god of fortresses" vividly describes Islam with its emphasis on fighting and warfare. There is no remaining major religion on earth as tied to using violence in the advancement of its cause than Islam. The Koran ridicules Muslims who refuse to fight as not being true Muslims. They are described as frauds who will go to hell (Surah 9:44–57). As mentioned earlier, there are at least sixty-nine exhortations in the Koran to use violence to spread Islam. It is mandatory for all true Muslims to fight for the cause.

Daniel reveals additional important information as well. The fact he will show no regard for the "gods of his fathers" suggests to some that he may be a convert, in this case, to Islam. The early church father Iraneus stated his belief that he will actually be from Jewish heritage. He believed he would come from the tribe of Dan.[199] He cites an interesting prophecy in Jeremiah, that states in part,

> ... They heal the brokenness of the daughter of My people superficially, saying, 'Peace, peace,' but there is no peace ... *We waited for peace, but no good came; for a time of healing, but behold terror!* From Dan is heard the snorting of horses; at the sound of the neighing of his stallions the whole land quakes; for they come and devour the land and its fullness, the city and its inhabitants. For behold, I am sending serpents against you, adders for which there is no charm, and they will bite you,' declares the Lord. (Jer. 8:11,15–17)

Interestingly, this time of terror seems to follow a period when peace is earnestly hoped for. Could there be some similarities here to the situation we see today in the Middle East? This may indicate an attack led by a descendant of Dan. The prophet Jeremiah many times announced Babylon was an instrument of judgment against Israel. But here, amazingly, the instrument seems to be the tribe of Dan.

Also, Jacob prophesied about Dan that, "Dan shall judge his people, as one of the tribes of Israel. Dan shall be a serpent in the way, a horned snake in the path, which bites the horse's heels, so that his rider falls backward. For your salvation I wait, O Lord" (Gen. 49:16–18). Samson was likely the Danite who was to judge Israel. But then we see something very peculiar about Dan. He becomes a serpent in the way, a horned snake in the path. The serpent is often associated with sin and Satan in the Bible. Additionally, Jacob ends his prophecy about Dan by saying, "for your salvation I wait, O Lord." This is exactly what the people of Israel will cry out for as they are surrounded by the Beast and his armies immediately prior to the Lord's return (Zech. 12:9–13:2).

It should also be noted the tribe of Dan is not mentioned among the twelve tribes of the 144,000. Although rare, it is not unheard of for Jews to convert to Islam. Many did so at the time of Muhammad and some do to this day. Even today, orphanages are run in Muslim countries, and children are raised to be Muslims regardless of their original parent's background.

No Regard for the Desire of Women

What else characterizes this Beast? He shows no "regard for the desire of women." This could indicate a homosexual bent or a mere disinterest in women. More likely, it may indicate he is completely inconsiderate of what women desire. This is clearly the case with radical Islam as demonstrated by the Taliban. In radical Islam, women cannot leave their homes without husbands or male relatives. When they do, they must cover from head to toe, regardless of the heat. Some women pass out from heat stroke and wretch when forced out in hot conditions. Many choose to stay behind closed doors in their homes, which is exactly where they are preferred to be.

Professions and work outside the home is greatly restricted regardless of whether a woman is widowed or not. Under extreme Islam, schooling is out of the question, except studying the Koran and only then in segregated schools for females. Although some forms of *Sharia* law are a little less harsh than others, the general spirit is oppressive in its treatment of women.

Although men are restricted to four wives, they are free to have sexual relations with as many female slaves as they can purchase. Such things still happen today in Sudan and Saudi Arabia. Many Western women who marry Muslim men are appalled to discover that their husbands have wives back in their native countries.[20]

Unlike Christianity, that teaches different primary roles for men and women, Islam teaches not just role differences, but also that women are less religious and less intelligent than men are. There are laws in Islam that state that women are prohibited from looking a man in the eyes, wearing shoes that make noise, and becoming educated. Furthermore, Muhammad was quoted as saying, "Wives are playthings so take your pick."[201]

Of course, the complete covering of women is standard practice in fundamentalist families and fundamentalist ruled nations.

Perhaps the most appalling commandment in the Koran concerning women is as follows: "Men have authority over women because God has made the one superior to the other . . . As for those from whom you fear disobedience, admonish them and send them to beds apart *and beat them*. Then if they obey you, take no further action against them" (Surah 4:35) While living in an Islamic country, I heard of one Muslim woman, when talking to another woman friend say that her husband only beat her on occasion. "But this is OK," she said, "because if your husband doesn't beat you at least sometimes, then he's not really a man."[202]

Under *Sharia* law, women are not permitted to divorce their husbands, but husbands are free to do so by verbally making a statement. A male adulterer is to receive eighty flogging strokes, while a woman is to receive one hundred. Many have heard of the so-called "honor killings" of the Muslim world where wives have been killed for not getting home before dark. Young women have been murdered for marrying those whom their family did not approve of. Even in countries where this is illegal, the man is often only lightly punished with a few years in jail or sometimes no time at all, even though he committed cold blooded murder. Some women have even been shot in fundamentalist ruled countries for "exposing one-fourth of their iris in public."[203]

The Beast, likewise, will "show no regard for the desire of women" (Dan. 11:37).

No Regard for any Other God

Additionally, he shows "no regard for any other god, for he will magnify himself above them all." There will be no tolerance for other faiths under the final Islamic kingdom. As the Koran states, "He is but one God. I deny the gods you serve besides Him" (Surah 61:19). Here we come up with an apparent contradiction on the surface of the Bible verse, when we see him magnifying himself above all other gods. For, in the next two verses, we see him seeking the help of a foreign god, "a god of fortresses" (Dan. 11:38a). However, as we showed earlier, there is no contradiction with this if we consider him to be the Jesus of Islam. If he is originally from another faith or ethnic background, especially Jewish, the god of Islam could then be considered as a foreign god to him.

Using Wealth to Advance Spiritual Goals

Daniel is also informed that "he will honor him (the god his fathers didn't know) with gold, silver, costly stones and treasures" (Dan. 11:38b). This too is a vital part of Islam. Believers are repeatedly exhorted in the Koran to use their worldly goods and possessions to help in the fight for the cause of Allah. "Whether unarmed or well-equipped, march on and fight for the cause of Allah, *with your wealth* and with your persons. This will be best for you, if you but knew it" (Surah 9:41). The leader of Islam, Muhammad was a good example of this. The Beast of Daniel and Revelation will also lead the way in spending of his own possessions. Could it be he will do this using the oil wealth of the Middle East?

Land and Honor to Those Who Help Him

Also, ". . . he will give great honor to those who acknowledge him and will cause them to rule over the many, and will parcel out land for a price" (Dan. 11:39b). Likewise, the Koran states,

> They solemnly swear by Allah that if you order them to march forth, they will obey you, Say: Do not swear: your obedience, not your oaths, will count. Allah is cognizant of all your actions. Obey Allah and obey the Apostle . . . . Allah has promised those of you who believe and do good works (*jihad*) to make them masters in the land as He had made their ancestors before them . . . (Surah 24:54,55)

Those who fight on the Beast's side will be given authority and land to rule. Perhaps the abandoned homes and land of imprisoned, killed or fleeing Christians will be given to them.

He will Destroy Many While They are at Ease

Daniel also is told that, "he will magnify himself in his heart and he will destroy many while they are at ease" (Dan. 8:25a). Never before in the history of the world have people been as at ease, as people in the West are today. The Beast will greatly upset the apple cart.

The Anti-Christ Teaching of Islam, The Beast and The False Prophet

The spirit of Muhammad and Islam certainly fits a "horn" who has "a mouth uttering great boasts" (Dan. 7:20) and who has and "will speak out against the Most High and wear down the saints of the Highest One . . ." (Dan. 7:25). This spirit will be embodied in the Beast and the False Prophet. Look at some of the claims and teachings of Muhammad.

- He claimed to be the judge of men. "Come to be judged by that which Allah has revealed and by the Apostle (Muhammad)" (Surah 4:61).
- He claimed to be speaking the very oracles of the God of the Universe. "This Koran could not have been devised by any but Allah" (Surah 10:37).
- He claimed that his religion is the only true religion. "The only true faith in Allah's sight is Islam" (Surah 3:19).
- He taught the Islamic faith would be exalted above all others. "It is He who has sent His apostle with guidance and the Faith of Truth, so that He may exult it above all religions . . ." (Surah 61:9).
- He claimed to be Allah's apostle to purify the Gentiles. "It is He that has sent forth among the Gentiles an apostle of their own to recite to them His revelations, to purify them, and to instruct them in the Book and in wisdom . . ." (Surah 62:2).
- He also claimed to be the greatest prophet. "Muhammad is the father of no man among you. He is the Apostle of Allah and the Seal of the Prophets" (Surah 33:40).
- He even put many words in Jesus' mouth. For example, he claimed both Moses and Jesus prophesied about his coming in the Torah and the Gospel. "Jesus the son of Mary, . . . said to the Israelites: 'I am sent forth to you from Allah to confirm the Torah already revealed, and to give news of an apostle that will come after me whose name is Ahmad" (Surah 61:6). Ahmad is another name for Muhammad. Then he had the audacity to say in almost the next breath, "And who is more

wicked than the man who invents a falsehood about Allah when called to submit to Him?" (Surah 61:7).

- He claimed to be an example of a true follower of God that all men should follow. "There is a good example on Allah's apostle (Muhammad) for those of you who look to Allah and the Last Day and remember Allah always" (Surah 33:21).
- He claimed that ultimately God would judge all those who didn't follow his religion by sending them to eternal hell (Surah 21:97–98).
- He promised eternal life to true followers of Islam who fight for Allah's cause (Surah 9:22–23).
- Muhammad also said that claiming that God had a son was the greatest blasphemy anyone could claim. ". . . Admonish those who say that Allah has begotten a son . . . a monstrous blasphemy is that which they utter. They preach nothing but falsehood" (Surah 18:4,5). He adamantly denied the divinity of Jesus Christ. "Never has Allah begotten a son . . . Exalted be Allah above their falsehoods!" (Surah 23:89,90).
- Muhammad demanded his followers kill multitudes, whereas the Lord Jesus Christ sacrificed his own life to save the lives of others.
- He also denied that Jesus was crucified. "We have put to death the Messiah, Jesus the son of Mary, the apostle of Allah.' They did not kill him, nor did they crucify him, but they thought they did" (Surah 4:157).

Time and space do not allow us to get into the many other outrageous claims he made. Yet we can see here in this last one that the significance of the Resurrection is also lost by the denial of the Crucifixion. Paul identified the gospel message as being "delivered to you (the church) as of *first importance* . . . that Christ died for our sins according to the Scriptures, and that He was buried and that He was raised on the third day according to the Scriptures . . ." (1 Cor. 15:3).

The Spirit of Anti-Christ Permeates Islam

The apostle John clearly identified the denial of Christ's divinity as being the spirit of antichrist. Even the Roman Catholic Church, in its days of greatest doctrinal darkness never did this. John states "Who is the liar but the one who denies that Jesus is the Christ? This is the anti-Christ, the one who denies the Father *and* the Son" (1John 2:22). Again look at what the Koran declares, "Unbelievers are those who declare: 'God is the Messiah, the son of Mary'" (Surah 5:17). The word *Christ* is simply the Greek translation of the Hebrew word *Messiah* that means the Anointed One. The Anointed One was identified as having origins "from long ago, from the days of eternity" (Micah 5:2b) and is thus, necessarily one with God and divine. Thus, the one who denies Jesus the Christ, denies his divinity, and is the anti-Christ. This is why John states clearly, "Whoever denies the Son does not have the Father; the one who confesses the Son has the Father also" (1 John 2:23).

There have been many little anti-Christs who have done this. Once again this will be an identifying trait of the greatest of all anti-Christs, the Beast. No major faith, outside of Islam, has so directly, violently, consistently and adamantly made a major issue of denying the divinity of Christ. It is hard to find another ideology that has come up with as many explicit, blatantly hostile blasphemies as Islam. Although denying the divinity of Christ and the Bible's message, no communist ever claimed to speak for God. Although in severe error, neither Mormonism nor Jehovah's Witnesses nor Hinduism or Buddhism officially proclaim violence as a pillar of faith against those who refuse their teachings.

Although, at one time it advocated violence against those who disagreed with it, the fact is that Roman Catholicism *never* denied Christ's divinity, humanity or his death and resurrection. Humanism may deny the Gospel, but it does not openly advocate violence to enforce its doctrines. Most New-Age practitioners and Wiccans are peaceniks, as are those who worship nature or feminism. There is no faith on the planet that commands the undying, fanatical and violent devotion of so many adherents to its violently anti-Christ message as

Islam. Is there really any other system in the world today so ready-made for the Beast and the False Prophet?

For a summary of the similar characteristics of the Beast (anti-Christ) of the Bible and the Islamic Jesus consult Appendix B in the back of the book. We have now arrived at another question. What will be the sign that the Beast has actually seized power over the world? What will be the sign that the end is finally at hand?

Chapter 12

The Sign of the End: The Beast Rears His Ugly Head (Rev. 13:4–15)

The Beast will use two primary tools to obtain worldwide worship. John identifies the first when he quotes the world's response, ". . . they worshiped the beast, saying, Who is like the beast, and *who is able to wage war with him*?" (Rev. 13:4). The Beast uses absolute fear. The world cries out, ". . . who is able to wage war with him?" Apparently, there is no military option available that can defeat him.

The devil and men under his direct inspiration do not fight fair. They don't follow the Geneva Convention's rules. Radical followers of Islam could care less about such rules. They are merely the laws of men and not the laws of Allah as given in *Sharia* Law (Islamic Law). "Muhammad is Allah's apostle. Those who follow him are ruthless to the unbelievers . . ." (Surah 48:29) the Koran openly states.

In Islam it is not simply allowable to obtain and use chemical, biological and nuclear weapons in a first strike. If useful, it is demanded. One must use any and all weapons at one's disposal in fighting for the cause of Allah. "Whether *unarmed or well-equipped*, march on for the cause of Allah, with your wealth and with your persons. This will be best for you . . ." (Surah 9:41) How can one wage a winning war with such an opponent? Communism, with its entirely materialistic ideology religiously refused to believe in the world to come. Yet it was, nevertheless, greatly successful for a time. It quite nearly enveloped the world. Unlike Communism, radical Islam assures its followers that the only truly important world is the one you join after this one.

It's not surprising to see why the world will say, "Who is able to wage war with him?" Will we be able to keep weapons of mass destruction away from the radicals? We will try for a time, but we will ultimately fail.

There are thousands of tactical nuclear weapons in Russia. Some are literally the size of a suitcase. There are already Chechen and Dagestani Muslim rebels with Russian citizenship. They do not need passports to enter that nuclear country. Iran, a nation fabulously rich in sunshine, wind, natural gas and petroleum, is building and constructing nuclear power plants supposedly for its energy needs. Many US officials and others believe the real reason is to build nuclear weapons.

Pakistan has a very active and vibrant radical Islamic movement already and it also has nuclear weapons and nuclear weapons technology. As mentioned earlier, the current President of Pakistan, Pervez Musharef, basically a secularist, is engaged in a struggle for the heart and soul of government policy with Islamic radicals. In the recent election for Parliament, when the Islamist parties made great gains, they even took over the governing of Peshawar, one of the northern provinces.

According to former US government official, John Neihaus, "Pakistan is the most turbulent and unstable country. It is sheltering Taliban. It unilaterally aided North Korea's nuclear program."[204] As this book is being written, both Iran and North Korea continue to pursue nuclear weapons programs. North Korea threatens to sell its technology and weapons to whoever will pay money. It is not a question of whether or not Islamic terrorists will get these weapons of mass destruction; it is only a matter of time. The United States now knows that prior to 9/11 there were Pakistani scientists meeting with Al-Qaeda.[205] Time is what the radicals have on their side, for they believe that whatever temporary setbacks may come, they will ultimately triumph.

What will be the trigger that indicates the Beast is ready to seize control? What will be the sign that he has finally been given authority over the world? When will we know that the Great Commission has finally been fulfilled? Jesus told us what would happen and Jesus told us what the sign would be.

What will be the Outward Sign of the Coming of the True Jesus? (Matt. 24:1–51, Mark 13:1–37, Luke 21:1–37)

When asked about the sign of his coming and the end of the age, Jesus gave his disciples a very distinct answer in Matthew 24. Here he specifically mentioned the key sign that will indicate the end of the age has arrived. He first warned them against being deceived. Many would come falsely claiming to be Christ. History has already seen this happen. Many gurus and cults make that claim. Islam declared a different Jesus as well. Many will be misled, Jesus said (Matt. 24:4–5). And many have been.

Furthermore, Jesus said we would witness wars and rumors of wars. Nations would rise against nation and kingdom against kingdom. This seems to amply describe the epic conflicts of the collapse of Rome, the Barbarian invasions, the Viking invasions, the conquests of Islam, and the invasions of the Mongol hordes. This seems to fit the crusades, the upheaval of the Reformation, the Renaissance, the conquests of Napoleon, and the two great World Wars, as well as the rise and fall of Communism. He foresaw gigantic conflicts. He also predicted famines and earthquakes in various places. We have had many over the past two millennia. But this would be only the "beginning of birth pains." God has worked through these upheavals, or birth pains, furthering his kingdom and moving us closer to the day when the Gospel will have finally been preached in all nations.[206]

These things are preparing the way, but they do not yet represent the end. He referred to troubled times in history when saints would be delivered into tribulation. They would be hated by all nations because of being Christian. Furthermore, "at that time (when persecution breaks out) many will fall away and will betray one another and hate one another. Many false prophets will arise and will mislead many. Because lawlessness is increased, most people's love will grow cold. But the one who endures to the end, he will be saved" (Matt. 24:10–13).

This is the testimony of history. All of the momentous struggles mentioned have witnessed Christians taken captive and martyred for the faith. Many Christians were killed in invasions of the barbarian tribes of Europe. The Vikings decimated Christian churches and monasteries. They took many Christian girls to be their slaves. The brutal Sunni Muslim Mongol ruler of China, Tamerlane, was responsible for slaughtering hundreds of thousands of Christians and burning hundreds of churches in Central and Western Asia. He almost single-handedly decimated what was left of the Eastern Church in Central Asia. Some Muslim rulers have shown some tolerance. Still, the history of Islam is filled with violence and martyrdom for Christians who refused to convert or pay the *Jizzya* (Infidel tax), who dared to share the Gospel with Muslims, or who dared to leave Islam to follow Christ.

When crusaders retook Jerusalem and parts of Judea, it was not only Muslims who suffered. Many Christians not loyal to Rome were also killed. We are all familiar with the brutal inquisition and subsequent martyrdom of many Protestant brethren during the reformation period. Some Catholics also perished at that time. World War I witnessed the brutality toward the Armenian community. Many evangelicals lost their lives. World War II saw the imprisonment and death of Christians who tried to help protect the Jews from Hitler's wrath. Others died resisting Hitler's rule. Each of these conflicts witnessed periods of lawlessness and brutality. It certainly made people's blood and love run cold. In each case, many fell away from the faith. Many betrayed one another and hated one another.

All these things would happen, Jesus said, and they have. Yet still, the end hasn't come. However, in the final generation, all these things will happen again (Matt. 24:34). But the final generation will witness more than the usual kingdom clashes. The final generation will witness the final clash of kingdoms. Conflict will not endure forever. What we have seen recently is the beginning of a clash between Islam and the West? Could this be the final clash of civilizations? Are we part of that final generation?

The final generation will be different. Unlike previous ones, it shall likely witness all of Matthew 24 (Matt. 24:34). But what shall be the sign when we will know for sure that we are the last generation and this conflict of civilizations is the last? Right after verse 13 comes that pivotal scripture, "this gospel of the kingdom shall be preached in the whole world as a testimony to all the nations, and then the end will come" (Matt. 24:14).

But we will not be able to know with certainty when this time of great completion has happened. Or will we? Certainly, at first only heaven will know when this has occurred. But fortunately, we will not be left without a clear sign on earth that the time has arrived. This sign will confirm for us that the Great Commission has been fulfilled. Both the Lord Jesus Christ and the apostle Paul gave us fair warning what will happen just *before* the Lord returns.

The Abomination of Desolation and the Apostasy

Jesus told us in his next breath what would happen immediately after the great completion. He said, "therefore *when you see the abomination of desolation* which was spoken of through Daniel the prophet *standing in the holy place*—let the reader understand—, then *those who are in Judea must flee to the mountain*" (Matt. 24:15).

Paul referred to this same incident. He referred to the abomination of desolation standing in the holy place in his second letter to the Thessalonians. Wanting to dispel a disturbing rumor circulating among the disciples that Jesus had already returned, and "the day of the Lord" had already come, Paul assured them several things must happen *before* Jesus' coming.

"Let no one deceive you in any way, for it will *not* come *unless the apostasy comes first, and* the man of lawlessness is revealed, the son of destruction, who opposes and exalts himself above every so-called god or object of worship, so that he takes his seat in the temple of God, displaying himself as being God" (2Thess. 2:3–4).

Paul asserts that before the Lord can come, the "man of lawlessness" must be revealed. This dovetails with what Jesus said in Matthew 24:15. It also fits neatly into Islam's teachings. Under Islamic thinking, the Mahdi will come. He will be the interpreter of Islam and the one who sets up Islamic rule of the world. He will be under no law, except what he interprets Islamic law to be.

As mentioned earlier, it is interesting to see how Muhammad changed the Koran to suit his own personal preferences and whims. Undoubtedly, this pretend Jesus will do similar things if needed. He will show no respect for the laws of other countries or international law or protocol. He will appear on the Temple Mount at the Dome of the Rock. He will declare himself to be Jesus, the one to establish Islamic rule. He'll put down all idol worship and all true forms of Christianity that will never acknowledge him. Where else does the Bible point to this?

Daniel's Vision and Gabriel's Explanation

Jesus referred to the abomination of desolation as having been spoken of by Daniel the prophet. Let's turn then to Daniel to understand what he was talking about. Here is the setting and context. At the end of Daniel 8, Daniel is frustrated by a prophecy he had received. He was astounded because he couldn't understand the latter fulfillment of this prophecy. He found himself unable to know when it would happen. "There was none to explain it" (Dan. 8:27b). Shortly after this, Daniel also realized the time for the fulfillment of Jeremiah's prophecy (the 70 years captivity) was fast approaching. So he determined to fast and pray for Jerusalem and for his people (Dan. 9:1–3). Following prayer and fasting he received a most remarkable insight about the earlier vision of chapter 8 (Dan. 9:23).

In answer to his intercession, Daniel is given some of the most remarkably detailed prophecy in scripture.

Gabriel declares,

> Seventy weeks have been decreed for your people and your holy city, to finish the transgression, to make an end of sin, to make atonement for iniquity, to bring in everlasting righteousness, to seal up vision and prophecy and to anoint the most holy place. So you are to know and discern that from the issuing of a decree to restore and rebuild Jerusalem until Messiah the Prince there will be seven weeks and sixty-two weeks, it will be built again, with plaza and moat, even in times of distress. Then after the sixty-two weeks the Mes-

siah will be cut off and have nothing, and the people of the prince who is to come will destroy the city and the sanctuary. And its end will come with a flood; even to end there will be war; desolations are determined. And he will make a firm covenant with the many for one week, but in the middle of the week he will put a stop to sacrifice and grain offering; and on the wing of abominations will come one who makes desolate, even until a complete destruction, one that is decreed, is poured out on the one who makes desolate (Dan. 9:24–27).

Here Gabriel declares seventy weeks for God's people. A prophetic day is often equated with a year. If so, then there are 490 prophetic years declared for God's people and the holy city Jerusalem to accomplish a list of things. Why are all these prophetic years needed? They are declared necessary to "finish the transgression" of the Jews in their rejection of Messiah. Their rejection would usher in a time of a separation from God for the nation of Israel.[207] Ultimately then, the time will come to "finish the transgression." Messiah will finally take away the sins of Israel as they repent at his return (Zech. 12:10–13:2).

But this will also include a prophetic time to make atonement for iniquity and bring in everlasting righteousness. This speaks, of course, of the sacrifice of Messiah on the cross. It also prophetically spoke of the Jewish sacrificial system for sin being discontinued. This system was outward and temporary, unlike the blood of Christ that is permanent and everlasting.

From the time the decree would be issued to restore Jerusalem until Messiah the Prince, there will be seven weeks and sixty-two weeks. This rebuilding of Jerusalem from its first destruction would take place in a time of distress and be rebuilt with plaza and moat (Dan. 9:25b). Historical fact documents that Nehemiah got his decree to rebuild Jerusalem from King Artaxerxes in 445 B.C.[208] Thus, we must go forward in time seven weeks and sixty-two weeks (or sixty-nine weeks) from 445 B.C. to find its prophetic fulfillment.

What significant year does this bring us to? The sixty-nine weeks are equal to 476 years of 365.25 days.[209] If we subtract 445 from 476 we arrive at A.D. 31. However, since there is no year 0 and we go from 1 B.C. to A.D. 1, we must add two years back on to A.D. 31 that causes us to arrive at A.D. 33. What would happen after 476 years? "After the sixty-two weeks, the Messiah will be cut off and have nothing . . ."(Dan. 9:26a)! Thus, Gabriel gave Daniel the exact time when Jesus would be crucified and appear to "have nothing"!

The First Post-Messiah Desolation of the Temple

What would come after the Crucifixion of Christ? There is still the seventieth prophetic week awaiting us. What is to happen in that seventieth week? Does it reach to our time? And where is this abomination of desolation that Jesus said Daniel referred to?

Daniel is told about "the people of the prince who is to come." It is these people who "will destroy the city and the sanctuary. And it will come with a flood; even to the end there will be war; *desolations* are determined" (Dan. 9:26). These desolations are desolations that come *after* the Messiah is cut off. Thus, they are not the same desolation that Antiochus brought in 169 and 167 B.C.[210]

It is during this seventieth prophetic week that the "*people* of the prince who is to come" will destroy the city and the sanctuary. This destruction of the sanctuary and cessation of sacrifices happens at the midpoint of this prophetic seventieth week (Dan. 9:27). However, is "the prince who is to come," the *latter prince,* responsible for this cessation of sacrifices? No. In actuality, the prince who oversees this initial desolation of Jerusalem and cessation of sacrifices is *not* the same as the latter prince. How do we know he is not the same? This is the second time Daniel has been told specifically about this prince "who is to come," this latter prince. He was also talked about in Daniel 8.

According to Daniel 8:25, this prince will:

1) oppose the Prince of princes
2) magnify himself
3) destroy many who are at ease
4) and finally be broken without human agency (Dan. 8:25).

Also, it is not the latter prince, but the *people* of this latter prince who will come and destroy the city and the sanctuary in the middle of the seventieth prophetic week. It is his *people* and not he himself who will destroy the city and sanctuary. In other words, this latter prince comes after his people, *his ancestors*, have already destroyed the sanctuary and temple. The latter prince is not the same prince who oversaw the first post-Messiah destruction of the sanctuary and Holy City that the Roman soldiers did in A.D. 70.

The *Latter Prince* Brings a *Latter* Desolation

Gabriel continues to clarify this point. He gives Daniel a prophetic picture of what the latter prince "who is to come" will do. He reiterates the reality of another desolation. Remember it is after the city and sanctuary are destroyed that war would happen, and "*desolations*" would be determined. Notice these desolations are plural and not singular. This makes it absolutely clear there will be *more than one desolation* of the holy city and the sanctuary. A future desolation will be done by a future, latter prince. [211]

On the other hand, it was Emperor Vespasian[212], an earlier post-Messiah prince who made "a firm covenant with many" to come against Jerusalem. He used promises of great spoils to gather together the troops of various vassal kings within the Roman Empire to battle. Of course, at the time this covenant was made, the Jewish-Roman War's duration was unknown. Yet history tells us it would last for exactly one prophetic week, or seven years. It was the same length of time as one prophetic week, the seventieth week.

The Jewish War against Rome lasted from A.D. 66 to A.D. 73 with the final defeat at the fortress of Masada in A.D. 73. It was at the midpoint of this conflict, in the middle of the week, in A.D. 70 that the temple sacrifice was abolished and the sanctuary destroyed. It was just as Daniel was told it would be (Dan. 9:27a). Thus, the *people* under the authority of the first prince, Emperor Vespasian, who made the firm covenant with them, did the first desolation. Interestingly, they destroyed the temple *in defiance* of Vespasian's and his son, General Titus' orders. In a very literal sense, it was *the people* who destroyed it.

The People of the First Post-Messiah Desolation Produce the Latter Prince

The glaring question then becomes, just who are these *people* who destroyed Jerusalem and the sanctuary? It is from the descendants of these people that the latter prince will arise. At a glance one might assume they are Italians since Roman soldiers destroyed the city and sanctuary in A.D. 70. But we would be wrong to make such an assumption. Some were Roman *citizens*. Yet, as we have already seen, about half of the Roman Empire encompassed territory in Africa and Asia. So just what part of the Roman Empire did the troops come from? Once we answer that question, we answer the question of where the latter prince will come from.

Josephus, the Jewish Historian of the late first century witnessed firsthand the destruction of Jerusalem and the temple. He worked on the side of the Roman conquerors as a translator. Josephus gave us a very detailed description of where these conquering troops came from. Here we find out a most intriguing fact. Once again, we discover that this latter prince *cannot be* the same as the prince of the first desolation. Vespasian, who was emperor at the time of the first desolation, was ethnically Italian, having been born near Rome. But the people who destroyed the temple were *not* Italians. So just who are the ancestors of this latter prince who is to come?

These troops came from Alexandria in Egypt, Antioch and other regions of Syria, including parts of southeastern Turkey and northern Syria. Additionally, soldiers came from Arabia known today as Jordan and Saudi Arabia.[213] What do all these people have in common? All of these people groups are predominantly Muslim peoples today.

Take note of that. The descendants of the people who destroyed the temple and the sanctuary are today largely Muslim people. In a future fulfillment of this prophetic word to Daniel, the people who will gather against Jerusalem will be predominantly Muslim people. It is from these Muslim people that Daniel was told this latter prince would arise!

Setting the Stage for the Latter Desolation of the Temple

Daniel found out that "on the wing of abominations *will come one* who makes desolate, even until a complete destruction, one that is decreed, is poured out on the one who makes desolate" (Dan. 9:27b). Yet again we see that this "complete destruction" of "*the one* who makes desolate," the latter prince, could not have been fulfilled by Emperor Vespasian or his son, Titus. He was the earlier prince who made "a firm covenant with the many." Vespasian, and later his son, Titus (who became Emperor after his father), were relatively popular emperors who died many years after the battle with the Jews ended.

Vespasian died peacefully six years later in A.D. 79, and Titus didn't die until A.D. 81. The idea that he would make desolate "*until a complete destruction . . . is poured out on the one who makes desolate*" (i.e. on himself) seems to imply that the only thing that will stop him from his work of desolation of Jerusalem will be his complete destruction. However, both of these men died many years after the destruction of Jerusalem, and the temple and neither of their deaths undid or brought an end to that desolation. They also never persecuted the Church. Titus was especially tolerant. But this "one who makes desolate" will come "on the wing of abominations" and only his complete destruction will bring an end to the desolation he will bring. Thus, we discover that the demise of this latter prince will bring different results than the deaths of Vespasian and Titus did.

Furthermore, Gabriel told Daniel that a *plural* number of desolations would come. Thus, this "one who makes desolate" comes later and causes a latter desolation. Unlike Vespasian and Titus, a complete destruction comes on *the one* who brings this final desolation. No one has yet fulfilled the description of that latter desolation and then been completely destroyed, as the prophecy says he will be.

To review, we see the first three-and-one-half years of the final prophetic week completely fulfilled when the temple sacrifice was abolished. Here we summarize the seventieth prophetic week:

- Vespasian makes a firm covenant with his many allies. It ends up lasting seven years.
- His assault on Jerusalem brought an end to sacrifice and offering in the middle of the week when the people fighting for him destroyed the temple.
- Later one *will come* on the wings of abomination to fulfill the final three-and-one-half years of the prophetic week.
- Revelation tells us the Beast of Revelation will rule for exactly forty-two months, that is also 1260 days or three-and-one-half Jewish years (Rev. 13:5–7).
- This latter prince is the same individual as the Beast of Revelation. He is also the same Beast of Daniel 7 and 8:25. Thus, the Beast of Revelation will fulfill the latter half of Daniel's prophetic seventieth week.

We must now ponder yet another question. What is this "wing of abominations"? For the latter prince, the Beast, will come "on the wing of abominations." On the wing of the old temple in the courts of the Gentiles, a most interesting thing has happened in history.

Chapter 13

. . . .

On the Wing of Abominations

A bd Al-Malik seized control of the Muslim world and not long after, in a.d. 685, cleared off the Temple Mount and built the Dome of the Rock right on the Temple site. It was completed in a.d. 691. On its interior, written on a wall in the structure that was set up was a declaration that Islam had replaced Judaism and Christianity as the only true faith. How could this not be an abomination to the Lord?

If this is not prophetically significant, then it is certainly a most amazing coincidence at the very least! Yet Jesus said the thing *we* would need to watch for as the sign of his coming is when we see "the abomination of desolation which was spoken of through Daniel the prophet, *standing* in the holy place" (Matt. 24:15).

This object of defiance and the very faith that would cause desolation may very well have been symbolically and physically *set up* with the Dome of the Rock in a.d. 691. However, Jesus didn't say the sign of the coming of the end of the age would happen when the abomination is set up. He said the sign to look for would come when *the individual* for whom it was set up is literally "*standing* in the holy place." This is the one who Daniel said is coming on the wing of abominations. It is to this statement in Daniel 9:27 that Jesus referred us when he said that this abomination was mentioned by the prophet Daniel (Matt. 24:15).[214] It is this event that has not yet occurred.

In any case, in the future when the one who makes desolate is standing in the holy place, then those in Judea especially, and we as well, should beware. The Beast will make his announcement of the Islamic kingdom and the end of all other religions, including Judaism and Christianity, in apparent "fulfillment" of the words written on the Dome of the Rock. He may literally traverse the Temple Mount and eventually stand right on the spot of the Holy of Holies itself. The Beast will mistakenly proclaim Islam's superiority and reign over Judaism and Christianity. Perhaps there will be an image of the Beast placed here to commemorate Islam's triumph. Maybe this will remain standing during his reign.[215]

A Warning for the Jews to Flee

We know that this abomination of desolation is yet future because Jesus himself made it clear that there would actually be at least two desolations of the temple building and not just one. How is that so? Follow this carefully. When the sanctuary was destroyed in A.D. 70 and the sacrifice abolished, nothing was set up or established. Nothing was left "standing in the holy place." However, it is only *after* the "abomination of desolation" is found "*standing* in the holy place" that Jesus told those in Judea to flee to the mountains.

For years I mistakenly believed that Matthew's warning was for Jews and believers concerning Jerusalem's first destruction by the Roman Empire. However, a careful look at history and this text makes it clear this is not the case. If this warning was meant for believers in Judea at the time of Rome's destruction of Jerusalem, then it was a poor warning. The fact is that by the time the temple was trampled on by Roman soldiers and destroyed virtually all of the remaining starving inhabitants were slaughtered in the push to take what was left of the city.[216] Waiting until the temple was destroyed before leaving would have been very poor advice indeed!

But, didn't Jesus give a clear warning to his disciples? He most definitely did. Jesus gave clear advance warning to the Jews of the Roman attack and a detailed escape warning. However, that warning is not found here in Matthew or in the parallel passage in Mark 13. So what was the warning given to Jews of the first century?

According to Josephus, the first Jewish territory attacked by Vespasian was Galilee. With the fall of the last Galilean City, many rebels fled to Jerusalem and spread the news of the approaching Roman armies. A dispute broke out among the Jews as to whether or not to surrender. Some infighting began. For this reason, the armies of Vespasian paused north of Jerusalem for a time. They hoped that the Jews would kill more of their own number and make the battle easier later.[217]

Thus, the only time a warning would have been useful and people could have escaped relatively safely would have been *before* the attack on Jerusalem began. Certainly *not after* the temple had been trampled on. After completely surrounding the city of Jerusalem and pausing for a time, Vespasian used Josephus to appeal to the Jews to surrender. Many people *did* choose to leave the city, Josephus tells us.[218] Thus, the impending attack and gradual surrounding of Jerusalem by Roman armies would have been a far better time for escape.

Did Jesus give such a warning? To find out let's compare Luke's end-time dialogue with the Matthew/Mark passages. The passage in Luke 21:1–24 most probably took place while Jesus was in the temple among throngs of Jews. In verses 1–4 we see Jesus talking to people in the temple about the widow and her two mites. Shortly after talking about the poor widow, some people start talking about the beautiful stones in the temple. Right then and there, Jesus comments "as for these things which you are looking at, the days will come in which there will not be left one stone upon another which will not be torn down" (Luke 21:6).

The Sign of the Temple's *First* Post-Messiah Desolation

Then he is asked, "Teacher, when therefore will *these things* happen? And what will be *the sign* when *these things* are about to take place?" (Luke 21:7). At this time, as he was leaving the temple and possibly still addressing a broad Jewish audience, he talked about the destruction of the temple and when to expect its imminent demise.

Then, mysteriously, he mentioned his Second Coming. In Luke (not Matthew or Mark) Jesus specifically says Jerusalem would be surrounded by armies and days of vengeance and wrath would come "to *this* people." In other words, this wrath would only come upon the Jewish people he was talking with (Luke 21:20–24), *not* the whole world. At least, not yet.

Although similar in some ways to Matthew's passage, Luke describes this destruction while making no reference to the Great Commission being completed. It also declares that the trampling of Jerusalem would continue *until the times of the Gentiles are fulfilled* (Luke 21:24). This may have very well been a public declaration to Jesus' friends and foes that judgment would fall upon those Jews who had rejected his coming.[219] As he had earlier stated

> If you had known this day, even you, the things which make for peace! But now they have been hidden from your eyes. For the days will come upon you when your enemies will throw up a barricade against you, and surround you and hem you in on every side and they will level you to the ground and your children within you, and they will not leave in you one stone upon another, because you did not recognize the time of your visitation. (Luke 19:42–43)

In Luke 21, he mercifully gives them and anyone else who was listening, clear instructions as to what they should do to avoid the slaughter.

At first, the early part of this discourse (Luke 21:8–19) sounds very similar to the exhortations and warnings of troubles and persecutions given to the disciples in Matthew and Mark concerning life prior to the "abomination of desolation standing in the holy place." Yet, in Luke he describes hardship believers would face *before* the destruction of the temple as well. The different discourse in Matthew and Mark probably relate to what believers will face throughout Church history. But history also testifies that the wars and earthquakes, difficulties and persecutions that the apostles and early disciples endured mirrored closely those problems faced by believers *after* the destruction of Jerusalem and down through the Church Age until now. Thus, the early parts of these discourses have many similarities.

But in Luke, Jesus is quite possibly speaking directly to a large Jewish audience in public. Large audience or not, Luke's recorded discourse speaks solely in terms that provide an answer to their question about when the Temple would be destroyed. He addresses issues that have a direct impact on the Jews. He warns them of the wrath coming on the Jews because of their rejection of him. He tells them to leave Jerusalem. He warns them to flee to the mountains and not come back when they see armies surround the city (Luke 21:20–24). These instructions to the Jews made complete historical sense, for there was time to safely escape Jerusalem while it was becoming surrounded by Roman armies. Remember that Vespasian paused in his attack. Then he appealed through Josephus for surrender before beginning the attack.

After describing the horrific destruction that would hit Jerusalem, Jesus spoke of events leading to his Second Coming. Again, he describes what would lead up to his Second Coming in terms directly relevant to the Jews. He stated quite clearly that, "Jerusalem would be trampled under foot by the gentiles *until* the times of the gentiles are fulfilled" (Luke 22:24b).

Thus, we see there is a time of Gentiles trampling Jerusalem. This must take place *before* Christ's return. It is *after* this trampling by the Gentiles has been completed that we see "signs in sun and moon and stars, and on the earth dismay among *the nations . . .*" (Luke 21:25a). These signs in the heavens and dismay on the earth among the nations transport us from a localized judgment on the Jews to a worldwide event. Thus, the time of the Gentiles will end just prior to Christ's return. This of course has significance for the whole world. It is shortly after these and other divine judgments that we ". . . see the Son of Man coming in a cloud with power and great glory" (Luke 21:27). But why did Jesus refer to his Second Coming when answering a question about the temple's destruction? Isn't that a rather peculiar topic to talk about in reference to the destruction of the Temple?

A Warning to the Last Generation: The latter desolation is still to come

Even though Jerusalem was retaken by Israel in 1967, the fact is that half of the city is largely Palestinian and the Palestinians also still lay claim to it as their capital city as well. Indeed, this was the main sticking point that sank the Camp David Accords and the peace process that President Clinton tried to finalize in the summer of 2000. Israel is still restricted in what it can do there and continues to endure the monstrosity of the Dome of the Rock on the Temple Mount. So what will be the ultimate sign that the times of the Gentiles are about to come to an end? It will be when we see "the abomination of desolation that was spoken of through Daniel the prophet standing in the holy place" (Matt. 24:15).

Again, it is when this event happens and the Beast stands at the Dome of the Rock proclaiming himself to be Jesus that those in Judea should flee to the mountains (Matt. 24:16). This type of warning makes sense only now because only half of Jerusalem is fully under Israeli control today. Thus, those who are in Judea (most of what is today the nation of Israel) and Jerusalem will have adequate time and opportunity to flee to the mountains only if they move swiftly. The split of the Palestinian and Israeli halves run right through the Temple Mount. Thus, the Beast will be able to stand on the Temple Mount without having to overrun all of Israel or even the Jewish half of Jerusalem.[220] Indeed, overrunning all of Israel will actually prove impossible.

The Sign of Christ's Second Coming Drawing Near

This revealing of the "man of lawlessness" in the Temple of God (2Thess. 2:3–4) on the Temple Mount will be the sign for the Church that the completion of the Great Commission has happened. Also, it will be a sign for Israel that the times of the Gentiles are about to come to a close and deliverance from their Messiah is at hand. As this second desolation happens, it will also be a sign to the Church of the beginning of the Great Tribulation. An initial attack will be launched on Israel, but successfully thwarted. As we shall see later, this attack may very well coincide with an attack on Babylon. After the thwarted attack upon Israel, she will flee to the place prepared for her in the wilderness to be nourished and protected by God. Then the Church will receive the bulk of the Beast's wrath (Rev. 12:12–17).

As Jesus warned,

> Whoever is on the housetop must not go down to get things out that are in his house. Whoever is in the field must not turn back to get his cloak. But woe to those who are pregnant and to those who are nursing babies in those days! But pray that your flight will not be in the winter, or on a Sabbath. For *then* there will be a *great tribulation*, such as has not occurred since the beginning of the world until now, nor ever will. Unless those days had been cut short, no life would have been saved; but for the sake of the elect those days will be cut short. Then if anyone says to you, 'Behold, here is the Christ,' or 'There He is,' do not believe him. For false Christs and false prophets will arise and will show great signs and wonders, so as to mislead, if possible, even the elect. Behold I told you in advance. (Matt. 24:17–25)

The fact that Jesus mentions to pray that flight won't happen on the Sabbath emphasizes the fact the flight of those living in Judea will have to be particularly swift. This will be harder to do if the day lands on the Sabbath. Perhaps this is because public transportation is more difficult to procure on that day in Israel.

Not One Stone will be Left on top of Another

There is another important distinction between the Olivet discourse of Matthew and the temple discourse in Luke concerning his coming. It gives us greater clarification about a second desolation to come to the temple building. Notice that only in Matthew do the disciples ask Jesus about his coming *and* the end of the age. However, in Luke, while likely just outside the temple, the only question that he is asked about is the destruction of the temple.[21] If they only asked about the temple's destruction in Luke, why does Jesus go on to tell them about the end of the age as well? Again, why would Jesus include in his answer details about his return when he was only asked about how they would know the temple was about to be destroyed?

The answer to that question lies in a statement that Jesus made that prompted the question in the first place.

Look at this carefully. "And while some were talking about the temple, that it was adorned with beautiful stones and votive gifts, He said, 'As for these things which you are looking at, the days will come in which there *will not be left one stone upon another which will not be torn down*'" (Luke 21:5–6). The disciples then asked him when that specific thing would happen. When would it be that "there will *not be left one stone upon another?*" (Luke 21:6b).

This question about when the temple would be torn down without one stone left upon another was asked in the Matthew-Mark discourse and in Luke as well. As stated before, many assumed this prophecy of the temple's destruction was fulfilled when the temple was destroyed by the Romans in A.D. 70. If so, both passages are completely parallel. The problem is that such an assumption is wrong. *There are still stones from the temple that Jesus and the disciples looked at that are still standing on top of one another, just as they were when they were constructed!* The Jews call these stones the Wailing Wall. They are remnants of the Western Wall of the temple. This continues to be the most holy site in Judaism. Many Jews gather there to pray and read scripture and even kiss the stones. Thus, the full destruction of the temple is not yet complete. And therefore, the curse against the Jews for rejecting their Messiah is still not completed.

Yet it will be completed after the times of the Gentiles are fulfilled when the Beast reveals himself at the temple initiating the final and second desolation of the temple in Jerusalem, just as Matthew states. The Beast, in his rage, will literally tear down the remaining stones of the temple found at the Wailing Wall. This will indicate the completion of the times of the Gentiles. Shortly afterwards, God's judgment will fall just as Luke states. It is then that the Lord Jesus says he himself will return.

The Two-step Destruction of the Temple

After leaving the temple and going to the Mount of Olives, Matthew records a detailed discourse spoken on Olivet where Jesus is asked, "What will be *the sign of your coming and of the end of the age?*" (Matt. 24:3b). Why was Jesus asked about the sign of his coming here on the Mount of Olives and not in Luke while he was just outside the temple? Because in Luke he only answered the question about the destruction of the temple. Thus, the answers given in Luke were only related to the event of the temple's destruction and how that related to the Jews.

The complication in understanding was caused by the fact that that event (the destruction of the temple) would actually take place in two stages. The second destruction would not happen until shortly before Jesus' return. That would happen *when* the times of the Gentiles were fulfilled and the Great Commission completed. Thus, when speaking of the temple's destruction, Jesus had to speak of his Second Coming as well. Later, on the Mount of Olives, the disciples wanted more details about when the times of the Gentiles would be fulfilled so they would know when his Second Coming would be. Whereas the first post-Messiah destruction was described in Luke, in Matthew we get a description of a second destruction of what remains that will signal his coming.

When the Beast reveals himself, he will also have the remnants of the Wailing Wall—holy to the Jews—torn down. Ironically, this action will finish the curse that was spoken against Jerusalem and the temple by the Lord Jesus. This final desolation is one of the desolations that Daniel referred to. In the case of Luke, where Jesus was addressing the Jews, there is no mention of a Great Tribulation after the times of the Gentiles are fulfilled. This is because Revelation tells us that after the initial assault, God shall mostly shield the Jews from the attacks of the Beast (Rev. 12:12–16).[222]

The Abomination of Desolation Unleashes the Great Tribulation

However, in the Matthew-Mark discourse, we see a different situation. After the abomination of desolation is found standing in the holy place, there is a Great Tribulation that will begin. It will be a tribulation such as the world has never known. Here Jesus warns his

Church via the apostles of the follow-up action to this final desolation. Again, the warning in Matthew is specifically applicable to a future desolation of the temple. It did not apply to the first post-Messiah desolation. This latter desolation comes after the initial desolation by the Romans. Unlike Luke's message, this message was made to the disciples privately while on the Mount of Olives.[23] The privacy of this message to the twelve further indicates the Lord's intention to give this warning to future followers through the written gospel message.

This is strongly suggested by the note enclosed in the message of verse 15 about the abomination of desolation. That special note (likely inserted by Matthew) says, "Let the reader understand" (Matt. 24:15b). Conservative scholars date the distribution of the gospel of Matthew as being sometime in the 60s.[24] By the time this gospel was well distributed and widely available to believers, the temple and Jerusalem had probably already been destroyed. So we see this warning has been placed there for a reader of future generations, especially the last one.

Furthermore, after the destruction of the temple by the Romans in A.D. 70, there was *not* a Great Tribulation against followers of Jesus immediately following. There had been tribulation under Nero up until about A.D. 68. However, Nero died before the destruction of the temple. The persecution of Christians under the new emperor ceased. Christians were not to experience martyrdom again at the hands of Rome until about A.D. 95–96, toward the end of the reign of Domitian. Yet, Matthew and Mark make it clear this final Great Tribulation will actually break out immediately after the abomination of desolation (Matt. 24:15–21), and it will make all other tribulations pale in comparison. Nearly twenty-five years passed after the first destruction of the temple before a major persecution broke out. Clearly the events of Matthew 24 still await a future fulfillment.

"For *then* there will be a great tribulation, such as has not occurred since the beginning of the world until now, *nor ever will*" (Matt. 24:21).

The future final desolation will be the opening salvo of the Great Tribulation. The chart on the next page illustrates the timing of the two desolations.

What Have We Learned of this "One Who Makes Desolate" So Far?

With the establishment of the Dome of the Rock, Islam announced that it had become a major player in the quest for world dominion. In its own view, it is the only player. Eventually, most Muslim peoples will rally behind their false prophet to support the false Christ, the Beast, in order to establish world dominion. He will have his dominion, but only for a three-and-a-half year time period. Thus, that prophetic seventieth week of Daniel will yet have its second

1st Destruction of Temple (Luke 21)	2nd Destruction of Temple Remains (ie. The Western Wall) (Matthew 24 & Mark 13)
• Church history prior to 1st destruction of the temple (Luke 21:7-19) ^	^ ^ ^ ^ ^
• 1st Destruction of temple & Jerusalem – 70 AD (Luke 21:20-24) • Jews scattered to the nations (Luke 21:24) • Beginning of the times of the Gentiles (Luke 21:24) ^	• Church history prior to the 2nd complete destruction of the temple. (Mt. 24:4-13) ^ ^
• Times of the Gentiles are fulfilled (Lk 21:24b) ^ ^ ^ ^ ^ ^ ^	• Great Commission is completed (Mt 24:14) • Abomination of Desolation found standing in the holy place (i.e. 2nd destruction of the temple & Jerusalem) (Mt 24:15) ^ • The Great Tribulation of the Church (Mt 24:15-26) ^ ^
• Time of judgment falls on the earth (Lk 21:25-27) ^ ^	• Time of judgment falls on the earth (Mt 24:29-30) ^ • Rapture of the Church (Mt 24:27-31)
• Christ's return (Lk 21:27) • Israel is redeemed (Lk 21:28)	• Christ's return (Mt 24:31)

half fulfilled. During these last three-and-a-half years, the Beast will rule and subdue the rest of the world "until a complete destruction, one that is decreed, is poured out on the one who makes desolate" (Dan. 9:27b).

It may be that sometime prior to accomplishing his goal of uniting the Muslim world; an attempt will be made to assassinate this individual. For he is later identified as "the first beast, whose fatal wound was healed" and "the beast who had the wound of the sword and has come to life" (Rev. 13:12b, 14b). Some time after this apparent fatality, he will amazingly recover and succeed in uniting the world of Islam.

Following this, he will overrun the Palestinian half of Jerusalem. He will destroy the remainder of the Western Wall of the outer court of the Temple. He will also announce to the world at the sight of the Temple Mount at the Dome of the Rock that he is Jesus who has returned "to break all crosses" and establish Islam as the only religion of the world.

He will say Christians falsely declared him dead on the cross. He will probably lie and say he was lifted into heaven and has now returned. His seeming ability to defy death will surely be seen as a sign of his invincibility. He will then attempt to try to overrun the rest of Israel and succeed in taking Jerusalem. But he will fail to take all of Israel. The Lord himself will come to Israel's defense and use the earth to swallow up the flood of his forces (Rev. 12:13–16). He will then attempt to force Islamic conversion on the whole world. He will make war on all who oppose him, especially, true Christians (Rev. 12:17).

Challenge of the Great Tribulation

Daniel also prophesied the actions of this man when he stated that "the king will do as he pleases, and he will exalt and magnify himself above every god and will speak monstrous things against the God of gods; and he will prosper until the indignation is finished, for that which is decreed will be done" (Dan. 11:36). He will have great success initially.

For "it was also given to him to make war with the saints and to overcome them, and authority over every tribe and people and tongue and nation was given to him. All who dwell on the earth will worship him, everyone whose name has not been written from the foundation of the world in the book of life of the Lamb who was slain" (Rev. 13:7–8).

It is here that John sees that armed resistance, outside of Israel, will fail for "if anyone is destined for captivity, to captivity he goes; if anyone kills with the sword, with the sword he must be killed"

(Rev. 14:10a). It is quite likely there will be few POW's from the combatants. Probably mostly only noncombatants will be afforded the "luxury" of prison, capture and a time to consider becoming Muslim. It seems military resistance will be futile. Those who choose to go down fighting will not prevail militarily. The dominant means of execution of the saints will be beheading (Rev. 20:4), a common means of execution under *Sharia* (Islamic) law. This will be a trying hour for the Church. John saw it, declaring, "Here is the perseverance and the faith of the saints" (Rev. 14:10b).

Chapter 14

The Islamic False Prophet: The Chief Enforcer (Rev. 13:11–18, 14:9–13)

The false Jesus Christ will not be alone in his efforts. He will have at his right hand the false prophet. John sees "*another beast coming up out of the earth, and he had two horns like a lamb and he spoke as a dragon*" (Rev. 13:11a). His coming up from the earth may signify he will claim to be one who never left the earth.

How might this fit with Islam? As mentioned earlier, in Shiite Islamic circles[225], Shiites believe true imams (leaders of Islam) are chosen at birth. Many Shiites believe the twelfth imam who descended from Ali (Muhammad's son-in-law) never actually died. This belief is fed by the fact that he mysteriously disappeared, and no one knows what became of him. Because of this, many Shiites believe he is hiding on the earth and will return one day to establish true Islam on the earth.[226] The groundwork has been carefully laid for a false prophet to come. Perhaps through the appearance of Jesus, as well as this twelfth imam as the False Prophet (in accordance with Shiite theology) these two major Islamic sects will finally be re-united demonically.

This so-called prophet is brutal, for he speaks as a dragon. Since the dragon is identified as the devil and Jesus labeled him as a liar and a murderer, it is no surprise this false prophet will have the same voice. Having two horns like a lamb, he will outwardly appear to be the picture of holiness and piety, as he will tirelessly serve the Beast. He will do his bidding, much as Jesus the Lamb of God did whatever he saw the Father doing.

He may possibly declare himself to be the twelfth imam or be declared by others to be so. The Koran states that apostles always come with signs. When this false apostle comes,

> He performs great signs, so that he even makes fire come down out of heaven to the earth in the presence of men. And he deceives those who dwell on the earth because of the signs which it was given him to perform in the presence of the beast, telling those who dwell on the earth to make an image to the beast who had the wound of the sword and has come to life. And it was given to him to give breath to the image of the beast, so that the image of the beast would even speak and cause as many as do not worship the image of the beast to be killed. (Rev. 13:13–15).

This will be his primary job, to insure worldwide worship of the Beast. For "he exercises all the authority of the first beast in his presence. And he makes the earth and those who dwell in it to worship the first beast, whose fatal wound was healed" (Rev. 13:12).

This false prophet—much as the magicians of Pharaoh temporarily succeeded using false signs—will succeed in deceiving much of the world with his false signs. This will be more than sufficient to convince devout Muslims. If any in the "rational" West remain skeptical, they will nevertheless submit, saying, "Who is able to wage war with him?" (Rev. 13:4b). In the name of self-preservation, they too will worship him.

The Image

John makes an interesting statement here about an image. This image may actually be what is ultimately left standing in the temple. John refers to the image having breath. It may be demonically enlivened, a genetic clone, or on the other hand, it may be that John is merely limited by his first-century vocabulary in describing the image. Perhaps this image is nothing more than a film footage of the Beast making his blasphemous declarations and reading from the

Koran. Then this image might be broadcast continuously throughout the world. To enforce allegiance to Islam, all that need be done is the flicking on of a television to the right station or a computer to the right website. All those watching could then be ordered to bow down to the image and declare acceptance of the message of this fake Jesus.

Amazingly, the Koran also seems to talk about a beast doing very much the same things this false prophet will do. It states,

> On the day when the Doom overtakes them (the unbelievers), We will bring out *from the earth a monster* that shall speak to them. Truly, men have no faith in our revelations.

> On that day We shall gather from every nation a multitude of those who disbelieved our revelations (the Koran). They shall be led in separate bands, and He (the monster) will say to them: 'You denied My revelations although you knew nothing of them. What was it you were doing?' The Doom will smite them in their sins, and they shall be dumbfounded. (Surah 27:83–85)

The context of this verse is talking about a judgment day when the mountains will pass away (Surah 27:88). Incredibly, the Koran asserts that a monster will arise out of the earth. The monster itself will speak to the unbelievers and announce their doom! And he will gather them from every nation! Perhaps the devil was peeking at Revelation and in his arrogance couldn't help boasting about what he was going to do.

The Economic Plan and the Number of his Name

The False Prophet will also undertake another project to ensure allegiance to the Beast's kingdom. In addition to fear and deception, there will be a powerful economic incentive.

> . . . He causes all, the small and the great, and the rich and the poor, and the free men and the slaves, to be given a mark on their right hand or on their forehead, and he provides that no one will be able to buy or to sell, except the one who has the mark, either the name of the beast or the number of his name. Here is wisdom.

Let him who has understanding calculate the number of the beast, for the number is that of a man; and his number is six hundred and sixty-six. (Rev. 13:16–18)

Ever since its beginning, Islam has used economics as a powerful means of arm-twisting to encourage conversion and submission to its rule. The Koran states:

Fight against such as those to whom the Scriptures were given as believe neither in God nor the Last Day, who do not forbid what God and his apostle have forbidden, and do not embrace the true faith, *until they pay tribute out of hand (the Jizya) and are utterly subdued.* (Surah: 9: 29)

Whenever they conquered a region, those who were not Muslims were given a few choices. They could convert to Islam. If they chose to not convert, then they would have to pay the *Jizya* (or the unbeliever's tax), that Muslims did not have to pay. They would also have to refrain from proselytizing Muslims. Those who refused either of these two choices would be imprisoned, and ultimately they could be killed.

According to Sunni *Sharia* (Sunni Islamic Law) texts: the

. . . capitation-tax is a sort of punishment inflicted upon infidels for their obstinacy in infidelity, (as was before stated;) whence it is that it cannot be accepted of the infidel if he send it by the hands of a messenger, but must be exacted in a mortifying and humiliating manner, by the collector sitting and receiving it from him in a standing posture. It is specifically a punishment for "infidelity"—i.e. for not being a Muslim. It is levied only on non-Muslims. *The aim of the tax is* not to safeguard the rights of the payee, but *to demonstrate the superiority of one religious confession over another.* Often *when paying the tax, the dhimmi (non-believer) was struck on the head or the neck, and had to wear a parchment proving payment* or face sanctions.[227]

It is not difficult to see how such a system could be adopted and modified under the reign of the Beast. A type of economic proof of subservience already exists in Islam through the *jizya* tax. Even the system of putting identification on the payer as proof, has also already been a practice of Islam under *Sharia* law. It doesn't take a rocket scientist to see that when worldwide Islam is established, this practice could be adapted to guarantee submission of the whole world to the Beast. Perhaps this will become something like an Islamic sales tax number. It could be placed on the end of all account numbers of people who receive the outward physical mark on their person.

It is particularly chilling to note that one of Muhammad's followers, Abu Huraira reported what the prophet said would happen when the Islamic Jesus returns to earth to establish worldwide Islam. He quoted the prophet as saying that "He (the Islamic Jesus) will break the Cross, and kill the swine, and *take away the poll-tax . . .* and fight for the religion of Islam until Allah shall destroy in His (Jesus') day the people of every other faith except Islam, and worship shall be Allah's alone."[228]

Notice that unlike past practice where infidels were allowed to pay the *jizyah* (also known as the poll-tax) in place of converting to Islam, the Islamic Jesus will come to bring an end to all other religions except Islam. Thus, he will "take away the poll-tax" since there will no longer be any need for it. The only choices will be conversion to Islam or death. The inability to buy and sell without the mark will be the mechanism used to force all to make a choice.

The Number of the Beast is the Name of the Beast or the Number of his Name (Rev. 13:16–18)

The number of the Beast is 666 and the mark must include his name or his number. Having the mark signifies complete submission to his reign. Much has been stated about electronic chips. Still, it is possible this mark may be something as simple as a requirement to show a tattoo with the Beast's number, 666, before every purchase. Perhaps the tattoo is only given after making a pledge of allegiance by bowing down to the Beast's image and reciting the basic Islamic creed, "There is no god but Allah and Muhammad is his prophet."

Might there be computer checks involved in the system? Might there be 666's added to the end of all account numbers? Certainly many things are possible. But the important thing is that it will be obvious to all what it is and what it signifies. No one will take this mark because they were fooled into doing it.

This number 666 is especially interesting for several reasons. First of all, numbers are of great significance in Islam. Allah is said to have ninety-nine revealed names. According to one tradition, only the camel knows the one-hundredth name. Muslim prayer beads have thirty-three or ninety-nine beads. The ninety-nine names are well known to Islamic scholars.

Some of Allah's names sound reasonable to Christians when they think of God, such as Allah, the Creator. However, others seem distinctly out of place for the God of the Bible whom we worship. For example, he is also called Allah, the Proud, and Allah the Eternal who begets not and is not begotten, and Allah the Killer at His will. Some names are just plain peculiar, but perhaps significant, such as Allah, the Computer who numbers everything and Allah, the Seizer.[229]

There is some disagreement among Muslim scholars about the number of verses in the Koran. However, it is widely said and believed that the Koran contains 6,666 verses. On the other hand, some Islamic scholars believe there are actually 6616 verses.[230] The Koran says Jesus is the "word of Allah and His spirit." As such, might not the personal number of this Islamic Jesus be given as 666? Or perhaps the verses of the Koran that mentioned him will be manipulated to show there are 666 verses about him. This could readily be done since some verses are unclear as to which apostle is being talked about.

Another possibility also revolves around the Islamic Jesus being the "word of Allah and His spirit." If it is accepted that there are 6616 verses, then he could declare that the number one represents Allah's number as the one and only true God. This false Jesus, being the word of Allah, contains all that Allah says and is the spirit of all that he is. Thus, the six at the beginning represents the false Jesus' number, since he is the beginning of Allah's word. He is the second six found in the middle, since he is the substance of all that is contained in Allah's word. Last of all, he is the last six because he is the end of Allah's word. Although this is speculative, it is not difficult to see how the Jesus of Islam can be easily identified with the number 666, in one way or another.

This might seem counterintuitive to Westerners since this number has long been associated with evil. We might think the Beast would loathe associating himself with a number so widely known to represent satanic significance. However, even for Muslims aware of what the Bible says, this fits perfectly into the Muslim belief that Christians have deliberately changed key texts in the Bible to hide "the truth" about Muhammad and Jesus. This could easily be seen as just another Christian conspiracy to smear Islam.

Muslims would not consider it an act of worship to take a mark to prove their devotion to the newly established Islamic kingdom with the false Jesus at its head. Yet it will certainly be considered as worship for the Christian. It will undoubtedly require bowing down to or praising and honoring the "image" of the false Jesus and a public acceptance of the Koran as the revelation of God and Muhammad as his prophet. Such behavior will be anathema to true Christians. Besides, the Bible forbids it. An angel warns John,

> If anyone worships the beast and his image, and receives a mark on his forehead or on his hand, he also will drink of the wine of the wrath of God, which is mixed in full strength in the cup of His anger; and he will be tormented with fire and brimstone in the presence of the holy angels and in the presence of the Lamb. And the smoke of their torment goes up forever and ever; they have no rest day and night, those who worship the beast and his image, and whoever receives the mark of his name. (Rev. 14:9–11)

This trial will require creativity for Christians and God's help to get food to eat and clothes to wear. Of course, it always has. But this time it will be more obvious. The words of Jesus will take on extra meaning:

> Do not worry then, saying, 'What will we eat?' or 'What will we drink?' or 'What will we wear for clothing?' For the Gentiles eagerly seek all these things; for your heavenly Father knows that you need all these things. But seek first His kingdom and His righteousness, and all these things will be added to you. So do not worry about tomorrow; for tomorrow will care for itself. Each day has enough trouble of its own. (Matt. 6:31–34)

This will be a time of testing of our faith. John recognizes the difficult trial this will engender and states, "Here is the perseverance of the saints who keep the commandments of God and their faith in Jesus" (Rev. 14:12). However, a voice from heaven is quick to add this encouragement, "Blessed are the dead who die in the Lord from now on!' 'Yes,' says the Spirit, 'so that they may rest from their labors, for their deeds will follow with them'" (Rev. 14:13). For a summary comparison of the characteristics of the False Prophet and Islam's end-times theology consult Appendix C.

Still, we have left an important characteristic of this Beast's program unmentioned until now. Daniel states that "he will take action against the strongest of fortresses . . ." (Dan. 11:39a).

He will not be afraid to take on the strongest of fortresses in the name of Allah, for in the Koran, Allah guarantees ultimate success. Those who capitulate to him and acknowledge him will be given positions of authority. Perhaps seized property will be used as an incentive to help buy allegiances. Speaking of the "strongest of fortresses," how will it be that America and her allies will give in? Is America ever talked about in prophecy? Won't America come to defend her old ally Israel?

Chapter 15

What Will America Do?

T he voice on the other end of the phone sounded agitated, if not downright panicky. "Mr. President have you seen the announcement on television?" blurted out a frantic Secretary of State, Thomas Franks.

"What announcement?" asked President Burns.

"It's a security threat to our nation . . . to the world . . . like none we've ever seen. It's just as we feared Mr. President. I have Aysha wheeling down a TV to the situation room as we speak. I'm heading there right now myself."

No sooner had these words gotten out of Frank's mouth that both men hung up the phone and scurried over to the situation room. There the television was already tuned on to CNN. A somber news reporter summarized the video just shown on Al-Jeezirah television. Suddenly the film clip was running again.

Just as he had feared, on the television that dreaded face appeared. He was a bearded man with white robes and a head covering, appearing to be in his thirties. The President immediately recognized him. He was President Isa Abdullah, of the newly formed United Kingdom of Islam, a united confederation of Islamic states spread across North Africa from Mauritania to the Arabian Peninsula up to Turkey and across Central Asia to Pakistan.

Abdullah personified the President's worse nightmare. His exact origins were unknown. Some rumored he had been an orphan of Jewish parents who had lived among the tiny Jewish community in Baghdad. According to this story his parents were killed accidentally during the second Iraqi war by an errant US bomb. Some sources identified him as going to a Madrassa School for orphans formed after the deposing of Saddam Hussein in Iraq. It was believed that there he converted to Islam and became a devout Muslim.

His personal mentor, a powerful Madrassa teacher, was actually a Jordanian with strong connections in Jordan. Other rumors popular in the Muslim world were that he had mysteriously come down out of the mountains to join this Madrassa School. In any case, it was known that as a young man he received training in terrorist tactics against the US backed regime in Iraq. During this time he made friends with many international terrorists.

He later moved to Jordan to assist in the ongoing *intifada* (uprising) against Israel. It was here that he eventually obtained his Jordanian citizenship and gathered a following among the fundamentalists. The last major world economic downturn hit Jordan hard. In the unrest, the Jordanian Hashemite kingdom came to a sudden end with the assassination of the Jordanian King and his son while vacationing together. In the ensuing chaos, Abdullah, by now a popular Islamic cleric, who frequently spoke out against America and Israel in the Jordanian parliament, gained the upper hand and seized power. He promised to establish a true Islamic state. He immediately called for a *jihad* to remove all false Muslims from power in all Muslim countries. He demanded a truly Islamic state for the entire world. Many in the US State Department hoped his revolution would go the way of the Iranian revolutionary government that moderated somewhat since its establishment in 1980 (in spite of acquiring nuclear weapons in 2009). It was not to be.

Abdullah had a number of close friends in Saudi Arabia. His first wife was also a well-connected Saudi whose family had strong links to the fundamentalist movement in Saudi Arabia. Encouraged by Abdullah's success and aided by Jordanian agents and the state of Jordan, within weeks—before the West could respond—a swift, bloody coup removed the house of Saud from power in Saudi Arabia. Saudi Arabia had fallen.

A close associate of Abdullah, a Saudi with dual citizenship in Saudi Arabia and Jordan, Imam Muhammad Al-Barakat came to power in Saudi Arabia. He was behind the coup lead by fundamentalists in the armed forces. Owing his success to Abdullah and given Abdullah's popularity in Saudi Arabia, the Islamic Revolutionary Council chose Abdullah to become ruler of the newly named United Islamic Kingdom. The merger of Saudi Arabia and Jordan was complete. Abdullah immediately encouraged other oppressed Muslims to overthrow their governments, establish true Islamic states and unite with this larger Islamic Kingdom.

Abdullah promptly declared he would put the interests of Islam first. No longer would they be held hostage to the West's demand for cheap oil. Oil supplies to America were immediately cut, due to its support for the "Zionist" state and unwillingness to become Muslim. Before the United States could respond, the situation escalated rapidly.

Deeply inspired by a leader willing to stand up against the United States, Pakistanis in the street rose up and overthrew their pro-Western government within a matter of days. Excited by the vision of a resurrected Islamic kingdom, the new Pakistani Islamic revolutionary council, stacked with old friends and confidantes of Abdullah from his terrorist days, recognized Abdullah as their supreme ruler. They quickly announced that any attempt by outsiders to interfere in the affairs of Muslim countries would be seen as meddling in the internal affairs of the United Islamic kingdom. This kingdom quickly declared itself to be the only legitimate ruler of the Islamic world. Outside interference would mean certain nuclear retaliation. Spontaneous pro-United Islamic Kingdom demonstrations were now springing up in countries throughout the Islamic world. The world watched in stunned amazement.

In the meantime, Abdullah continued working secretly behind the scenes with his network of friends from his terrorist days. The world braced itself in astonishment as in one nation after another; the dominoes fell in rapid succession, much as when Communism rapidly collapsed in Eastern Europe and the Soviet Union. Coups and brief civil wars lead to new fundamentalist Islamic states. Abdullah's cronies were awarded positions of authority in these new Islamic regimes.

Syria fell. Then Iraq, Lebanon, Uzbekistan and one state after another in both Central Asia and Northern Africa succumbed to radical Islam. As each one was toppled, it pledged allegiance to the Islamic World Kingdom. As each Muslim country with oil fell under Abdullah's authority, oil supplies were cut off, not only to America, but also to all non-Islamic nations. Gasoline prices surged more than a thousand percent in only three-and-a-half years. Gas shortages sprung up. Western economies were teetering on the brink of total collapse as stock markets crashed and discretionary spending and investment dried up.

Within two years from his rise to power, only Egypt, Turkey, and surprisingly Libya and Iran, still held out. In spite of harsh government crackdowns, each experienced protests and unrest daily. Turkey tried desperately to stay neutral and out of the whole fray, but its own fundamentalist movement had hidden allies in the government and military. They encouraged the radicals to act, and they became increasingly emboldened and restive. Along with a flood of liberal Muslim refugees, radicals from the newly fundamentalist nations were infiltrating these holdout countries fomenting greater unrest and daily terrorist attacks. Such attacks in the West were also on the rise, occurring almost daily now.

An unlikely bunch of allies, Egypt and Turkey, were trying desperately to maintain a quietly pro-Western semi-democratic system. Mammuar Qhadafy, the leader of Libya—by now an old man—was against the West but also quite unwilling to submit to Abdullah's authority. Abdullah had become extremely popular on the Arab street and within the holdout countries. He was increasingly looked to as the political and spiritual leader of the entire Islamic world. He was seen as the one individual who could end the domination of the wealthy north and restore the honor and power of the Islamic peoples.

The Iranian Islamic Revolutionary Council, as a Shiite group, was also holding out in the vain hope of wresting control of the Islamic world. As Shiites, they chaffed at the thought of coming under Sunni Muslim leadership. These four countries with rather formidable armies and Iranian nuclear weapons appeared as difficult nuts to crack for the new United Islamic Kingdom. The West, not so secretly, helped supply weapons to Egypt and Turkey. At first it seemed these countries might hold out. Things stabilized for about six months and attacks began to decrease.

That was until an Iranian Shiite cleric, the magnetic Muhammad Rafsanjani Al-Mahdi began to make public appearances in Saudi Arabia alongside Abdullah imploring Shiites everywhere to unite behind Abdullah's United Islamic Kingdom. Rafsanjani was an old friend of Abdullah's from his days in Iraq. He was one of the first influential Shiites to openly advocate burying differences with Sunnis to fight for the good of Islam. He was an Iranian Shiite by birth popular in both Iran and Iraq. He had moved to Iraq as a child, and was fluent in both Farsi and Arabic. Rafsanjani was a rare charismatic figure who enjoyed trust from Sunni and Shiite Muslims.

For his support Rafsanjani was rewarded the number-two position in the United Islamic Kingdom as the foreign minister of World Islamic Propagation. Due to his public support of Abdullah, and his promotion to the number-two position in Abdullah's government, many Shiites buried their dislike of Sunnis and agreed to unite for the greater cause of Islam. Abdullah declared that the Islamic leaders in each Islamic state and Shiite and Sunni communities would be free to interpret some of the finer, less important details of Islamic law for the populations within their states.

Only the most important issues of Islamic law would be decided by Abdullah. Most importantly, Shiites would be free to continue to celebrate their Shiite holidays. Emboldened and encouraged by these declarations, Shiites who decided to throw their lot in with Abdullah and Rafsanjani Al-Mahdi rapidly purged out the older conservatives in the Iranian government who refused to submit to Abdullah's authority. Soon Iran was in the United Islamic Kingdom.

This left Turkey, Egypt and Libya as the last stubborn holdouts. Greatly outnumbered, Turkey and Egypt, nevertheless, had some of the most powerful militaries in the region. The United States and some in Europe pleaded with Turkey and Egypt to receive large numbers of NATO troops for support. But because of their own growing fundamentalist movements both felt that asking foreign "Christian" soldiers to come and help fight Muslims would prove counterproductive. Abdullah had already threatened that any large scale deployment of Western troops would be grounds for nuclear war.

Incredibly, the small contingent of American NATO soldiers already in Turkey was asked to leave. They insisted on fighting alone, though they welcomed Western aid that the West was more than anxious to give. Frustrated, the West was reduced to threatening nuclear retaliation should nuclear weapons be used on Turkey, Libya or Egypt.

Many secular and democratic-minded Muslims fled to Turkey and Egypt as refugees. They pleaded with these governments to do something to take back the Islamic world. By combining forces with Libya and moving quickly before he had a chance to fully centralize his control, they decided to try to catch Abdullah off guard. They hoped to deal a deathblow to his messianic dreams before they could take full root. Perhaps they could knock him off balance with a quick strike. Millions of liberal Muslims held out hope of a backlash from liberals in these states and a counterrevolutionary overthrow of this fundamentalist cancer. But by now most liberals had already been jailed or killed or gone into hiding. The West held its collective breath wondering what would happen next.

The two-pronged attack began in the spring and originated in the southeast from Egypt into Jordan and Saudi Arabia and in the north from Turkey into Syria and Iraq. The whole world was riveted to this cataclysmic battle. It looked hopeful at first, but after several months, to the great horror of the West the tide began to turn badly. The fanatical support of untold millions of Muslim troops, including many young volunteer vigilantes, proved too much. Additionally, both Pakistan and Iran once again threatened the use of nuclear weapons if the West should try to intervene by sending troops. They even threatened to use them on Turkey and Egypt if necessary to prevent their victory. The only restraint on using the nuclear option now was the millions of "faithful Muslims" in those countries whom Abdullah did not want to harm.

By now the world economy had sunk into an economic depression far deeper than the Great Depression. Unemployment reached well above thirty percent in most developed countries. Many poor nations suffered unemployment rates as high as ninety percent. As it became clear that the United Islamic Kingdom would triumph, the situation grew even worse.

The impact on the world was devastating. During the year of Islamic consolidation (as it was later called) all remaining government foreign aid from the West to the poorer countries had to be cut off, and private aid slowed to a trickle. Without funds to finance many vital medical and food programs, famine and disease was hitting historically monumental proportions in Africa and parts of Latin America. Government authority in many of the poorer nations was in total breakdown with the subsequent spread of virtual anarchy and lack of any basic government services.

In some nations governments had virtually ceased to exist. In other places there was no government left at all. Cholera and other diseases were spreading unchecked. Violence, looting and rioting was spreading unchecked, as was famine. Even in the West, crime had spiked greatly with a growing number of homespun Islamic street gangs carrying out their own jihadi inspired crimes and terrorist acts. It seemed that many criminal gangs were using Islam as a justification for more and more wanton acts of violence.

In the meantime, to the horror of the West and liberal Muslims, Egypt and Turkey were about to lose. Within a year, first Egypt on February 19, then Libya on March 1, and finally Turkey on April 2, fell under the spell of the Islamic tide. The last of the majority Muslim nations had fallen under the control of the United Islamic Kingdom. Turkey saved some face by agreeing to join the Kingdom under one condition. That was if Abdullah agreed to not execute its leaders and allow Turkey to share regional leadership of the Western and Central Asian portion of the United Islamic Kingdom. Abdullah agreed, and Turkey joined this federation of Islamic states. Shortly after, he promptly broke his word and executed its leaders declaring that investigations had revealed they were apostates.

The shock for secular Muslims was nearly as great as it was for the West. Many millions wanted to flee to Europe and America. However, these regions were wary to allow more than several thousand carefully screened refugees to come. They feared that fundamentalists would slip in among them. Indeed many had previously succeeded in slipping into Egypt and Turkey. When millions of secular liberal Muslim refugees came, so did thousands of undercover fundamentalists. They had operated successfully as a fifth column, undermining and sabo-

taging the efforts of Turkey and Egypt to resist. Once he had control
in Turkey and Egypt, thousands of secular Muslims were thrown into
jail. Many hundreds were executed and millions more were quickly
silenced and repentant because of fear of the same.

The surrender of Turkey emboldened many Islamic minorities to
press their demands further for the right of independence to join the
United Islamic Kingdom. Indeed Abdullah threatened to send troops
to liberate these areas. The Muslim Russian Republics of Chechnya
and Dagestan declared independence and alliance with the United
Islamic Kingdom. Tired of decades of civil war and not wanting to
start a large-scale war with the entire Islamic world, Russia granted
the secession.

Even Ethiopia, with a Muslim minority of only thirty-three percent, backed by state support of the United Islamic Kingdom pulled
off a *coup d'etat* that established an Islamic state over its Christian
majority. The whole world was spinning. Within days, Nigeria
and Eritrea—with their populations half Muslim—also fell under
Abdullah's power. In just under three-and-one-half years, the entire
Islamic world had fallen under the control of an Islamic fundamentalist dictatorship.

It was against this backdrop that the President found himself
watching Isa Abdullah deliver a message of warning to the West.

After making a number of religious statements, Abdullah continued, "Israel and America and all like-minded infidels must accept
Islam. They must recognize that Allah has declared there is only
one religion. All must bow and pledge allegiance to the religion of
Allah. There is only one government for the world. It is the holy
government of *Sharia* Law. It is the Law of Allah. As Allah's apostle
and representative I have come to establish true Islam. I demand the
United States, Israel and all infidel states accept eleven conditions to
demonstrate their allegiance and submission to Allah.

"All governments will be given thirty days to state in writing and
by public proclamation their acceptance of these conditions. On Janu-
ary 6, the anniversary of Muhammad's, peace be upon him, assent
into heaven above Jerusalem, I will make a very public declaration
officially proclaiming formation of a worldwide Islamic state. At this
time, governments that have not proclaimed unconditional accep-

tance of all of these conditions will be at war with us. We consider use of nuclear weapons to eliminate infidel cities to be acceptable if needed for the establishment of Allah's Kingdom. Following written acceptance of these eleven conditions, all governments will have sixty days to fully comply with all announced requirements. Non-compliance will warrant death and eternal fire."

1) "In past years all who refused to become Muslims could agree to pay the infidel tax in order to buy and sell and receive the protection of the Islamic government. This will no longer be acceptable since the time has arrived for Islam to be established in the entire world as the only religion. From now on my personal number, 666, shall be added to the end of all financial accounts of individuals who have converted to Islam and confirmed their loyalty to Allah's Islamic government. Thus all purchases will be tracked for compliance. Those not complying will be arrested and if found guilty killed.

2) "A mark must be clearly distinguished on one's hand, or forehead should an individual not have hands. This will be outward proof on their persons that all financial accounts have been registered. Persons without this outward mark will be unable to conduct financial transactions. Individuals may not obtain this mark until all financial accounts are amended with the number that represents my name. I repeat, refusal to comply or attempts to use accounts without three sixes at the end will mean death for violators.

3) "When submitting to this, each individual must outwardly and verbally declare allegiance to Allah and myself as his apostle and head of the United Islamic Kingdom. Exact details will be given at the end of this month when we declare the official beginning of the worldwide rule of Islam.

4) "Receiving this mark demonstrates a willingness to submit to Allah, his apostle and Islam as the supreme Faith. I have returned to the earth to establish the Islamic kingdom over the

entire earth. Therefore, by taking my name upon their hand or forehead and saying the creed of Islam, they will be demonstrating loyalty to Allah, the prophet and the United Islamic Kingdom that is perfect Islam. All pre-existing Muslims must also be marked with my name in order to verify their identity as true Muslims in submission to Allah's government.

5) "All governments must openly state they will no longer support any Zionist, Crusader, Christian, or similar elements that try to resist the rule of Islam. All non-Islamic places of worship will be closed and converted to mosques or destroyed. All crosses and pigs wherever they are found must be destroyed.

6) "All governments must surrender command and control of all police and military forces. All police and military will be required to convert to Islam. They must swear allegiance to me to keep their positions. Along with this, governments must agree to accept the authority of one of the ten regional governors appointed by the United Islamic Kingdom to have final authority over the affairs of the nations. Each of the ten governors reports directly to me. These governors will assist the leaders of the subdued nations in implementing a process to bring Islamic law into practice. Their word will be final on all matters of Islamic law.

7) "All children must henceforth be raised as Muslims. Anyone caught propagating any other faith to children or adults will be imprisoned and put to death.

8) "All governments must agree to enforce provisions of Islamic law upon all of their citizens. To maintain government positions, all government employees will be required to accept Islam and take an oath of allegiance to enforce the policies of the United Islamic Kingdom.

9) "In return for accepting these terms, subdued nations will receive protection and a guarantee of peace from the United Islamic Kingdom. All submissive subjects will be granted the

right to prosper and conduct all business consistent with the dictates of Islam. Local rulers who have sworn loyalty to Islam will be free to establish laws and policies for their own areas, as long as they do not run counter to Islamic law. The only way of peace is the way of Islam. By accepting Islam, world leaders will guarantee peace, safety and prosperity for their nations.

10) "If any governments should resist this decree of Allah, they shall remain in the Realm of War with Islam. Every non-Muslim in their kingdom not submitting to the Islamic kingdom shall be subject to the most horrible of murders. We will feel free to use all weapons and means at our disposal to enforce Allah's will. All Muslims, wherever found, will be duty bound to fight against those governments and individuals until they are subdued.

Any Muslim who does not agree to fight will be treated as an unbeliever and receive the most horrible of punishments. Governments who do not accept my terms will have their cities targeted by martyrs armed with tactical nuclear weapons. Every citizen of every nation that accepts Islamic rule will be expected to submit to Islamic law. Non-compliance will be met with the severest of punishments. However, if nations and people should repent and receive Islam, they will be pardoned, for Allah is all merciful.

11) "Thirty days from today I will announce the establishment and official beginning of the Worldwide United Islamic Kingdom that will include all nations. At that time I shall officially declare my absolute authority as Allah's apostle over the entire world. In preparation for this time, individuals are immediately forbidden to seek the aid of any god but Allah. Any gatherings of idol worshippers will be subject to attack by our holy warriors. I call on all true Muslims to enforce this decree.

My second in command, Muhammad Rafsanjani Al-Mahdi shall demonstrate, with signs, the power of Allah throughout this month. There will be no doubt as to the true religion of Allah. You have one month to choose submission to Islam or death and hellfire. In the name of Allah, the merciful and beneficent."

The President sat in stunned silence, paralyzed by the growing feeling of absolute fear slowly seeping into every corner of his brain. For a minute the only voice heard in the room was that of a news commentator interviewing an analyst. Everyone was staring at the ground or off into space. It was the President who finally broke the silence.

Turning to his Chief of Staff, he said curtly, "Give a text of the statement to all members of my cabinet immediately. Have them look at the text. Have everyone convene in the war room in one hour."

With that said, he turned to his private secretary, "Aysha, get me a copy of the statement right away and uhh . . . I don't want any visitors or interruptions for the next hour, I need to think." Turning the rest of the way around, he marched straight into his private office closing his door.

As he stared at the portrait of Bill Clinton that hung on the wall, he could not avoid a feeling of helplessness welling up deep in the pit of his stomach. Resistance would certainly mean nuclear attack. There was no question that Abdullah's threat was not idle. Suddenly the world seemed to be spinning in unreality. The entire world was teetering on the edge of a bottomless abyss. He felt like a figure in a Salvador Dali painting beginning to melt and slip off a cliff. His thoughts were interrupted by a crisp knock on the door. Aysha entered with the copy of the text. They exchanged weak smiles as she turned and left.

As a devoted Muslim, she was a good example of the diversity that he and his government had continued to work hard to promote. After all, he campaigned as the President of diversity. He was proud of his great efforts to promote a diverse society. To show his commitment to fighting discrimination and promoting diversity, he had appointed the first openly homosexual Secretary of State as well as a liberal Muslim as Secretary of Transportation. But soon social progress would be forgotten under the suffocation of Islam. The American way of life was threatened with extinction. The US was in danger of ceasing to exist. All that America stood for was in danger of disappearing from the earth.

Why couldn't Abdullah negotiate with him? Didn't he see America's balanced approach to the Israeli-Palestinian problem and his serious attempt to be fair minded toward Muslims? Hadn't he listened to the protests of the peace community and kept American soldiers out of the Islamic Wars that had only recently subsided? Abdullah didn't seem to care.

Many Americans and indeed the entire world would be looking to him, as President, to resist. But what would that lead to? It would unquestionably lead to the unchecked use of nuclear weapons. The slaughter would be in the hundreds of millions, perhaps billions of persons. The world economy would be wrecked, perhaps irrevocably, for centuries to come. As it was, it was already teetering on total collapse. On the other hand, peace would mean the restoration of cheap oil and economic recovery.

What if America submitted? Perhaps Americans would be able to keep some measure of local authority. Perhaps they could preserve enough of their lifestyles to enjoy peace and a measure of prosperity. Didn't the very survival of the world hang in the balance? Wasn't his primary obligation to protect the American public? Fighting would almost certainly lead to wholesale slaughter of much of the nation in ongoing nuclear attacks. If he resisted, the whole world could be plunged into a blood bath. Would that really be the best way to defend Americans? Perhaps by surrender and submission, America could eventually liberalize the United Islamic Kingdom by working from within. Perhaps they could gradually restore greater rights and freedoms as the years passed and the initial revolutionary fervor mellowed. Wasn't it inevitable that the inward cry of freedom in the human heart would ultimately triumph? It was a dangerous gamble, but either way danger seemed overwhelming. At least by suing for peace, it would guarantee the lives of most Americans.

After all, who could possibly militarily resist an ideology that loves and values death and martyrdom above all else? Hadn't Israel and the West been trying unsuccessfully for years? It hadn't stopped the Muslim radicals. They seemed to thrive on conflict. Fighting now would mean the obliteration of the world. On the other hand, if he consented, it would simply mean an outward conformity to Islam. What could be the harm in that when compared to the alternative of obliteration? Although humiliating, no one said you had to really believe in Islam in your heart. One could continue to secretly practice his own faith while outwardly submitting to Islam.

Probably the only ones who would dare to defy outward submission would be a handful of fundamentalist Christians. Those troublesome fundamentalists! Surely Abdullah's use of the number 666 would rile them up. It seemed that Abdullah had picked that number just to pick a fight with them. There was no question he hated them. But then again, he seemed to hate anyone who wasn't a radical Muslim.

Still, surely many within the evangelical community would agree with the necessity of submission. Hadn't a significant portion of them voted in his favor last election because of his economic platform? This was true in spite of his enthusiastic support for the "Sexual Rights For All" Act. Many evangelicals had seen the wisdom in his overall policy to get beyond single issues like this. Hadn't most finally acquiesced on the abortion issue as well?

Surely, any clear-minded individual would realize the blackmail he, the nation and indeed, the world faced. All they had to do was outwardly submit. Anyone with common sense could do that! Any Christians refusing would be absolutely foolhardy and probably irrational and fanatical anyway. In fact, if too many of them refused to accept Abdullah's reign; they could endanger the rest of Americans by inciting attack due to their resistance.

Suddenly, it struck him. He felt it creep over him like a fog rolling in off the sea. He felt a growing urge to pray. Perhaps he should call the nation to pray for this decision. He had never been a religious man, but hadn't George Washington, and Abraham Lincoln and Franklin Roosevelt asked the nation to pray during times of national distress? Abraham Lincoln had even called them to repentance.

But then he caught himself. How could such an irrational act help at a time like this? Besides hadn't Abdullah threatened against praying to another god? Americans need me to think clearly, not irrationally he told himself. How could prayer possibly help with such a serious decision as this? This was no time for Bible stories. No, this was the twenty-first century. Tough decisions required clear and rational thinking. The American people would appreciate that. A call to national prayer would only increase the terrorist attacks.

Suddenly his intercom buzzed. Aysha's voice came over the speaker, "Mr. President, your cabinet is waiting for you in the situation room."

"Tell them I'm on my way Aysha," President Burns responded. He took a deep breath and exhaled slowly as he looked at the portrait of former President Clinton hanging on the office wall opposite his desk. Then with resolute determination he headed out of the room and down the hallway to the situation room, holding the fate and blood of the world and its Christians in his hands.

Chapter 16

The Destruction of Babylon (Rev. 14:6–8, 17:1–18:24)

W e have found ourselves face to face with two perplexing questions before us. What will happen to Israel during this time? And what will happen to America? Surely, as the unchallenged superpower in the world, America could never allow a worldwide Islamic kingdom. Or could it?

We have looked at a hair-raising, yet not entirely inconceivable scenario. In fact, the Bible says the world will look at the whole situation as nothing short of incredible. They *will* be stunned! The situation described in Revelation *is* amazing and surreal. The Bible states, ". . . the whole earth was *amazed* and followed after the beast" (Rev. 13:3b). It *is* amazing but not difficult to imagine radical Muslims, perhaps even a suicide bomber with a suitcase size nuclear bomb, blowing up a large and important city. As one Al-Qaeda spokesman stated, "To achieve a level playing field will take about 4 million dead Americans."[231] Once nuclear weapons are in terrorist hands, what could stop them from taking twenty-five or so bombs and strategically planting them in cities around the world? If the world refuses *Sharia* law, couldn't they threaten to dispose of those cities one at a time? It would be the ultimate blackmail.

Would they do such a bloodthirsty thing? Not only would they, but the Koran commands they use everything at their disposal to fight for the cause of Allah. Could such a thing happen? Many experts now say it's not a question of if, just a question of when they will obtain weapons of mass destruction.[332] Aware of the grave nature of the threat, President Bush has stated we are at war with those who want to bring on another period of the Dark ages. He has frequently stated that we won't give in to the blackmail of terrorism. Yet, what world leader would be willing to risk the systematic destruction of the world's cities? Much of the struggle we witness today is a frantic attempt to prevent terrorists from ever getting to a place where they could do such things.

The terrorists themselves have declared that the greatest weakness of the West is that we love life, whereas they, the *Islamists*, love death. However, if the West refuses to give in to *Islamists* with large quantities of nuclear weapons, the only thing the West would guarantee is wholesale destruction and death of all but a smattering of mankind. The Bible tells us that politicians and the world will finally conclude, "Who is able to wage war with him?" (Rev. 13:4b).

After seeing the establishment of the kingdom of the Beast and hearing a description of what it will look like, John sees the 144,000, perhaps some of the first martyrs from the Beast, in heaven worshipping. But we also see another powerful picture. We see an angel flying in mid-heaven. He has an "eternal gospel to preach to those who live on the earth, and to every nation and tribe and tongue and people; and he said with a loud voice, 'Fear God, and give Him glory, because the hour of His judgment has come; worship Him who made the heaven and the earth and sea and springs of waters" (Rev. 14:6–7).

With the Beast having just established his kingdom and begun his execution program,[333] we see an angel of God flying in mid-heaven with a message for the world's inhabitants. This is God's final warning to a world that has already had the gospel of salvation preached to it.

Literal angels physically announced to shepherds Jesus' first coming to earth. That was a relatively humble announcement to humble people for his first humble coming. That coming brought salvation. However, his next coming will bring judgment on the whole earth and "salvation without reference to sin, to those who eagerly await Him" (Heb. 9:28b). When, Jesus comes a second time "every eye shall see him." Revelation suggests that through these angelic announcements many ears will also be forewarned of the coming judgment.

Babylon Falls

A second angel follows the first with another disturbing announcement for earth dwellers, "Fallen, fallen is Babylon the great, she who has made all the nations drink of the wine of the passion of her immorality" (Rev. 14:8).

Notice that Babylon falls right after this heavenly warning to worship God. Chronologically Babylon's destruction occurs with this angelic announcement. However, the detailed description of that destruction isn't given until Revelation 17 and 18 to which we shall now turn.

Who is Babylon?

An angel who had just announced one of the seven bowls of judgment in Revelation 16 calls John aside to show him the specific judgment that will befall "the great harlot who sits on many waters . . ." (Rev. 17:1b). What do we know about that Babylon from the Scriptures? Is there a city in America with overwhelming similarities to the Biblical Babylon of Revelation?

She is a City of Harlotry

Peter makes an interesting remark in the closing of his first epistle saying, "*She who is in Babylon*, chosen together with you, sends you greetings . . ." (1 Pet. 5:13a). There are some important things to see here. First of all, Peter mentions Babylon as an actual location and city. However, the original Babylon did not exist in Peter's day. Thus, this city is a real city, but is Babylon in a spiritual sense. It is not literally Babylon, but has simply captured her spirit and role.

In Peter's day, there was a clearly dominant immoral city of great wealth, world power and luxurious opulence. The city that Peter referred to was in all likelihood, Rome. The worldly spirit of immorality and luxury and power that had resided in Babylon now resounded from that great city, the center of the Roman Empire. It is important to realize that Peter identified Rome as Babylon many hundreds of years before there was ever any connection between the church and state. It seems that Peter saw the spirit of Babylon as essentially of man's attempt to have dominion over the earth apart from submission to God.

What city best embodies this spirit today? What nation has essentially become like an empire in its world wide economic, political and military dominance? What system represented in a nation has attempted to establish man's dominion over the earth apart from submission to God? There is no other nation in recent years that has so eloquently embodied such secular values and exported them to the world as the United States. Given recent court cases against the pledge of allegiance, even the days of the empty verbiage found on our currency, "In God We Trust," are numbered.

The "great harlot" of Revelation is just that. In the Bible, harlotry represents immorality. However, it is also a symbolic description of following false gods, even as a harlot takes the place of a legitimate wife. Babylon of Revelation epitomizes both. She represents a lifestyle and way of thinking, a system that tries to be a substitute heaven. She works hard to seduce people (even God's people) away from love for the Lord Jesus. She tries to convert them into lovers of pleasure and lovers of self (2Tim. 3:1–4). Paul prophesied to Timothy that this pleasure seeking spirit would be a significant problem in the Church in the last days (2Tim. 3:5–8). What is this great harlot like?

She is a City of Luxury and Greed

Not surprisingly, Revelation describes a place filled with luxury and greed. We see a city that is fabulously wealthy and fabulously immoral. It is this economic system, focused on materialism and sensuality that will be adopted by the world and become its economic engine. The world economy is tied into her and business people all over the world are becoming fabulously wealthy through her. Quite specifically "the merchants of the earth have become rich by the wealth of her sensuality" (Rev. 18:3b).

Compare this scripture with these modern-day facts. "If it were a nation, Wal-Mart would be China's eighth largest trading partner."[234] America runs gigantic trade deficits in the many billions of dollars with nearly all nations of the world. The trade deficit with China alone was expected to hit $130 billion in 2003.[235] The result is that America is pumping incredible amounts of income into the nations of the world.

Meanwhile, the world looks in jealous awe upon the success of the American system and seeks to duplicate it, while at the same time resenting its dominance. The United States has a Gross Domestic Product in Billions of dollars nearly three times larger than the second largest economy, Japan.[236] The economy of the entire European Union combined is almost $1,000,000,000,000 (that's $1 trillion or 1,000 billion) less than the United States.[237] The United States consumes three times more energy than the next closest competitor, China.[238]

She is the Largest City in America

Now let's ask ourselves which city in America most vividly captures the heart and soul of America in the world's eyes. Having lived overseas for a number of years, I can confidently say that the city most closely associated with America in the mind of the people of the world is New York City. It is, by far, the most famous and well known of American cities. The world equates New York City, with the Statue of Liberty at the entrance to her port, as the ultimate symbol of America. I remember quite well a number-one pop song in the Muslim country I lived in for years. It was about the adventure of going to America. The made-for-TV video featured shots of the music star touring the sights in New York City, including the Statue of Liberty and the former World Trade Center.

This city is the largest in the United States. It is twice as large as any other US city with a population of about eight million people. It is home to the largest, most wealthy stock exchange in the world. It is home to many of the world's largest and most powerful corporations and banks. In terms of dollars, this port has generated the greatest amount of trade of any port city in America. In terms of shipping tonnage it is third for the country and number one on the East Coast.[239] It is the number-one port for the importing and exporting of automobiles. And it is the home to more office space than any city in the entire world.[240]

Her Destruction will Economically Devastate the World

At her sudden destruction, the merchants of the world will be overwhelmed with mourning and weeping. Part of their weeping will be selfish because of the economic disaster they will experience, for "no one buys their cargoes anymore" (Rev. 18:11b). The impact of Babylon's destruction will cause an economic crash of horrific proportions. The unbelievable volume of financial trading and physical trading that goes on in this city of the wealthiest nation in the world means that absolutely no city today, or in the entire history of the world, has ever been more economically and symbolically important. New York City's sudden obliteration would be like an economic and psychological tsunami slamming into the entire world with an obliterating force of unparalleled proportions.

John describes for us the mourning of "every shipmaster and every passenger and sailor, and as many as make their living by the sea" for ". . . all who had ships at sea became rich by her wealth . . ." (Rev. 18:17b, 19b). They exclaim there has never been a city like the great city. If the greatest generator of wealth the world has ever known was suddenly destroyed; such a reaction as described here would be exactly what one would expect. September 11 was just a small foreshadowing of what awaits.

She has Incredible Cultural Influence for Greed and Immorality over the Whole World

The woman Babylon is described as "sitting on many waters." What are these waters? John is told by the angel that "the waters which you saw where the harlot sits are peoples and multitudes and nations and tongues" (Rev. 17:15). This indicates that she will dominate many people in the world. She is the one "with whom the kings of the earth committed acts of immorality, and those who dwell on the earth were made drunk with the wine of her immorality" (Rev. 17:2).

Not only common folk, but also leaders of nations will be seduced by her lustful way of life, epitomized by her extreme sensuality and immorality. Richard Brookheiser, the Senior Editor of the conservative magazine, *The National Review*, put it this way; "This country grew

and grew. Our influence is worldwide. People speak of our hegemony .
. . . Maybe we don't like the sound of it, but I think it is in our DNA."[241]
Our founding fathers foresaw our growing influence in the world.
Thomas Jefferson, when purchasing the Louisiana Purchase, spoke
of expanding an "empire of liberty."[242] George Washington spoke of
America as "this rising empire."[243]

David Gergen, Director of Public Leadership for Harvard University, summarized the goals of this American Empire when he said,
"We want to extend our values of democracy and capitalism."[244] The
problem is that the rest of the world is not always embracing all aspects of Americanism with a smile. They resent certain things about
our growing impact on their lives. Most Muslims associate democracy with sex and drunkenness. Radical Muslims see democracy as
an enemy of true Islam.

Still, the world is undergoing a cultural transformation. According to results from the Pew Global Attitudes Project, "people
everywhere also strongly believe that their traditional way of life is
getting lost."[245]

"Majorities in every nation surveyed report that over the past five
years, there has been increased availability of foreign movies, television programs and music. And in more than half of those countries,
the globalization of culture has been intensive with people saying
there is a lot more foreign culture available to them."[246]

Not surprisingly, the most prominent cultural exporter in the
world is the United States. "There is global agreement on the importance of children learning English. Solid majorities in every country
surveyed believe that 'children need to learn English to succeed in the
world today.' Nine-in-ten Indians (93%) and Chinese (92%) agree . .
." "Even those people who say they dislike American culture, or say
they are concerned about the future of their own culture, believe it
is necessary for children to learn English."[247]

"In most countries, younger respondents are more positive than
older ones about the effect of foreign television, music and movies
on their families."[248] This signifies that our cultural impact on beliefs
is on the upswing with the up-and-coming young of the world.

Majorities in most nations blame the erosion of traditional ways on
commercialism and consumerism. This leads to resentment. "There

is a widespread sense that the rapidly changing world represents a major threat to people's traditional way of life."[249] And what culture are these old cultures being replaced with? Clearly it is American culture, consumerism and immorality. These are byproducts of our notion of democracy and capitalism that we actively promote around the world.

Our modern notions of democracy are increasingly being used to push immoral agendas. Although we ought to oppose vigilante violence against immorality and its participants, the moral and legal trends are disturbing. While writing ABC recently, complaining about the increasingly pro-homosexual message of its TV shows, including *The Practice*, one viewer was shocked at the response he allegedly received. It read as follows,

> How about getting your nose out of the Bible (which is ONLY a book of stories compiled by MANY different writers hundreds of years ago) and read the *Declaration of Independence* (what our nation is built on), where it says "All Men are Created equal," and try treating them that way for a change! Or better yet, try thinking for yourself and stop using an archaic book of stories as your lame crutch for existence. You are a minority in this country and your boycott will not affect us or our freedom of statement.[250]

One show that debuted in the summer of 2003 on the Bravo channel was called *Queer Eye for the Straight Guy*. A Los Angeles Times reporter, Lynn Elber, gave it raving reviews. The show tells the story of gay men giving straight men the once over to help them improve their appearances and appeal. She quotes the producer as saying, the ". . . straight guy, gay guy perspective is at the heart of the show. We're trying to break down some walls here."[251] Elber makes only passing reference to the Traditional Values Coalition criticizing it. She also advertises another Bravo show that debuted as a gay-theme series, entitled *Boy Meets Boy*. Here a gay leading man will choose from fifteen potential mates—with the twist that some are actually heterosexual.[252]

Recently some state governments have begun rewarding homosexual behavior with the same benefits as marriage. Homosexual unions have been given recognition by the state of Vermont and Massachusetts now recognizes gay marriages as having the same validity and rights as heterosexual marriage. Mayors in cities throughout America are issuing gay marriage licenses as the supposed constitutional right of gay marriage is being espoused. Seven more states have lawsuits and laws on the verge of doing the same thing. It seems only a matter of time before homosexual marriage or something approximating that will become the law of the land throughout America.

According to the Pew Global Attitudes Project, a majority of people in every Western nation, including the United States, believe that homosexuality should be accepted by society.[253] Not surprisingly, Africa and the Islamic nations sharply disagree that homosexuality should be acceptable.[254]

However, immorality is a problem for straights in America as well. According to the 2003 World Almanac, almost one out of ten boys (9.3%) had their first sexual intercourse *before* age thirteen. About one out of twenty-five girls (4.0%) could say the same. That means that about two students in an average eighth-grade class have had sexual intercourse.

The numbers jump rapidly once they have finished their first year of high school. By the end of ninth grade, two out of every five boys (40.5%) and about one out of three girls (29.1%) have had sexual intercourse. By the end of their senior year of high school the numbers even out. 61.0% of all boys and 60.1% of all girls have committed fornication and engaged in sexual intercourse. In fact, by the twelfth grade, more girls (50.1%) than boys (44.6%) were actively fornicating![255]

The Bible says "Do not be deceived; *neither fornicators*, nor idolaters, nor adulterers, nor effeminate, nor homosexuals, . . . will inherit the kingdom of God" (1 Cor. 6:9b,10b). Our blatant snubbing of God-given standards and warnings clearly reveals we are not a moral society. Fortunately, God has given us an opportunity to be forgiven through the sacrifice of Jesus Christ. Many of us can say along with the Corinthians, "Such were some of you (us); but you (we) were washed . . ." (1 Cor. 6:11a). Still our nation is clearly in moral trouble as many not only refuse to turn away from such behavior, but strongly encourage and advocate these practices.

And these are only our teenagers. The above statistics make no mention of the millions who will go on as adults to have immoral lifestyles. They also do not take into account many who have yet to have sexual intercourse outside of marriage but who participate in deviant sexual behavior or the millions who have exposed themselves to pornographic materials on television, and the Internet or other sources.

She is a City of Sorcery and Drugs

As "Babylon the Great, the Mother of Harlots and the Abominations of the earth" this city "has become a dwelling place of demons and a prison of every unclean spirit, and a prison of every unclean and hateful bird" (Rev. 17:5b, 18:2b). She has become home to demonically inspired depravity.

Not only is she immoral, she has become a haven for demonic activity. This is probably connected with her love and fascination with witchcraft and sorcery. For "all the nations of the world were deceived by her sorcery" (Rev. 18:23b). The word for sorcery here is derived from *pharmakeia* and means drugs (illicit and otherwise) and also casting spells. She has an intense drug problem and a fascination with witchcraft. Movies and books like *Harry Potter* have helped stir up a huge grass roots interest in sorcery.

She is a Workaholic Materialistic Culture

Babylon has captured not only human labor, but also people's very lives. This goes beyond labor. This system is a way of life to which the entire world has submitted. It is out of this mindset, this love of pleasure and bondage to a materialistic way of life that God is trying to call his people. A voice from heaven warns God's people saying, "Come out of her, my people, so that you will not participate in her sins and receive her plagues, for her sins have piled up as high as heaven, and God has remembered her iniquities" (Rev. 18:4–5). The Church is warned to not become seduced by Babylon and commit sin with her, lest we share in her judgment.

So how are we doing? Amazingly, although 120 million American adults regularly attend church, only seven percent identified spiritual wholeness and development as the factor that will produce a successful life. Only 15 million of the 120 million identified success as being something other than personal accomplishments and material possessions. A large majority of both adults and teenagers, confessing Christians and non-Christians contend that there is no absolute moral truth. "While most of these people describe themselves as followers of Christ and say the Bible is accurate in all of its teachings, they nevertheless believe that truth is based on feelings, experience or emotion." [256]

Christian pollster George Barna goes on to say,

> This is one of the greatest deceptions of our age. Embracing relativism under the guise of the Christian faith facilitates comfort with sin. By claiming the authority to determine right from wrong, we crown ourselves the kings and queens of reality, yet we have no such authority and we constantly pay the price for the arrogance of believing and acting like we are in control of our destiny and experience. What an affront it is to God for us to claim His name and protection but to resist His moral truths on the basis of human feelings. [257]

Is it any wonder God warns his people to come out of Babylon that they might not share in her judgments?

Why is Babylon Judged?

Heaven says,

> Pay her back even as she has paid, and give back to her double according to her deeds; in the cup which she has mixed, mix twice as much for her. To the degree that she glorified herself and lived sensuously, to the same degree give her torment and mourning; for she says in her heart, 'I sit as a queen and I am not a widow, and will never see mourning.' For this reason in one day her plagues will come, pestilence and mourning and famine, and she will be burned up with fire; for the Lord God who judges her is strong. (Rev. 18:8–9)

Here we see God judging her primarily because of her immorality, pride, and greed. The voice from heaven warned God's people to avoid immorality and greed. Paul warned the Church in the same way saying, "Therefore consider the members of your earthly body as dead to immorality, impurity, passion, evil desire, and greed, that amounts to idolatry. For it is because of *these things* that the wrath of God will come upon the sons of disobedience" (Col. 3:5–6). Paul repeats the same warning against greed and immorality in Ephesians 5:5–6, once again stating judgment is coming because of *these things*. Babylon the Great, the United States, is a primary exporter of this very mindset around the world.

She Serves the God of Wealth

This city that most epitomizes this system has made generating wealth its god. Its destruction will come quite rapidly, and the entire world will see it burn up in smoke. With the advent of CNN and international TV, this can now be literally fulfilled. This system is all encompassing in its reach. It has enveloped every corner of economic activity including:

- Cargoes of "gold and silver" representing **the financial sector**.
- Cargoes of "precious stones and pearls" representing **the jewelry industry**.
- Cargoes of "fine linen and purple and silk and scarlet" representing **the clothing industry**.
- Cargoes of "citron wood . . . ivory . . . very costly wood and bronze and iron and marble" representing **the construction industry**.
- Cargoes of "cinnamon and spice and incense and perfume and frankincense" representing **the cosmetics industry**.
- Cargoes of "wine and olive oil and fine flour and wheat and cattle and sheep" representing **the food and beverage industry**.
- Cargoes of "horses and chariots" that represent **the transportation industry**.
- And cargoes of "slaves and human lives" that represent **cheap labor and slave labor** and a workaholic, **materialistic mindset** on which this system thrives.[258]

She will have Tremendous Political and Military Power

John makes it clear that Babylon is not only an economic system and a way of life, but she ". . . is the great city, which reigns over the kings of the earth" (Rev. 17:18b). She has tremendous political influence and power. Babylon is a city that represents a nation, a political force, and a philosophy to the world. As the embodiment of an incredibly influential nation, this city and its ideas and way of life make it the most influential city in the history of the world.

New York City fits that bill today more than any other city ever has. While speaking to the United Nations General Assembly in New York City on September 23, 2003, President Bush essentially declared that the United States and its allies had saved the credibility of the United Nations by attacking Iraq. This statement was made on behalf of the nations of the world, even though the majority of them strongly disagreed with the war. They were powerless to stop it.

The Beast will Hate Her

John saw this woman Babylon "sitting on a scarlet beast full of blasphemous names, having seven heads and ten horns" (Rev. 17:3b). This woman, at least for a time, is holding down the seven-headed beast by riding on its back. As such, the Beast will hate it. For years, the United States has been working behind the scenes. It has been utilizing the United Nations and alliances over which it has great power to hold down radical Islam. It is also working openly through economic embargoes, war and political pressure to do what it can to prevent the rise of the Islamic kingdom of the Beast.

Resentment towards American meddling in Islamic affairs is reaching the bursting point. Of Islamic nations recently surveyed, Moroccans had the most favorable view of America. What percentage of them looked at America favorably? 60%? 45%? Actually, *only* 27% viewed America favorably. Most of the Islamic nations were significantly lower in the percentage that held a favorable opinion. In our NATO ally Turkey, only 15% of Turks had a favorable view of America, and in two countries, Jordan and the Palestinian Authority, only 1% of the population viewed America favorably.[259]

Look at the anti-American feeling dripping from these survey numbers. Huge majorities in many Islamic nations, Morocco (93%), Jordan (91%), Lebanon (82%), Turkey (82%), Indonesia (82%), and the Palestinian Authority (81%), expressed disappointment Iraq did not put up a greater fight against the coalition forces. This shows deep-seated resentment toward the United States and a deep emotional attachment with their Muslim brethren.[260]

Middle-East journalist, Fareed Zakaria is observing that "anti-Americanism is morphing from a purely anti-Bush phenomenon into a much broader cultural attitude."[261] Samar Fatamy, a Saudi woman who has lived in America and has a weekly radio show in Saudi Arabia has said, "If you (America) continue on your present path, you will have no partners in the Middle East . . . In this next generation, you are creating so much bitterness. They don't understand you (America), and they don't want to understand you. What will come of that?"[262]

Because of Babylon's opposition to the Beast's kingdom, the angel tells John,

> The ten horns which you saw, and the beast, these will hate the harlot and will make her desolate and naked and will eat her flesh and will burn her up with fire. For God has put it in their hearts to execute His purpose by having a common purpose, and by giving their kingdom to the beast, until the words of God will be fulfilled. (Rev. 17:16–17)

Amazingly, God will actually use the Beast and his allies to bring judgment upon Babylon. This desire to burn her with fire has actually been put into the heart of the Beast by God himself.

She has a Female Idol on a Pedestal

The Prophet Zechariah gives us further insight on this woman in Zechariah 5:5–11. Here he sees an *ephah* (a basket with a lid), going forth. It turns out that wickedness is sitting inside the basket in the form of a woman. This is quite likely the same woman John saw sitting on the kingdom of the Beast (Rev. 17:1–3).

Suddenly, Zechariah sees this woman lifted up by two other women wearing wings like a stork. They lift wickedness up in the *ephah* and carry her for a long distance in the air between the earth and the heavens. This is a picture of going somewhere on a trip with this symbol of wickedness. Zechariah is curious as to where they are taking her and asks the angel. Then the angel states a most peculiar thing. He tells Zechariah that they are going ". . . to build a temple for her in the *land of Shinar*; and when it is prepared, she will be set there on *her own pedestal*" (Zech. 5:11).

Where is Shinar? The land of Shinar is another name for Babylon (Gen. 11:2–9). Notice also that this wickedness is a woman and is carried by two women. Just as the Statue of Liberty was set on her own pedestal in New York harbor, so too this woman is set up on her own pedestal. Lady Liberty beckons to the nations proclaiming her two messages of freedom and riches. Just as the two women placed her on her pedestal, so too these twin freedoms earned the statue her spot. This city has historically been the port of entry for the greatest number of immigrants to enter our land. It continues to be a major port of entry for visitors and immigrants. It is here that the Statue of Liberty greeted many to the shores of America. "Lady Liberty" as she is called, on the shores of the Empire State, has come to be associated with freedom and opportunity for riches. Those two core values have been elevated as the greatest of American values.

Interestingly, when she was being set up on our shores over a hundred years ago, a number of Protestant ministers and evangelical Christians protested that it was wrong to be setting up a female idol on our shores since they considered us a Christian nation. Their protests were ignored.[263]

The artist who designed the statue designed her following a portrait of the goddess of "liberty" that was based upon the goddess Venus, also known as Aphrodite, Isis, and ultimately Ishtar, the primary goddess of ancient Babylon who was essentially a goddess of "love."[264]

Author R.A.Coombes found a number of other interesting similarities between the woman who sits on the beast and the Statue of Liberty. Here are some of the most intriguing ones:

- The woman on the beast is clothed in scarlet. The Statue of Liberty was originally robed in scarlet/purple.

- The woman on the beast has a golden cup in her hand. The Statue of Liberty originally had a golden cup in her hand until it was later changed to a torch.
- The woman who rides the beast wears purple robes denoting royalty in the ancient world. She also considers herself a queen. The Statue of Liberty is crowned like a queen as well.
- The woman on the beast sits on seven heads that are mountains. The seven spikes on the Statue of Liberty's crown represent the seven continents of the world. In the broadest sense, the continents could be considered as each a massive mountain.
- The woman on the beast represents Babylon the mega-city. The Statue of Liberty overlooks a suburb of New York City known as Babylon, Long Island. It was a town founded by Jewish immigrants.
- The woman on the Beast reigns over the kings of the earth. The Statue of Liberty also overlooks the United Nations Building.[265]

Freedom and Liberty Increasingly Equal Immorality and Greed

Today, freedom in America has come to mean freedom for homosexuals to practice sodomy without government interference according to a recent Supreme Court ruling.[266] Freedom means that consenting adults can engage in any form of immorality that pleases them, without government interference. In fact, with the push for civil unions and gay marriage, they are increasingly enjoying the government's blessings!

It is only a matter of time before the laws against pedophiles and the exposure of children to sex are eased. Indeed, it is already happening. It was with great difficulty that Congress was finally able to place a restriction on public-library computers to screen out pornography. In the name of freedom, the American Library Association adamantly and successfully opposed it for seven years. Even so, under the current law, adults only need to ask the librarian to disengage the filter, and she must do so, regardless of whether or not children may be walking around looking over shoulders.

Liberty and freedom has now been expanded to mean the freedom to *not* hear about Christ at any public gatherings. We have gone beyond mere separation of church and state (a phrase found nowhere in our constitution or any legal ruling before 1962) and have decided that separation of God and state is a foundational value of liberty. Christian students in Texas are no longer allowed to even ask the blessing of Jesus before public high school football games.

This new-found value of godlessness in our public speech has replaced the value of the gospel of Jesus Christ or the acknowledging of God in the affairs of men. Remaining vestiges of our Christian heritage and its impact on our governmental system are being relentlessly erased and suppressed all in the name of freedom. Government officials with Christian beliefs, such as judges or Attorney General John Ashcroft are vilified, often publicly, *because* of their outspoken Christian faith. They are now often questioned as to whether or not they could make competent government officials because of their Christian beliefs.[267] They are considered as potential threats to freedom!

In the name of freedom, Americans sell, buy and watch magazines, movies, songs and TV shows, that celebrate every form of immorality the human mind can imagine. In the name of freedom and economic opportunity we extort by manipulation nearly one trillion dollars each year in gambling receipts, usually from those who can least afford it. In the name of freedom and, economic opportunity, we have murdered over one million unborn babies every year since 1973. "We sing God Bless America," and I wonder if God doesn't ask us one haunting question, "Why should I?"

Our economic system has been adopted by countries around the globe as the surest way to economic wealth and development. The cultural impact of American music, television and movies upon other nations has been nothing short of a tidal wave in its force and effect. According to the French Ambassador to the United States, two-thirds of all movies seen by French moviegoers in 2002 were American movies. The same man said that American novels are fabulously popular in France, as well. Traditional cultures, including Islam, have had difficulty withstanding the assault on their traditional values from the West. America has been front and center stage in this cultural tsunami enveloping the world.

Today in Saudi Arabia, "up and down chic Tahliyah street, carloads of teenage boys, with baseball caps worn rakishly backwards and their ankle-length robes tossed aside in favor of baggy low-slung pants, idle alongside cars full of teenage girls driven by chauffeurs."[268] Girls and boys rapidly exchange papers with phone numbers on them. The girls anxiously wait for the boys to call them.

> Jeddah, in the middle of the night is the paradox of contemporary Saudi Arabia . . . 'We are being carried in two directions, at once, backward and forward,' says Sadi al-Yamani, a Saudi neurologist who sees, in her patients, the disorienting effects of changes that have rocketed a deeply conservative society from the seventh to the twenty-first century in the span of a few decades.[269]

> Modern in Saudi Arabia came to mean American modern—and more precisely, the outsize, mass-consumerism version of modern that American oilmen carried with them from the US Southwest, primarily Texas . . . The Arabian Peninsula has seen more change in the past six decades than in the previous 13 centuries.[270]

It is true that this has been done by peaceful means and largely for business reasons and secondarily political ones. Yet, we are convinced that our concept of Lady Liberty is the great hope of the world. The truth is that the great hope of the world is the gospel of Jesus Christ. God shall not share his glory with another.

Babylon with its fabulous hanging gardens, tremendous opulence and worldly wealth was one of the seven wonders of the ancient world. Ancient Babylon, caught totally unaware, was destroyed overnight by the Persians and Medes who dammed up the river entering the city through its channel. While the city partied, the Persians overwhelmed them before they knew what happened. Their riotous living on that fateful night is described in Daniel 5. Not unlike the future Babylon, they were busy praising the works of human hands when the prophet interpreted the handwriting on the wall. The future Babylon will be destroyed just as suddenly as the ancient one.

Is there any hope for America? In the short run, perhaps. In the long run, America will eventually decline just as every other great empire has. It is pride to think otherwise, particularly given the depth to which the Gospel and Christian values had penetrated our society and government in the past, and the fact that as a nation, we have largely willfully turned our back on these truths.

This doesn't mean we should desire America's punishment or take pleasure in it. Certainly not! For God takes no pleasure in the punishment of the wicked. But there is a far more serious question than the survival of America? The real question is: will the Church of Jesus Christ survive the temptation of America? John exhorts God's people to "Come out of her and not participate in her sins." God desires us to be salt and light in our societies.

The story of Josiah is very appropriate for the situation in America today. Even if America is the Babylon of Revelation, there is no reason to give her up as lost. Josiah didn't give up on Judah. Under the leadership of Manessah, Josiah's grandfather, Judah fell into gross immorality and wickedness. Manessah did "evil in the sight of the Lord according to the abominations of the nations whom the Lord dispossessed before the sons of Israel" (2Chron. 33:2). He even made Israel worse than the nations they had dispossessed (2Kings 21:9). He undid all the righteous reforms of his godly father Hezekiah and ignored the example of David his ancestor and ignored the law of the Lord.

How did Manasseh respond to rebuke? The Scriptures tell us that "The Lord spoke to Manasseh and his people, but they paid no attention" (2Chron. 33:10). Eventually God brought the Assyrians against them and Manasseh—under great duress—repented in his old age (2Chron. 33:12–20). Still the damage had been done as it has in America. How should we live in such a troubling situation?

Chapter 17

What to do with a Reprobate Nation?

Manasseh's grandson, Josiah, eventually became king as a child and seemingly against all odds had a heart that sought the Lord. He ultimately brought great reforms in his zeal for the Lord. Josiah had all Baals and female deities and astrological devices removed from the house of the Lord. He did away with the idolatrous priests on the king's payroll. He destroyed all high places to idols and defiled the idol worship location used for Molech. It was where men and women had brought their sons and daughters to be sacrificed. He burned up and destroyed every idol and place of idol worship he could find. Yet, when the book of the law was rediscovered and the prophetess was consulted, Josiah was told,

> . . . I bring evil on this place and on its inhabitants . . . because they have forsaken Me and have burned incense to other gods that they might provoke Me to anger with all the work of their hands, therefore My wrath burns against this place, *and it shall not be quenched.* (2 Kings 22:16a, 17)

How did Josiah respond? Did he just throw up his hands in despair? In response to this great judgment pronounced on the land, in spite of his many reforms, did Josiah become fatalistic or uncaring? No. Instead, he humbled himself more and with great zeal set about bringing even more reforms. The Scriptures say he re-instituted Passover, removed mediums and spiritists, and teraphim and all the idols and various abominations he could find. Josiah's example must resonate with the American church today.

Even if America is Babylon the Great, we cannot simply abandon her to God's judgment. We must do everything we can to bring revival and reform where possible. Undoubtedly, a remnant was powerfully touched by Josiah's reforms and turned to the Lord. So too, we may yet see a Josiah-like revival hit America, in what may prove to be the eleventh hour. Perhaps God will use films like *The Passion of the Christ* to help spark a final revival. Yet, even if revival comes, so much evil has been done that God's judgment is nearly certain. As hard as we work for reform, and as much as we shine as lights in the darkness, we must remember that our home is not America, but the kingdom of God.

Judgment will most definitely burn up all that is not of God. Indeed, within three months of Josiah's demise, Pharaoh Neco took control of Judah and exacted tribute. Eight years after that, King Jehoiakim was made subservient to Nebuchadnezzar. Three years later, Nebuchadnezzar removed him from power.

When explaining why Nebuchadnezzar succeeded in capturing Judah's king, the writer of 2Kings states,

> Surely at the command of the Lord it came upon Judah, to remove them from His sight because of the sins of Manasseh, according to all that he had done, and also for the innocent blood which he shed, for he filled Jerusalem with innocent blood; and the Lord would not forgive. (2 Kings 24:3–4)

God didn't forget, even though it was forty-four years after Manasseh's reign had ended. Not long after Jehoiakim was removed from power, the whole nation went into exile (2 Kings 24:14, 25:26). Has God forgotten America throwing prayer out of schools in 1962? Has God forgotten throwing out the Ten Commandments from schools in 1963? Has God forgotten the removal of references to Him and Jesus Christ from public monuments and buildings over the years? Has God forgotten the legalization of abortion and the subsequent slaughter of well over one million babies annually since 1973?

That's over 43 million babies murdered since 1973! Estimates tell us about 45 million people died in World War ll. As a nation we will soon surpass Adolph Hitler in the number of murders we are responsible for. The only difference is that many of his deaths were against adults, but we've chosen to kill more than 43 million helpless babies instead.

He gassed people because they were Jews and killed many soldiers and civilians in warfare. All we do is burn babies alive in chemical solutions, crush their skulls and suck their brains out in partial birth abortions. Or sometimes we choose to tear them limb from limb and chop them up in DNC procedures all to save ourselves from inconvenience. This is the way we "protect" babies from being unwanted. We murder them by slicing them up and burning them alive. Adolph Hitler led Germany into atrocious evil. But are we really any better?

Has God forgotten the loosening and removal of many laws restricting pornography and immoral sexual practices? Has God forgotten the wanton practice of immorality in the highest offices of our land? Has God forgotten the recent countrywide legalization of sodomy in July 2003? Is he ignoring the movement to grant equal status and government blessing to homosexual unions? Will God ignore these things? I think not.

It is important for us to see that God is patient, but also, God is certain to bring judgment to the unrepentant. This judgment fell, in spite of the Jeremiahs and Baruchs and Daniels and those like them. There were godly people in Judah when judgment fell, but God could no longer ignore the overwhelming willful sin of the majority of people to whom so much spiritual and material blessing had been given. They all should have known better. The only advice that God could give Jeremiah for those who feared the Lord was to come out of Judah for judgment was going to fall (Jer. 38:2).

The Blood of Prophets and Saints and All the Slain of the earth: Is it found in America?

Before we leave the subject of Babylon, there is yet one characteristic that we must observe about Babylon. It is stated that "in her was found the blood of prophets and of saints and of all who have been slain on the earth" (Rev. 18:24). How could this be America?

Isn't America the bastion of freedom where people are free to worship as they choose? Isn't America the nation that has sent out more missionaries than any other nation? Wasn't America instrumental in preventing the world from being overrun by godless Communism? All these things are most definitely answered yes.

However, one must also ask some other questions. Wasn't Israel the nation to whom the Ten Commandments were given? Wasn't Israel the source of nearly all the prophets and virtually the entire word of God? Wasn't Israel God's chosen nation to bring his light to the Gentiles? Wasn't it through Israel that the Messiah eventually came? All these things are most definitely answered affirmatively as well.

But there are other truths. Didn't Israel fall into gross idolatry and immoral perversion and reject the word of God? Didn't Israel regularly ignore her own prophets that were sent to her? Didn't the bulk of Israel and her leaders ultimately reject the Messiah sent to her? In spite of a significant minority of Jews who did believe in Jesus as their Messiah, wasn't Israel once again judged, Jerusalem sacked and the Jews sent into exile because most in leadership and many common folk refused to recognize his coming? The answer to all these questions is also yes. Couldn't similar things be said of America?

It is not just the future Babylon that will be judged for the blood of all the prophets and all the saints. While pronouncing judgment upon the scribes and Pharisees, Jesus told them, ". . . upon you may fall the guilt of all the righteous blood shed on earth, from the blood of righteous Abel to the blood of Zechariah, the son of Berechiah, whom you murdered between the temple and the altar. Truly I say to you, all these things will come upon this generation" (Matt. 23:35–36). And they did thirty-seven years later when Jerusalem and the temple were demolished.

Remember these Jewish leaders led a nation that had produced many great men of God, the Holy Scriptures, and the Messiah himself. Yet, a fearful judgment was prophesied. Furthermore, they were blamed for the guilt of "*all* the righteous blood shed on the earth." This seems rather extreme at first glance. Weren't believers free to worship in the temple? Wasn't the word of God freely read and preached from the pulpits of the synagogues of the land? Weren't there many genuine followers of the God of Abraham in this nation?

Undoubtedly, there were more genuine followers of the God of Abraham in this nation than in any nation in the world. Also, these Pharisees had not literally killed Abel; in fact, they hadn't literally killed any of the prophets. They weren't even directly responsible for John the Baptist's death, although they ignored his message. Why would they, the leaders of a nation with such a godly heritage, be found guilty for *the blood of all the righteous blood shed on earth*?

Because Jesus knew what was in their hearts. He knew that the same spirit that was in the murderers of the prophets resided in these leaders. He knew they would murder him, even though he was the Messiah sent to them. They would be found guilty because they would choose to ignore the many lessons of Bible history about what happened to those who had murdered the prophets. The Bible is full of stories of judgment that fell upon those who killed the prophets. The Word of God is clear on this. Yet the leaders of the Jews still chose to ignore every one of those lessons. In spite of multiple lessons, they received the same spirit that inspired those before them, and killed the prophesied Messiah, of which the prophets spoke.

Babylon's Guilt and The False Peace

What final sin might immediately precede this judgment on Babylon that ultimately releases God's wrath? Why will she be held responsible for all the blood on the earth? There may be nothing else at all. It may simply be that Jesus realizes that this indulgent, immoral, greedy system would never welcome his kingdom. Just like the Jewish leaders before, they would seek to kill him to prevent it, if they could. Certainly, just like the Jewish leaders, the leaders and people of America have the great witness of history before them and a rich, godly heritage and exposure to the Word of God. America has plenty of access to the Bible and the history of God's dealings with men to warn them of what happens to those who reject God's messengers and the Messiah himself. That may be sufficient as far as God is concerned.

Might Babylon Seek to Preserve Herself at any Cost?

Yet, it may be there is one final straw that Babylon will break. When discussing how they might kill Jesus, the chief priests and Pharisees revealed what was in their heart. They surmised about Jesus that "if we let Him go on like this, all men will believe in Him, and the Romans will come and take away both our place and our nation" (John 11:48). Thus, it was not only because of jealousy the Jewish leaders wanted him crucified. They wanted to get rid of Jesus for reasons of self-preservation, not only for themselves, but also their nation.

Even though they completely despised the Roman Empire and what it stood for, when faced with what they saw as a threat to their personal survival and the survival of their nation they decided to surrender Jesus to the Romans. Rome was an opportunity to get rid of Jesus of whom they were jealous. When asked by Pilate, "Shall I crucify your king?" the chief priests answered, 'We have no king but Caesar'" (John 19:15b). They were willing to admit and declare their complete submission to much-hated Rome and deny God their King, all to preserve their place and their nation. They were not only willing to allow the Romans to kill Jesus; they were shouting, "Crucify Him! Crucify Him!" (John 19:15a).

Perhaps in the face of a nuclear weapons suicide bomber threat, with their lives, their nation and their material wealth threatened, Americans will be given a final choice when face to face with a nuclear Islamic kingdom. Adopt *Sharia* law and pledge allegiance to the Beast, at least superficially, in return for a promise of safety, peace and prosperity. Paul wrote the Thessalonians saying, ". . . the day of the Lord will come just like a thief in the night. While they are saying, 'Peace and safety!' then destruction will come upon them suddenly like labor pains upon a woman with child, and they will not escape" (1Thess. 5:2b–3).

After watching the terrifying rise to power of this Beast, it is hard to imagine us holding out for long against such a threat. At least "rational" materialists who didn't believe in an afterlife led the Communist Soviet Union. There is no such luxury with fundamentalist Islam. Is it possible the Beast will appear to offer America a way to avoid nuclear obliteration? Could it be that many Americans will be upset with Christians who threaten America's survival by refusing to submit to the Beast?

Unwilling to take a stand on matters of principle that many Americans no longer believe in, terrified Americans will probably eventually give in to the wishes of the Beast. America, worshipping the idol of greed and "peace" and thus, wanting peace at any cost, will submit to *Sharia* law. Ignoring the testimony of God's word and history itself, she may willingly surrender the world, and true Christians everywhere to face the reality of martyrdom.

In the same way that leaders of the Jews sold out Jesus in order to retain their place and their nation, America's leaders may sell out Jews and Christians for the same self-preserving, greedy reasons. The country most able to mount a successful fight may capitulate because of a love for this world. Relieved by the prospect of averting nuclear annihilation, the world will breathe a collective sigh of relief, crying out in jubilation, "Peace and safety!"

However, for alert Christians this would be further confirmation of who this Beast really is and what is soon to follow. As Paul stated, "But you, brethren, are not in darkness, that the day would overtake you like a thief; for you are all sons of light and sons of day. We are not of night nor of darkness; so then let us not sleep as others do, but let us be alert and sober" (1Thess. 5:4–7).

Perhaps in response to America's weakness and unwillingness to stand and fight, remaining rulers of the world may quickly acquiesce to the Beast in the interest of their own survival as well. The Beast will probably set up a system whereby the world will be divided into ten administrative regions. Governments in those regions will need to submit to these regional rulers. Once these ten rulers are firmly in place, the hysterical fears and seething hatred that the Islamic kingdom feels for America will want to find expression (Rev. 17:16–17).

Babylon gets Burned Anyway

Perhaps, it may also be clear to the Beast that his greatest potential for future trouble remains in America. Maybe America's participation in this system will seem too begrudging. The Koran gives Muslims the right to break a treaty any time they fear the other side might violate it. "If you fear treachery from your allies, you may fairly retaliate by breaking off your treaty with them" (Surah 8:58).

Notice, no proof is needed, only fear of the possibility. Daniel states that the future beast-king will slaughter many solely on the basis of rumor. "But rumors . . . from the North will disturb him, and he will go forth with great wrath to destroy and annihilate many" (Dan. 11:44). This may speak of an attack on the wealthy north in Babylon (New York City).

Historically, Muhammad temporarily made treaties when not yet in a position of sufficient strength to impose his will. Later, he violently and without warning broke them. In any case, it will be his desire to wipe out American power. Hatred will be the core reason. The decision will be made to make an example of Babylon and annihilate her biggest, most powerful city in one hour.

The Beast and his ten horns conspire to "make her desolate and naked and will eat her flesh and will burn her up with fire" (Rev. 17:16). God himself has "put it in their hearts to execute his purpose by having a common purpose and by giving the kingdom to the beast, until the words of God will be fulfilled" (Rev. 17:17).

This attack sounds eerily similar to the nuclear attack on the Japanese cities of Hiroshima and Nagasaki at the close of World War II. It is quite sudden, done "in one hour" and produces a cataclysmic fire that "will burn her up." "Her" of course refers to the entire city. Also, this destruction apparently originates with man's weapons, thus making the massive destruction almost certainly the product of a nuclear attack.

The one nation to use the atomic weapon will itself receive it. This attack is likely to come fairly early in the reign of the Beast, as the text suggests (Rev. 14:6–13). Whenever its exact timing, the absolute horror it produces will create a reign of terror similar to Stalin's or Hitler's, only worse. This Beast's reign will encompass the entire earth. No one will dare to defy the orders of the Beast, except those who only bend the knee to the Lord Jesus Christ and the remnants of Israel up in the Judean mountains.

Closing in on the End: Six Bowls of Wrath and Har-Megeddon (Revelation 15:1– 16:16)

A t the start of Chapter 15, in Revelation, we see John witnessing another spectacular sight in heaven. Seven mighty
angels hold seven plagues, the final plagues of God. They
prepare to cast them onto earth. After seeing them, he sees ". . . a sea
of glass mixed with fire, and those who had been victorious over the
beast and his image and the number of his name, standing on the sea
of glass, holding harps of God" (Rev. 15:2b).

The intensity and speed with which these final plagues are announced suggests a rapid succession. The earthly time frame over
which these first five bowls are poured out is probably only a few
weeks or a few months at most. At least four of the first five bowls
of wrath seem to be somewhat similar to plagues done through the
two prophets and seem to approximate those things done by these
two witnesses. The five bowls will be as follows:

- The first bowl of wrath involves loathsome sores that appear
  only "on the people who had the mark of the beast and who
  worshipped his image" (Rev. 16:2). Thus, we have assurance
  that once again, even as with the Egyptians and the Israelites,
  these plagues will only fall upon those who have rejected the

Lord and chosen to follow the Beast. The Church won't be the direct target of any plagues of God.

- The second bowl of wrath turns the sea into blood, and the entire sea dies (Rev. 16:3). Unlike the second trumpet that saw one-third of the sea perishing, this plague finishes the job. There is no indication any visible sign from heaven will precede this. Perhaps a prophetic declaration from one of the two witnesses will be the only warning.

- The third bowl is poured onto the rivers and springs of water turning them into blood, as well, just as the waters in Egypt became blood during one of the plagues of Moses (Rev. 16:4–5). The angel cannot help but comment on its appropriateness when he says, "Righteous are You . . . O Holy One . . . for they poured out the blood of saints and prophets and You have given them blood to drink. They deserve it" (Rev. 16:5b–6). Again there is no apparent sign from heaven. Perhaps the two witnesses will announce it. Drinking water may now only come from newly dug wells. Those who have only the hope of this current world will be desperate.

- The fourth bowl is poured out on the sun and scorches men with its fierce heat (Rev. 16:8–9). But rather than repent at God's further judgment, we see the utterly depraved nature of unbelievers still alive on the earth at this time. They choose to blaspheme God.

- The fifth bowl plunges the throne of the beast and his kingdom into darkness (Rev. 16:10–11). The fourth trumpet brought darkness to one-third of the earth; however, this bowl brings darkness upon the Beast's entire kingdom. Since the Beast now rules the entire world, except for a few mountains and rural areas in Judea, this suggests a nearly worldwide darkness. This is exactly what Jesus stated would happen immediately before his return.

> "But *immediately after the tribulation of those days*, the sun
> will be darkened, and the moon will not give its light, and
> the stars will fall from the sky, and the powers of the heavens
> will be shaken" (Matt. 24:29).

People will still be suffering from the previous bowls of wrath,
gnawing their tongues in pain from the malignant sores. Once again,
rather than repent, they choose to blaspheme God, confirming the
evil in their hearts and the justice of his judgments.

Very little light will be able to penetrate the earth at this time. Perhaps, there will be clouds of cosmic meteoric dust, that will blow into
the atmosphere and block out sight of the stars and obscure the sun
and the moon. Perhaps it is due to the upheaval of dust from previous
meteoric impacts. The "powers of the heavens will be shaken."

- Following this, the sixth bowl is poured out and the Euphrates River dries up in time for the kings coming in from
  the East to make their way down to Israel (Rev. 16:12–16).
  These kings of the east may, or may not be related to armies
  released earlier after the sixth trumpet sounded. These kings
  will be joined from kings around the whole world. They will
  assemble their armies and troops in response to messages and
  signs performed by three demonic spirits. These spirits have
  gone forth from the Beast, the False Prophet, and the Dragon,
  Satan himself. Perhaps these signs are meant to give the kings
  assurance of an ultimate victory.

The Days are Cut Short

Martyred saints who have overcome the Beast gather together
to sing a special song of worship *before* the release of the bowls of
wrath. This suggests the end is very much at hand (Rev. 15:1–8). It
also suggests that the Great Tribulation of persecution and martyrdom will have largely come to an end. Why else would they all be
singing and rejoicing at this time? This bowl suggests these kings
from the east were previously on the move toward Israel. It strongly

implies kings and armies coming forth from the whole earth to battle against Israel. Possibly frustrated from his inability to defeat Israel, the Beast will literally muster together all remaining able-bodied armies from around the world to finish off Israel. This draining of military manpower may very well lead to a suspension of his religious cleansing program and give respite to those Christians still alive on the earth. It may cut short his program to wipe out all Christians as he tries to muster all forces to overrun the stubborn pocket of Israeli resistance.

Jesus may have alluded to something like this when he said, "Unless those days had been cut short, no life would have been saved; but for the sake of the elect those days will be cut short" (Matt. 24:22). It's true the saints will be given in to his hand for three-and-one-half years or 1260 days. Yet, toward the end probably not all of those 1260 days will be utilized for killing saints. Perhaps he will make the faulty assumption that eliminating the remaining number of Christians is assured in any case. The more serious issue will become stubborn Israel. If so, with this suspension the number of martyrs will have reached its fullness. Those who have overcome the Beast and are in heaven will break into song, realizing the end is truly at hand. Those who have overcome the Beast and successfully kept their faith even unto death partake in special worship. They rejoice that God is justly dealing with their persecutors and establishing his kingdom on the earth among all nations (Rev. 15:3–4).

Har-Meggedon

The prophet Ezekiel saw two future assaults on Israel. The first is at the end of the worldwide reign of the Beast and is the battle of Har-Meggedon. Another assault will be attempted at the end of the millennium when the devil is once again let loose for a time (Rev. 20:7–10). That latter assault at the end of the millennium is described in detail in Ezekiel 38:8–16a as taking place "in the *latter years*" (Ezek. 38:8a). On the other hand, the assault we are speaking of now at the end of the Beast's reign is described with its aftermath in Ezekiel 38:16b–39:29. It is distinguished as taking place "in the *last days*." Both assaults will involve the nations mentioned in Ezekiel 38:1–7.

Those nations are identified as the following: Gog of the land of Magog, prince of Rosh, Meshech and Tubal, Persia, Ethiopia, Put, Gomer, and Beth-togarmah from the remote parts of the north. Ezekiel summarizes that there shall also be "many people with you" (Ezek. 38:6b). The phrase, "many people with you" confirms what Zechariah said because essentially all nations of the world will come against Israel. Still, Ezekiel makes it clear where the backbone of these troops will come from in this final assault. From where do the bulk of participants in the final battle against Israel come? The chart[271] below details the places:

The Nations of Armageddon

Biblical People Identified	Modern Day Location
Gog of the land of Magog	Western Turkey
Rosh	Northwest Iran (home of mostly Kurds), and Azerbaijan
Ancient Persia	Iran (the old Empire also included the Central Asian Repubics of the former USSR, Pakistan, Afghanistan, Western China & Northwest India)
Meshech	Turkey
Tubal	Turkey
Ethiopia	Ethiopia and/or Eritrea
Put	Libya and/or Sudan
Gomer (originally Aryans from the Caucasus from a region in Southern Ukraine and southern Russia just north of the Black Sea who settled in Eastern Turkey and became know there as Cimerians)	Southern Crimea of Ukraine, home of the Muslim Tatars + Muslim Russian Republics of Dagestan & Chechnya and/or Eastern Turkey
Beth-Togarmah	Southern Turkey and Northern Syria

Once again, we see that the main nations directly identified in this conflict are all Muslim peoples. The only exception is Ethiopia and Eritrea. Nevertheless, both have very large Muslim populations. Ethiopia is about one-third Muslim and Eritrea is about one-half Muslim.

It is interesting that the bulk of the troops massed for this final assault come from Muslim nations farther away from Israel. Could it be that so many troops from the nations closer to Israel have already been killed in the initial and ongoing attacks against Israel during the three-and-a-half years of fighting since the start of the Beast's reign and the Great Tribulation began? Again this may indicate the Beast is now drawing upon all his reserves in a final attempt to overwhelm Israel.

Probably in connection with this final campaign, and perhaps because of the incredible severity of the plagues from the bowls of wrath, the False Prophet personally makes war on the two witnesses. If they can be eliminated, victory over Israel and the "peace" of Islam will be assured. Much to the delight of the subjects of the Beast, the False Prophet is able to overcome them and kill them (Rev. 11:7).

Their bodies are left in the middle of Jerusalem, perhaps at the dividing line of East and West Jerusalem. By not permitting them to be buried, the Muslim inhabitants will signify they are cursed. The subjects of the Beast from all the peoples and tribes and tongues and nations around the world will gaze upon their dead bodies rejoicing they have finally been killed. For it is these two prophets who tormented those who dwell on the earth. This is a strong indicator that the plagues and bowls of wrath will be associated with them. For three-and-a-half days they are left out in the open. The world celebrates by sending each other gifts (Rev. 11:8–10).

It seems now that the troublesome Achilles heel for the Beast and his kingdom, the two prophets, has been eliminated. The Islamic Kingdom seems poised for triumph. The only religion of the world will finally be Islam as the Koran declared. Or will it?

Just when triumph finally seems secure, doom awaits. An ominous sign of the impending end of the Islamic kingdom occurs next. After lying dead for three-and-a-half days, the two prophets are called up into heaven as their stunned enemies look on. As they ascend, an earthquake hits Jerusalem wiping out one-tenth of the city, killing seven thousand people. Terrified residents actually give glory to the God of heaven (Rev. 11:11–13). This may speak of some last-minute conversions, or perhaps more likely, the terrified realization that God's just judgment has come upon them. What will happen next? What will happen to the Church? How will Jesus defeat the Beast?

Chapter 19

The Harvesting of the Earth and the Return of Christ (Rev. 16:15)

After the sixth bowl of wrath has been poured out, we see the kings of the earth massing troops on the plains of Har-Meggedon. This is believed by many to be a valley in northern Israel north of Jerusalem.

The Rapture of the Church

As this is taking place the Lord Jesus gives us an inserted warning. He says "Behold, I am coming like a thief. Blessed is the one who stays awake and keeps his clothes, so that he will not walk about naked and men will not see his shame" (Rev. 16:15). It is no accident that this warning is placed here. For it is in these days, as the troops gather, the Bible declares the Lord Jesus Christ will return to call his bride to the wedding. The saints, the Church of the Living God, will meet him in the sky, and then he will physically return to overwhelm the armies of the Beast.

When will we finally know we are within days, at the most weeks or a few months of his return? Jesus said,

> But immediately *after* the tribulation of those days the sun will be darkened, and the moon will not give its light, and the stars will

fall from the sky, and the powers of the heavens will be shaken.

And then the sign of the Son of Man will appear in the sky, and then all the tribes of the earth will mourn, and they will see the Son of Man coming on the clouds of the sky with power and great glory.

And He will send forth His angels with a Great Trumpet and they will gather together His elect from the four winds, from one end of the sky to the other. (Matt. 24:29–31)

Luke also records Jesus as saying; ". . . the powers of the heavens will be shaken. Then they will see the Son of Man coming in a cloud with power and great glory" (Luke 21:26b).

Mark notes Jesus saying,

. . . *After* that tribulation, the sun will be darkened and the moon will not give its light, and the stars will be falling from heaven, and the powers that are in the heavens will be shaken. *Then* they will see the Son of Man coming in clouds with great power and glory. And *then* He will send forth the angels, and will gather together His elect from the four winds, *from the farthest end of the earth to the farthest end of heaven.* (Mark 13:24–27)

Here we learn detailed information about when we will be gathered together to meet the Lord. Jesus described a darkness obstructing view of the sun and moon throughout the whole earth. This is identical to what is described in the fifth bowl of wrath in Revelation 15:10 when the whole kingdom of the Beast, probably most of the earth (minus what is left of Israel), is plunged into darkness. This means the Rapture follows sometime shortly *after* the fifth bowl, but prior to the wrath of the seventh bowl hitting the earth. Given the warning issued to the Church *after* the sixth bowl, the Rapture must then take place sometime during the time when the troops are gathering north of Israel.

A further indication of a late Rapture is that both Mark and Matthew record this gathering of the elect as happening immediately "*after* the tribulation" of those days. This tribulation is mentioned earlier in both of those passages as "the *Great Tribulation*" (Matt.

24:21). This is a tribulation greater than any to (Mark 13:9) ever hit planet earth. The gathering occurs *after* this.

Thirdly, we also see this gathering together of the saints occurring *after* the "sign of the Son of Man" appears in the sky. Specifically, Matthew records for us that "every tribe of the earth will mourn, and *they will see* the Son of Man coming on the clouds of the sky with power and great glory" (Matt. 24:30b). All the nations see Jesus in the heavens *just prior* to our gathering together with him in the sky. Jesus will be seen by the world *prior* to the gathering of the Church. The Bible is clear he will be seen by *all* of the earth. The fact the world will be mourning this coming makes it clear these are unbelievers. They will see and observe this return of Christ in the sky that precedes the gathering of the saints. This will not be a secret coming for the Church. This will be the most public event in the history of the world for "every eye shall see Him."

Fourthly, we see that when Jesus sends fourth his angels to collect his bride, he sends them to gather his "elect from the farthest end of the *earth* to the farthest end of *heaven*" (Mark 13:27b). Just who are the elect that Jesus is gathering? The Greek word used for "elect" is the exact same Greek word that Paul used when he said, "Who will bring a charge against God's *elect*?" (Rom. 8:33). Thus, "elect" is the same word used for *all* believers in Jesus Christ.

Fifthly, the fact that he will gather his beloved from the farthest end of the *earth* is crystal clear evidence that there will be saints (i.e. the Church) waiting on the *earth* for his return *after* the Great Tribulation. The indication that he will also gather them from the farthest end of heaven indicates that those saints on the earth will meet up with those who have gone before them.

Paul affirms this when he says

> . . . that *we* who are alive *and remain until the coming of the Lord,* will not precede those who have fallen asleep. For the Lord Himself will descend from heaven with a shout, with the voice of the archangel and with *the trumpet of God,* and the dead in Christ will rise first. *Then we* who are *alive and remain* will be caught up *together with them* in the clouds to meet the Lord in the air and so we shall always be with the Lord. (1Thess. 4:15–17)[372]

This brings us to a sixth important detail concerning the Rapture's timing. Matthew indicates this gathering will take place with the sound of "a great trumpet." Paul also mentions it happening in connection with "the trumpet of God." He's even more specific when he says, "I tell you a mystery; we will not all sleep, but we will all be changed, in a moment, in the twinkling of an eye, *at the last trumpet; for the trumpet will sound*, and the dead will be raised imperishable, and we will be changed" (1 Cor. 15:51–52).

Here Paul tells us that this Rapture—or gathering to meet the Lord in the air—will happen at the sound of the *last trumpet*. Fortunately, the book of the Revelation gives us a very clear description of when *the seventh and last trumpet* will sound. We see in Revelation chapter 11 that immediately following the taking up of the two prophets into heaven the second woe of the two prophets has passed and "the third woe is coming quickly" (Rev. 11:14). That third woe happens with the seventh angel sounding the seventh *and* last trumpet. There is no trumpet after this one.

Thus, the last trumpet will sound *after* the ministry of the two prophets has ended. It will happen at the very end of the reign of the Beast *immediately* preceding Jesus' reign on the earth. Precisely when the seventh angel sounds his trumpet, heaven breaks out in a shout of loud voices saying,

> The kingdom of the *world* has become the kingdom of our Lord and of His Christ; and He will reign forever and ever . . . And the twenty-four elders . . . fell on their faces . . . saying, '. . . You have taken Your great power and have begun to reign.
>
> And the nations were enraged, and Your wrath *came* and the time came for the dead to be judged, and the time to reward Your bond-servants the prophets and the saints and those who fear Your name, the small and the great, and to destroy those who destroy the earth. (Rev. 11:15b–18)

After the saints have been gathered in the largest gathering of people ever, the time will come for their reward. The "gentle will inherit the earth" (Matt. 5:5b), and they shall return with the Lord and his holy angels to follow-up the rout of the armies of the Beast and "those who destroy the earth" (Rev. 11:18b).

John also referred to the Lord Jesus gathering his Church to himself *after* the period of the Great Tribulation ends. In Revelation 14:9–13, the world is warned not to worship the Beast and not to take the mark. The saints are also encouraged to persevere through this time and are encouraged there will be a special blessing in store for all Christians who endure. *Following this*, in verse 14 John says,

> Then I looked, and behold, a white cloud, and sitting on the cloud was one like a son of man, having a golden crown on His head and a sharp sickle in His hand.
>
> And another angel came out of the temple, crying out with a loud voice to Him who sat on the cloud, 'Put in your sickle and reap, for the hour to reap has come, because the harvest of the earth is ripe.
>
> *Then* He who sat on the cloud swung His sickle over the earth, and the earth was reaped. (Rev. 14:14–16)

Thus, not only are there no scriptures that indicate a Rapture prior to the Great Tribulation, *all* scriptures that specifically discuss the Rapture place it afterward. The chart on the next page summarizes the timing of the Rapture according to the Bible.

The Marriage of the Lamb

In Revelation 19 we see heaven rejoicing at this time of union with the Church.

> I heard the voice of a great multitude and like the sound of many waters and like the sound of mighty peals of thunder, saying, 'Hallelujah! For the Lord our God, the Almighty, reigns.
>
> Let us rejoice and be glad and give the glory to Him, for the marriage of the Lamb has come and His bride has made herself ready.
>
> It was given to her to clothe herself in fine linen, bright and clean, for the fine linen is the righteous acts of the saints.

The Timing of the Rapture

After:	When:	Just Before:
• The Great Tribulation. (Mt 24:21,29-31) (Mk 13:19,24-27)	• The angels are sent to gather together the elect from earth and from heaven to meet the Lord in the air (Mk 13:27) (Mt 24:31)	• Har-Magedon (Re 16:15-16)
• The sun and moon are darkened (Mt 24:29-31) (Mk 13:24-27)		• All the mountains of the Earth are leveled (Re 16:15,17,20)
• The stars fall from the sky (Mt 24:29-31) (Mk 13:24-27)	• The Last trumpet call sounds, which is the 7th trumpet (1 Th 4:15-17) (1 Co 15:51-52)	• All the islands disappear (Re 16:15,17,20)
• The powers in the heavens are shaken (Mk 13:25-27) (Mt 24:29-31)		• All the cities of the nations fall (Re 16:15,17,19)
• The Son of Man is seen coming in the clouds by the entire world. (Mt 24:30-31) (Mk 13:26-27)		• Huge hailstones of 100 pounds fall on mankind (Re 16:15,17,19)
• The two prophets have been killed by the false beast (Re 11:7-18)		• The wedding of the Lamb (Re 16:7-8)
• The sixth bowl of wrath is poured out (Re 16:12-15)		• The return of Jesus to the Earth (Re 19:11-15)
• Moments after the resurrection of the Christian dead (1 Th 4:15-17) (1 Co 15:51-52)		

Then he said to me, 'Write, 'Blessed are those who are invited to the marriage supper of the Lamb.' (Rev. 19:6b–9a)

At this marriage of the Lamb, the bride is clothed in fine linen. We already saw the martyrs of old get their white robes when the fifth seal was opened. Then we saw those who were martyred during the Great Tribulation receive their white robes. Finally, white robes will be given out again, because all the other brethren now join the martyrs. This includes the ones whose bodies have just been changed and gathered from the earth. The return and reclamation of earth follow this joyous time, probably almost immediately. The fine linen probably comes as an immediate covering on the changed heavenly bodies given to believers who were left alive on the earth at the Lord's coming. This meeting in the sky is the marriage of the

Lamb with his bride, the Church. The two become one and shall be together forevermore.

Some have felt that this must also be when the marriage supper happens; however, the Bible does not say explicitly that the marriage supper occurs at exactly this same time. It only says, "Blessed are those who are *invited* to the marriage supper of the Lamb" (Rev. 19:9). A blessing is declared for all those who get the invitation. They include all those who are the bride of Christ and who are married to the Lamb at this time. However, like all weddings, if the wedding supper is a literal banquet, it will occur *after* the wedding, probably not long after the Lamb has returned and destroyed his opponents. After all, one of the Lord's wedding presents to his bride will be the newly cleansed earth.

This return will coincide with the opening of the temple of God in heaven and "flashes of lightning and sounds and peals of thunder and an earthquake and a great hailstorm" (Rev. 11:19b). We see all of these exact same things happen at the pouring out of the seventh bowl of wrath, only with greater detail.

Then "a loud voice *came out of the temple* from the throne, saying, 'It is done'" (Rev. 16:17b) as the Lord Jesus himself cries out in triumph just as he cried out "It is finished" on the cross.

> There *were flashes of lightning and sounds and peals of thunder*; and there was *a great earthquake*, such as there had not been since man came to be upon the earth, so great an earthquake was it, and so mighty. The great city was split into three parts, and the cities of the nations fell. Babylon the great was remembered before God, to give her the cup of the wine of His fierce wrath. And every island, and the mountains were not found.
>
> And *huge hailstones*, about one hundred pounds each, *came down from heaven upon men*; and men blasphemed God because of the plague of the hail, because its plague was extremely severe. (Rev. 16:18–21)

Here we see that the events right after the sounding of the seventh trumpet coincide perfectly with the events of the seventh and final bowl of wrath. The chart on the next page compares the similarities between the sixth seal, the last trumpet and the last bowl.

There is a massive thunder and lightning storm and a massive earthquake that decimates the mountains, the nations and all their cities. The great city, that is either the remnants of New York City or Jerusalem, is remembered by God and split into three parts. "Babylon *the Great*" (as opposed to simply Babylon) is probably a reference to all of the United States and not just New York City. It is remembered before God and is thoroughly devastated in the earthquake and hailstorm.

COMPARISON OF 6TH SEAL, 7TH TRUMPET AND 7TH BOWL		
Mentioned in all three: 6th Seal, 7thTrumpet & 7th bowl	Mentioned in both the 7th trumpet & 7th Bowl:	Mentioned in both the 6th Seal & 7th Bowl:
• Great Earthquake • Final destruction of all of Jesus' opponents	• Great Earthquake • Final Destruction of all of Jesus' opponents • Flashes of Lightning & sounds and peals of thunder • Great Hailstorm	• Great Earthquake • Final Destruction of all of Jesus' opponents • Every island and mountain is destroyed • (the 5th bowl occurring shortly before the 7th bowl, mentions darkness covering the Beast's kingdom, just like the 6th seal)

Christ Returns

The martyrs in heaven got to see a preview of this in Revelation 6 when the sixth seal was opened. There we saw the sun become blackened and the moon look like blood, and the stars fall to the earth (Rev. 6:12). These all seem to closely resemble what happens at the fifth bowl of wrath and the verses of Matthew 24:29–31, Mark 13:24–27 and Luke 21:25–28. Shortly *after* this the

> . . . sky is split apart like a scroll when it is rolled up, and *every mountain and island were removed out of their places.* Then the kings of the earth and the great men and the commanders and the rich and the strong and every slave and free man hid themselves in the caves and among the rocks of the mountains; and they said to the mountains and to the rocks, 'Fall on us and hide us from the

presence of Him who sits on the throne, and from the wrath of the Lamb; for the great day of their wrath has come, and who is able to stand? (Rev. 6:14–17)

Again, stars falling from the sky to the earth may speak of another meteor shower. This could explain the darkening of the sun and moon and the gigantic hailstones due to large amounts of dust and particles in the upper atmosphere. The sky splitting apart like a scroll may be a direct reference to what will happen when Jesus appears on the clouds of the sky and Raptures his Church. It is evident that the massive earthquake immediately follows this. The entire world is desperate for a place to hide from the "wrath of the Lamb." It's interesting they say that the great day of "their" wrath has come. "Their" wrath once again indicates terrified unsaved humanity seeing the armies of heaven, the Church of Jesus and his angels, descending with the Lord Jesus to claim planet earth.

John sees the descent from heaven's perspective as heaven opens and he who sits on a white horse rides the sky.

He

. . . is called Faithful and True, and in righteousness He judges and wages war. His eyes are a flame of fire . . . He is clothed with a robe dipped in blood, and His name is called The Word of God.

And the armies which are in heaven, clothed in fine linen, white and clean, were following Him on white horses.

From His mouth comes a sharp sword, so that with it He may strike down the nations, and He will rule them with a rod of iron; and He treads the wine press of the fierce wrath of God, the Almighty.

And on His robe and on His thigh He has a name written, 'King of Kings, and Lord of Lords.' (Rev. 19:11–16)

What a fearful sight this will be for the Beast and his armies! Coming at them will be an army the size of which has never been seen before, full of soldiers who can never die! The Beast and his armies won't stand a chance. However, it will not be necessary for the heavenly armies to fight since the Lord himself will fight and destroy them by himself (Rev. 19:15, Zech. 14:3).[273]

> Then I saw an angel standing in the sun, and he cried out with a loud voice, saying to all the birds that fly in midheaven, 'Come, assemble for the great supper of God, so that you may eat the flesh of kings and the flesh of commanders and the flesh of mighty men and the flesh of horses and of those who sit on them and the flesh of all men, both free men and slaves, and small and great.
>
> And I saw the beast and the kings of the earth and their armies assembled to make war against Him who sat on His horse and against His army.
>
> And the beast was seized, and with him the false prophet who performed the signs in his presence, by which he deceived those who had received the mark of the beast and those who worshiped his image; these two were thrown alive into the lake of fire which burns with brimstone.
>
> And the rest were killed with the sword which came from the mouth of Him who sat on the horse, and all the birds were filled with their flesh. (Rev. 19:17–22)

From Israel's Vantage Point

What will Israel be seeing and doing as this is happening? Zechariah saw this day when he stated,

> . . . In that day I will set about to destroy all the nations that come against Jerusalem.
>
> I will pour out on the house of David and on the inhabitants of Jerusalem, the Spirit of grace and of supplication, so that they will look on Me whom they have pierced and they will mourn for Him, as one mourns for an only son, and they will weep bitterly over Him like the bitter weeping over a firstborn. In that day there will be great mourning in Jerusalem like the mourning of Hadadrimmon in the plain of Megiddo. (Zech. 12:9–11)

As enemy armies of an unprecedented size surround Israel, and the two prophets are killed, a Spirit of grace and supplication will overtake Israel. All Israel will begin to pray for deliverance from her enemies and the coming of Messiah like never before. The grace of God will be poured out on them and undoubtedly there will be much deeply felt confession of sin. They will be pleading for forgiveness and for Messiah to come. With the two prophets now gone, only Messiah will be able to rescue them. The ministry of Elijah will this time prove successful. The hearts of the children will be turned back to the fathers of the faith and the fathers to the children (Mal. 4:5–6). The remaining physical descendants of the entire house of Israel will genuinely repent in brokenness, crying out for Messiah (Rom 11:24–27).

Their crying and mourning will only increase as they see Messiah appear in the clouds. They will recognize him as the one "whom they have pierced," the Lord Jesus.

> In that day a fountain will be opened for the house of David and for the inhabitants of Jerusalem, for sin and for impurity. It will come about in that day,' declares the Lord of hosts, 'that I will cut off the names of the idols from the land, and they will no longer be remembered; and I will also remove the prophets and the unclean spirit from the land. (Zech. 13:1–2).

Here the Lord declares a cleansing and forgiveness of Israel and a removing of those "prophets" who claimed to be spokespersons for the Lord. That would of course mean unbelieving Rabbis, so-called spokesmen for God, who had taught them not to trust in Jesus as their Messiah. Zechariah goes on to say that both they themselves and their parents will be ashamed of what they did. They will try to cover up the fact this was their occupation.

The flow the battle takes is described in Zechariah.

> In that day His feet will stand on the Mount of Olives, which is in front of Jerusalem on the east; and the Mount of Olives will be split in its middle from east to west by a very large valley, so that half of the mountain will move toward the north and the other half toward the south. You will flee by the valley of My mountains, for

the valley of the mountains will reach to Azel; yes, you will flee just as you fled before the earthquake in the days of Uzziah king of Judah. Then the Lord, my God, will come, and all the holy ones with Him! (Zech. 14:4–5)

The Lord will set foot on the Mount of Olives that is the same spot from which he left when he ascended into heaven (Acts 1:12). The angels told the disciples this would happen right after Jesus left saying, "This Jesus, who has been taken away from you into heaven, will come in just the same way as you have watched Him go into heaven" (Acts 1:11). Just as the disciples saw the physically risen Christ ascend to heaven from the Mount of Olives in the same way he will return. In the same, literal, physical way, the glorified Christ will descend onto the Mount of Olives.

Zechariah speaks now of a massive earthquake as Messiah comes down. It is so gigantic it actually splits the Mount of Olives in half. This will coincide with that massive earthquake that will level the mountains of the world (Rev. 16:20) at his return. As this massive earthquake ends, they will flee down a newly created valley stretching down through the mountains of Judah to Azel that is at an uncertain location in Judah. Thus, a pathway will be created for the refugees who have been holding out in the wilderness in the mountains of Judea. There they can stay until the Lord has wiped out their enemies. The slaughter will be unprecedented.

Since the Beast will have made Jerusalem his capital, there will be great wealth in its environs. He also stole much spoil from the Jews in his initial taking of Jerusalem. The Jews will get it all back. As Zechariah saw, "Behold, a day is coming for the Lord when the spoil taken from you will be divided among you" (Zech. 14:1).

John also saw this final wrath of God being poured out immediately following the harvesting of the earth at the Rapture as pictured in Revelation 14:14–16. In verse 17–20 we see the angel swinging his sharp sickle over the earth gathering the clusters from the vine of the earth and then throwing them into "the great wine press of the wrath of God" (Rev. 14:19b).

"And the wine press was trodden outside the city, and blood came out from the wine press, up to the horses' bridles, for a distance of two hundred miles" (Rev. 14:20).

This refers to the slaughter of Armageddon. The winepress is trodden outside the city that is Jerusalem. The blood will rise chest high for two-hundred miles around. No slaughter has ever been like it. Ezekiel also saw the same vision and heard the calling of birds of the air and beasts of the field to this same feast (Ezek. 39:17–20). Ezekiel tells us that those who live in Israel will use all the military equipment for fuel for a period of seven years afterward (Ezek. 39:9). They won't need to use anything else for fuel that whole time.

Prior to this, the Beast and the False Prophet will be seized and thrown into the lake of fire. Their inspirer and prime mover, ". . . the dragon, the serpent of old, who is the devil and Satan . . ." will also be seized and bound with a great chain and thrown into the abyss where he will be sealed up (Rev. 20:1–3a). This will render him unable to ". . . deceive the nations any longer, until the thousand years were completed; after these things he must be released for a short time" (Rev. 20:3b).

So what will happen during these thousand years while the Dragon is bound? What will Christ do upon the earth once he has conquered and defeated the Beast, the False Prophet and the Dragon? What will the earth be like? Who will be living there?

Basic Chronology of the Revelation of Jesus Christ

- **GREAT COMMISSION IS COMPLETED (Re 4:1, 5:1-10, Mt 24:14, Mk 13:10, Lk 24:46-47, Ac 1:8, 2 Pe 3:8-9, Mt 28:18-20)**

- **THE FOUR HORSEMEN RIDE:** (White Horse released in Heavenlies) (Re 6:1-2)
- **Red Horses Ride** : World War / Jihad (Re 6:3-4, Ze 6:2a)
- **Black Horses Ride:** Economic Disaster Hits Wealthy nations (Re 6:5-6, Ze 6:2b, 6a)
- **FALSE PEACE**– Babylon / America might sell out Israel & Christians between now and world takeover of the Beast. (1 Th 5:1-3, Re 18:24)
- **White Horses Ride:** the Beast goes forth conquering the wealthy nations (Re 6:1-2, Ze 6:3a, 6a, 8)
- **Babylon (New York City) is obliterated** by nuclear attack. (probably around this time, maybe be just before or during attack on Jerusalem). (Re 14:6-8, 17:16-18:24)
- **Dappled/Ashen Horses Ride:** Death sweeps the poor world: (Re 6:7-8, Ze 6:3b, 6b)
  - sword, pestilence, famine + wild animals

- **BEAST SEIZES COMPLETE WORLD POWER (Re 13:1-10)**
- **Israel is attacked** / Jerusalem is overrun (Ze 14:1-2)
- The False Prophet arises declares himself to be Christ on the Temple Mount in the Dome of the Rock / the Wailing Wall is torn down. (Mt 24:15-20)
- **OFFICIAL START OF THE GREAT TRIBULATION** (Mt 24:21)
- The two prophets begin their ministry. (Re 11:1-6, Mal 4:1-6, Ju 15-16, Ge 5:24, 1 Ki 18:21, 36-37, 19:8, 2 Ki 2:11)
- **Worship of the Beast / Mark of the Beast** required to buy and sell. (Re 13:16-18, 14:9-11)
- **Slaughter of Christians** begins in earnest. (Re 14:12-13)

- 1st **Trumpet** – Hail + Meteors + 1/3 Grass & Trees burned up. (Re 8:7)
- 2nd **Trumpet** – Huge Meteorite Hits Ocean 1/3 of sea life killed. (Re 8:8-9)
- 3rd **Trumpet** – Comet enters atmosphere, pollutes 1/3 of springs & waters (Re 8:10-11)
- 4th **Trumpet** – 1/3 of sun, moon, stars darkened by cosmic dust and smoke from fires. (Re 8:12-13)
- 5th **Trumpet** – Locust Creatures attack unsaved for 5 months. (Re 9:1-11)
- 6th **Trumpet** – Armies go on rampage killing 1/3 of the earth. (Re 9:13-21)
- (possible lull in killing of Christians, as troops begin to gather for Har-Magedon) (Re 16:13-14, Ez 38.39, Mt 24:22)
- 1st **Bowl** of Wrath – sores, malignant growths on the unsaved. (Re 16:2)
- 2nd **Bowl** – all sea life perishes. (Re 16:3)
- 3rd **Bowl** – springs and rivers become blood. (Re 16:4-7)
- 4th **Bowl** – sun scorches men with intense heat. (Re 16:8-9)
- 5th **Bowl** – darkness falls on the Beast's kingdom. (Re 16:10-11)
- 6th **Bowl** – River Euphrates dries up / armies from east come. (Re 16:12)
- **CHRIST APPEARS IN THE SKY**
- 7th **Trumpet / RAPTURE**– angels harvest Christians from heaven & earth to meet Jesus (Mt 24:31, Mk 13:27, Re 16:16)
- 7th **Bowl** – massive earthquake & hailstorm. (Re 16:17-21)
- **Christ Returns** – Christ returns and wipes out his enemies. (Re 19:11-19, 2 Th 1:6-10)
- **Beast & False Prophet captured** and thrown in lake of fire. (Re 19:20-21)
- **Millennium begins** – 1000 year reign of righteousness / followed by brief rebellion (Re 20:1-10, Ez 38:1-16a)
- **The Great White Throne Judgment** – followed by New Heaven & New Earth. (Re 20:11-22:9)

· ·

Chapter 20

The Millennial Kingdom of Christ on Earth & The Judgment (Rev. 20:1–22:21)

J ohn describes a most wonderful sight after the devil has been bound.

> Then I saw thrones, and they sat on them, and judgment was given to them. And I saw the souls of those who have been beheaded because of their testimony of Jesus and because of the word of God, and those who had not worshiped the beast or his image, and had not received the mark on their forehead and on their hand; and they came to life and reigned with Christ for a thousand years.
>
> The rest of the dead did not come to life until the thousand years were completed. This is the first resurrection.
>
> Blessed and holy is the one who has part in the first resurrection; over these the second death has no power, but they will be priests of God and of Christ and will reign with Him for a thousand years. (Rev. 20:4–7)

Undoubtedly, to bring extra encouragement and strength to those who have to endure the Great Tribulation, John emphasizes they will rule and reign with Christ. Each one will be rewarded for their faithfulness. Since there will be believers and martyrs from every tribe and tongue and nation, we can be assured there will be worthy rulers who know their own people.

John heard the voice in heaven say, ". . . the time came for the dead to be judged, and the time to reward Your bondservants the prophets and the saints and those who fear Your name, the small and the great . . ." (Rev. 11:18). Thus, this first judgment of the dead will also be the resurrection and reward of all the righteous dead, the prophets, the saints and all who feared the name of the Lord. All believing dead will be raised to meet the Lord in the air.

John does not spend much time describing the millennium on earth, probably because there are so many lengthy passages in the books of the prophets to do that for us.[274]

King Jesus and his Capital Jerusalem

Isaiah saw this coming thousand-year reign of Christ:

The word which Isaiah the son of Amoz saw concerning Judah and Jerusalem.

Now it will come about that in the last days the mountain of the house of the Lord will be established as the chief of the mountains, and will be raised above the hills; and all the nations will stream to it.

And many peoples will come and say, 'Come let us go up to the mountain of the Lord, to the house of the God of Jacob; that He may teach us concerning His ways and that we may walk in His paths.

For *the law will go forth from Zion and the word of the Lord from Jerusalem. And He will judge between the nations, and will render decisions for many peoples*; and they will hammer their swords into plowshares and their spears into pruning hooks. Nation will not lift up sword against nation, and never again will they learn war. (Isa. 2:1–4)

It is no accident the Lord has situated Jerusalem and Israel to be at the crossroads of the three continents of Africa, Asia and Europe. It really has been strategically located at the center of the world. It will become the chief of the mountains, literally the political and spiritual capital of the world. Both the law and the word of the Lord will go forth from Zion.

Here we see that the peoples will come to learn of God's ways. Indeed, they seem eager to do so. Furthermore, since he will judge disputes and problems between the nations, there will be no need for war. His judgment will always be perfectly just and final. It will be a glorious time of peace and the gentle "shall inherit the earth" (Matt. 5:5b).

There will be no need for democracy, as Jesus shall rule them with a rod of iron. This shall be an incorruptible, benevolent dictatorship with a perfect balance of mercy and justice. There is much that can be said about the millennium, but the scope of this book doesn't permit a detailed look.

In short, during the millennium people, the angels and all creation will get to see what humanity and creation could be like without the devil. This will be another age. It will be a new epoch in God's dealings with man and his creation. The pre-Flood days differed from the post-Flood days. The times after the Mosaic Law differed from the days of the patriarchs. The age of the Church was different from the times that preceded the Resurrection and Pentecost. In the same way, this will also be a new age.

Certainly, life will be far more joyous with far less sickness, far less sin, and far lengthier in duration, along with far more justice and truth. Each age has proven to have greater blessings than the one prior to it. Certainly, the Church Age has proven a greater blessing than the previous ages. This coincides with the Bible that says, "There will be no end to the increase of His government or of peace . . ." (Isa. 9:7a).

Who will be the nations that the saints will rule (1 Cor. 6:2)? The Bible seems to indicate that some people will survive the Lord's return. They will probably be retarded people, small infants and children. The sick shall be healed and children raised by Christians to repopulate the earth.[275] Resurrected Christians will administer the government and ensure justice.

However, even under such ideal conditions, man will still be a sinner in need of God's salvation. The ways of the Lord and the proclamation of the Gospel will still need to be made. Zechariah 14:16–19 seems to suggest that man's obedience will be less than perfect. The fact sin cannot be eradicated, even under ideal conditions, will become clear from the fact that even though people will live longer lives, they will still die. The enemy of death will still be out there, even during the millennium. It's true the devil himself will be bound, but this problem of death because of sin, although weakened, will remain until the millennium is over. Yet, King Jesus will not leave the enemy of death alone forever.

At the end of the millennium, for a brief period of time, the devil will be let out. In spite of nearly paradise-like conditions, just as with Eve, he will once again deceive and manipulate people. This time it will be unregenerate people from the nations born during the millennium and alive at this time. Motivated by greed and lust for power, they will try to take the world capital, Jerusalem. They will ignore the warnings of God's people (Ezek. 38:11–13).

The reality of their deception will soon become evident as God rains "fire and brimstone" (Ezek. 38:22b) down upon them from heaven and devours them (Rev. 20:10). The devil will then be taken and thrown into the lake of fire and brimstone where the False Prophet and Beast have been hanging out. There they shall remain, tormented forever and ever.

Now that the devil's power has been forever abolished and all remaining rebels killed, death itself will be obsolete. It too will now be abolished forever and brought under subjection to the Lord Jesus Christ. Then "when all things are subjected to Him (Christ), then the Son Himself also will be subjected to the One who subjected all things to Him, so that God may be all in all" (1 Cor. 15:28). What will happen next? What will become of all those who opposed Him? W hat will happen to those who died during the millennium?

The Judgment

The first judgment and the time of giving out rewards to the prophets and saints of old came at the return of Christ and the start of the millennium. However, God is not finished with his judgments.

Following the millennium's end, the old heaven and earth flee away for there is "no place found for them" (Rev. 20:11b). They literally wear out their usefulness to God. The new age is preparing to begin. But before this can happen, the time has come to tie up some old business.

God loves us and desires that all of us will be able to enter this wonderful new age where love and goodness reign supreme. Fortunately, for the person who has come to faith in Christ, he or she has already had a time of judgment. This one's sins have been wiped away. Even so, he will be judged. For "each one of us will give an account of himself to God" (Rom. 14:12). The Bible indicates that the "Lord will both bring to light the things hidden in the darkness and disclose the motives of men's hearts; and then each man's praise will come to him from God" (1Cor. 4:5). Since his sin has already been wiped out, judgment for the believer will only involve rewards or loss of rewards. It seems that God will primarily be concerned at the motivation behind what we did, more than the actual outward actions. However, the Lord is not unconcerned with the outward actions, for Paul also states that "the fire will test the *quality* of each man's work."

Again, the main thing that is checked at the Great White Throne Judgment is an individual's deeds. Those individuals whose names are not found written in the Book of Life, who have not put their hope in Jesus Christ for their salvation from sin, will be thrown into the lake of fire. There is no return from this place called the lake of fire. Those already in Hades will be thrown in there.

John tells us the kind of people who go to Hades. They are ". . . the cowardly and unbelieving and abominable and murderers and immoral persons and sorcerers and idolaters and all liars, their part will be in the lake that burns with fire and brimstone, which is the second death" (Rev. 21:8). God will judge each individual according to his holy standards.

For example, God considers belief or lack of it to be a deed to be judged. The lake of fire is a place where the "unbelieving" will go. Why would God force someone who doesn't believe to go to heaven? Those relying in something other than faith in Jesus Christ to save them will be in trouble. Reliance on church attendance, church membership, good works, sincerity or belief in some other faith will be found wanting. Some may think of themselves as believers in God and consider themselves to be pretty good, but the Bible makes it clear that God will define them as unbelievers since they are relying on something other than belief in Jesus for salvation. Unbelief (lack of reliance) in Jesus Christ is unbelief in God's provision for salvation and forgiveness of sins (John 3:16–19, 1 John 1:8–2:2).

Not believing in Jesus Christ reveals pride and trust in our own abilities. It shows a willingness to reject the way that God Himself suffered so greatly to make available to us. There will be no good people in hell or heaven. God will only send the sinner to hell. He will forgive the remaining sinners who have acknowledged their sin and relied upon Jesus Christ for salvation. We'll see how he made this salvation possible in a moment.

Here in Revelation 20 the text seems to imply there will be some whose names are actually found written in the Book of Life at this second judgment after the millennium. Only people *not found* in the Book of Life are thrown into hell. If they would all automatically be thrown there anyway, why would someone bother to open up the Book of Life? The saved will certainly include those Jews who got saved at Messiah's return and any others who got saved during the millennium.

The New Heaven and New Earth (Rev. 21:1–9)

Finally, the judgment comes to an end and John is shown a new heaven and a new earth. There is no longer any sea. The New Jerusalem coming out of heaven is beautifully adorned as a bride for her husband. God chooses to permanently make his abode with men. He will freely move and live among them, just as a father would with his son. Every tear will be wiped from their eyes, death shall be forever abolished and all mourning, crying and pain will be absent in this place.

The New Jerusalem (Rev. 21:10–22:9)

As John is taken away to be shown the New Jerusalem, it is clear this is the place Jesus promised he was going to prepare for his followers. The city is filled with the glory of God and the brilliance of very costly stones and crystal-clear jasper. The scope of this book doesn't allow us a detailed look into this wonderful city. But it will be beyond spectacular.

The bondservants of God will serve him and see his face. His name will be on their foreheads. They shall reign with God forever and ever.

The nations coming in and out of this city will probably be the bondservants of God free to come and go as they serve the Lord. If that is the case, then they will always have a place to stay in this city. They will always be welcome, much in the same way that permanent residents of a country are welcome to return from excursions to other places.

A Warning and an Exhortation

As one approaches the end of Revelation, we are struck again by an important warning. Jesus wants us to realize that "Nothing unclean, and no one who practices abomination and lying, shall ever come into it (the New Jerusalem), but only those whose names are written in the Lamb's book of life" (Rev. 21:27). Clearly, those whose names are not written in the Lamb's Book of Life at the Great White Throne Judgment will have no second chances. As Hebrews states, "It is appointed for men once to die and after this comes judgment" (Heb. 9:27b).

There will be no second-chance purgatory payments to earn our way into heaven. Such doctrine is not found in the pages of the Holy Scriptures. Jesus makes the finality of this judgment clear when he states, "Blessed are those who wash their robes, so that they may have the right to the tree of life, and may enter by the gates into the city. Outside are the dogs and the sorcerers and the immoral persons and the murderers and the idolaters, and everyone who loves and practices lying" (Rev. 22:14–15).

Again, after all is said and done, we end up in one of these two places, the New Jerusalem or the Lake of Fire. The question is: where do *we* choose to go. Jesus tells us the blessed ones are the ones "who wash their robes." The martyrs of chapter 7 show us where to wash our robes. "They have their robes washed and made white in the blood of lamb" (Rev. 7:14b).

This refers to the cleansing and washing away of sin available for those who take their sins to the cross of Jesus Christ. The only thing that made their robes white and clean was the blood of the Lamb. It was not a matter of good deeds outweighing bad deeds.

The Bible says that ". . . whoever keeps the whole law (God's standards) and yet stumbles at just one point, he has become guilty of all" (James 2:10). This sin will doom us to the second death that Revelation talks about. "For the wages of sin is death . . ." (Rom. 6:23a). However, the good news is that ". . . the free gift of God is eternal life *in Christ Jesus our Lord*" (Rom. 6:23b).

Here's the bottom line. God loves us. Yet God is completely holy and absolutely good. Because God is like this, our sin produces a gigantic unbridgeable gulf between this Holy God and ourselves wider than any Grand Canyon. Although some leap farther toward the other side of the canyon than others do, even the best of us will fall pitifully and hopelessly short. We'll all wind up splatting on the canyon floor. It's not only that we sometimes *feel* guilty for doing wrong; the fact is we *are* guilty of sinning against the Holy God of Creation. ". . . For there is no distinction, for all have sinned and fall short of the glory of God" (Rom. 3:22b–23).

What does God mean by sin? The following Bible verse gives just a partial list of sin examples. Paul wrote,

> . . . Do you not know that the unrighteous will not inherit the kingdom of God? Do not be deceived; neither fornicators (people who have sex unmarried), nor idolaters (people for whom God is not number one in their lives), nor adulterers, nor effeminate, nor homosexuals, nor thieves, nor the covetous, nor drunkards, nor revilers (people who hurt others with their speech), nor swindlers, will inherit the kingdom of God. Such were some of you; but you were washed . . . (1Cor. 6:9–11a)

Fortunately God demonstrated His love for us when Jesus took our sins upon himself on the cross. It was there he built the one bridge that can take us to the other side. He made a way to get us over the canyon of separation from God that our sin has made. "He made Him who knew no sin to be sin on our behalf, so that we might become the righteousness of God in Him" (2Cor. 5:21). Even better yet, not only did Jesus live a sinless life of love to become the spotless sacrificial lamb to die for us, but he backed up his words. Unlike any other founder of any other religion, he proved the truth of his message, his life and his death by conquering death with his own power. For he ". . . was declared the Son of God with power by the resurrection from the dead . . ." (Rom. 1:4).[276]

Those of us who come to rely upon him for forgiveness and cleansing from our sins have the only credible Savior of the world. Because of the reality of his resurrection from death, we can be assured of the same eternal life he has. "O death, where is your victory? O death where is your sting? The sting of sin is death, and the power of sin is the law; but thanks be to God, who gives us the victory, through our Lord Jesus Christ" (1Cor. 15:55–57).

If you want to be assured of eternal life and desire heaven with Jesus Christ, you must become his believer here on earth. You can do that now. If you are unsure you have ever really done so, become absolutely sure that you are a true believer in Jesus Christ. If you have made a decision to rely on Jesus to save you and you want to start living for him, it may be helpful to verbalize this in prayer. Prayer is just talking to God. You could speak to God something like this:

Dear Jesus: I know I am a sinner. I can't even always keep my own standards perfectly much less your standards. I can't wash my sins away by my own efforts. Please have mercy on me! I am relieved to know you did what I couldn't do by dying in my place on the cross. How wonderful to know you love me and don't want me to go to hell. You have defeated death for me by rising again! From now on I'm relying on your mercy to receive forgiveness and an open door to heaven and a new life here on earth. Please take over my life. Help me live the way you want me to live. Thank you for keeping your promise to save me. In Jesus name I pray. Amen.

Having your robe washed in the blood of the Lamb is probably the most important message in Revelation for us as individuals. Be sure to read your Bible and talk to God regularly. This will help you to learn to live as a follower of Jesus Christ. Also, be sure to be a part of a church that teaches the Bible as God's true word and encourages people to live according to its message. There is a lot of spiritual benefit you can gain from other followers of Christ. You can also learn to serve and help them as well. For those of us who are disciples of Jesus Christ, what are some other important things that Revelation tells us?

. . . .

Chapter 21

Overcoming by the Blood of the Lamb (Rev. 12:11)

C hrist himself warned us to not become complacent about his coming, as did several New Testament writers. The theme of God's visitation to earth is even prevalent in the Old Testament as well. It wouldn't be wise to ignore the reality of his coming and its necessary implications for our lives.

Maintaining an attitude of expectancy is not only wise; it has a purifying effect on the Church. Becoming complacent and sleepy about his coming has the opposite effect. First and foremost, preparing for the Lord's return means maintaining an attitude of vigilance. Luke records the Lord saying: "Be dressed in readiness, and keep your lamps alight. And be like men who are waiting for their master when he returns from the wedding feast, so that they may immediately open the door to him when he comes and knocks" (Luke 12:35).

Secondly, Revelation clearly tells us how the Church will triumph over the devil while looking forward to and hastening the Lord's return. If we want to be part of the victorious Church of Jesus Christ, then we would do well to look at the way Revelation prophesies that victory is won. The voice from heaven told John of three ways we would overcome. ". . . (1) They overcame him because of the blood of the Lamb and (2) because of the word of their testimony, and (3) they did not love their life even when faced with death" (Rev. 12:11).

Applying the Blood of the Lamb

The blood of the Lamb speaks of reliance upon the payment of Jesus Christ for our sins. The peace with God that has been won for us came through it. It is this peace with God, won through the blood of the Lamb that enables us to endure hardship in this life. We know that trials only serve to make us more like Jesus who suffered for us. And we know that we needn't fear God's wrath, either on this earth, during the coming judgment, or on that day when we stand before God to give an account of ourselves.

Paul put it this way,

Therefore, having been justified by faith, we have peace with God through our Lord Jesus Christ, through whom also we have obtained our introduction by faith into this grace in which we stand; and we exult in hope of the glory of God.

And not only this, but *we also exult in our tribulations*, knowing that tribulation brings about perseverance, and perseverance, proven character, and proven character, hope;

And hope does not disappoint, because the love of God has been poured out within our hearts through the Holy Spirit who was given to us.

For while we were still helpless, at the right time, Christ died for the ungodly. For one will hardly die for a righteous man; though perhaps for a good man someone would dare even to die.

But God demonstrates His own love for us, in that while we were yet sinners, Christ died for us.

Much more then, *having now been justified by His blood, we shall be saved from the wrath of God through Him.* (Rom. 5:1–9)

It is especially important for the suffering Church (whether suffering now or during the Great Tribulation), to enjoy her friendship with God and the peace of knowing that everything will ultimately be okay. The Apostle Paul, who probably suffered more than many of us ever will (Great Tribulation or not) stated, ". . . momentary, light affliction is producing for us an eternal weight of glory far beyond all comparison, while we look at things which are not seen; for the things which are seen are temporal, but the things which are not seen are eternal" (2Cor. 5:17–18).

We will have to maintain an eternal view of things to endure tribulation. The blood of the Lamb enables us to have peace with God in the midst of the storm.

The Blood of the Lamb Must Apply to Others

Applying the blood of the Lamb to ourselves is critical. But the application of his blood has an even greater reach than us. Paul said, "Be kind to one another, tender-hearted, forgiving each other, *just as* God in Christ also has forgiven you" (Eph. 4:32). In the same way Jesus forgave us, we too must forgive others, including our brethren. Without learning to forgive others, we will be unable to walk in unity with our brethren. Overcoming by the blood of the Lamb must involve applying it to our brothers and sisters in Christ.

In Matthew 18 we see Jesus telling us how to reconcile with a brother who has sinned against us. He follows this by relating to us a parable about a king who had a servant who owed him millions, not unlike our debt to God. The king was about to have him thrown into jail, but the servant pleaded for mercy, much as we did when we came to Christ. The king had compassion on him and forgave his debt in full, just as God had mercy on us and forgave us. Soon after, this servant ran across a fellow servant that owed him a few hundred bucks. Like far too many Christians, he demanded payment in full, and when he didn't get it he had the fellow servant thrown into prison. Unfortunately, this servant had learned nothing about giving mercy, in spite of the incredible debt that had been forgiven him.

The king was so distressed with this servant's actions that he "handed him over to the *torturers* until he should repay all that was owed him" (Matt. 18:34). Jesus went on to say, "My heavenly

Father will also do the same to you if each of you does not forgive his brother from your heart" (Matt. 18:35). Older Christians are not exempt from the bitterness that can overwhelm a soul unwilling to forgive. As Jesus said, he "handed him over to the torturers." Bitterness is torture to one's soul.

Nearly twenty years ago, I remember going for an entire year with an unresolved hurt towards a brother. Because I did not respond according to Matthew 18, my soul literally felt tortured by the hurt. I could not be free as long as I had not forgiven from my heart. Finally, confronted by a friend of mine who wanted to know why I was so glum, I went to this brother with a determination to deal with the issue and restore our relationship. As I forgave him from my heart, my soul was released, and I felt my relationship with God renewed.

I learned that every word of God is true. I determined to never again allow bitterness to take root in my soul. We must not fall into the trap of the enemy. We must allow the forgiveness of the blood of the lamb to extend to those who have hurt us deeply, whether in the Church or outside it. As Paul said, "Be kind to one another, tenderhearted, forgiving each other, just as God in Christ also has forgiven you" (Eph. 4:32).

Jesus put it this way, ". . . Love your enemies, do good to those who hate you, bless those who curse you, pray for those who mistreat you" (Luke 6:27–28). Has somebody mistreated you? Then try to reconcile when possible (Matt. 18:15–17). But whether it is possible or not, every time the memory of hurt comes back we must forgive, again and again. At the same time we should pray for the one who has mistreated us. If we consistently pray for the one who mistreated us, God is free to work in our hearts to free us, and he is free to work in our opponent's heart. Satan surely doesn't want us to pray, and after a time he will eventually give up. But we must be ready, if he ever brings a reminder. We must be quick to forgive and pray again. Let's be one of those "who overcame him because of the blood of the lamb."

Walking in Unity: Not optional

I remember years ago watching a Monty Python comedy skit. The skit involved a race between men who had no sense of direction.

They all poised at the starting line awaiting the gun. As the gun fired they all took off in many directions running zigzag and bumping into one another and stumbling around in chaos. No one knew who was in front. It didn't take long for the race officials to lose track of the runners. Contestants were all running very rapidly in no particular direction.

Sadly, the Church endeavoring to run the race and complete the Great Commission without unity sometimes looks a little like this. As somebody once said, "If you aim for nothing you'll hit it every time." Fortunately, our efforts to complete the Great Commission need not continue to be this broken and haphazard. There are several excellent networks of churches and missions organizations now working together to organize and help focus our efforts.[277] But it will take a mature Church that has learned to walk in forgiveness to maintain unity and focus. Why must we slander and put down our brethren over doctrinal differences that don't keep anyone out of heaven?

As we attempt to move forward in what God has called us to do, the devil will not be cheering. When dealing with an issue of sin, Paul exhorted the Corinthian church to not let Satan take advantage of them. He said, "We are not ignorant of his schemes" (2Cor. 2:11). Could it be that our rational Western approach to things has made us less sensitive to the spiritual, even demonic side of the attacks on our unity? The devil's strategy is to take our eyes off the Lord Jesus and his Great Commission by sowing seeds of unforgiveness, disunity, and enmity. Somehow he has convinced us that undying love, forgiveness, and unity are optional. To speed the accomplishment of the Great Commission, we must recognize this lie and overcome it. Fortunately, the overcoming Church will overcome the devil. They'll be busy applying the blood of the Lamb over the faults and shortcomings of the brethren.

In his great priestly prayer for the Church, Jesus prayed,

As You sent Me into the world, I also have sent them into the world. I . . . ask . . . for those also who believe in Me through their word; that they may all be one; even as You, Father, are in Me and I in You, that they also may be in Us, so that the world may believe that You sent Me. The glory which You have given Me I have given to them, that they may be one, just as We are one; I in them and You

in Me, that they may be perfected in unity, so that the world may
know that you sent Me, and loved them, even as You have loved
Me. (John 17:18–23)

The context of this part of his prayer is talking about evangelism.
He prays for what will be a key in completing his commission. He
asks for unity of believers. Unity among believers will help the world
believe Jesus came from the Father. That unity finds its purest expression as we learn to forgive and love one another, just as he did to us.
The Church is called to be unified in one purpose to glorify Christ,
seek first his kingdom, and disciple all nations.

God is doing a new thing, increasingly networking churches and
mission agencies from a variety of doctrinal positions and views for
the purpose of completing the Great Commission. The fact is, no one
movement of God or denomination or people with certain doctrinal
views will be able to finish the Great Commission alone. As one
Chinese leader emphasized,

> "We refuse to be drawn into the spirit of denominationalism in any
> way. We are going to preach the Gospel and see sinners come to the
> feet of Jesus and experience the new life that he won for them on
> the cross. We don't want any part in promoting any denomination.
> We only want to promote Jesus and ask the Holy Spirit to confirm
> whether Jesus is alive or not."[278]

Of course, this doesn't mean being wishy-washy. As this same
brother stated, "Although we do have some strong convictions about
how God's work should be done, let us reiterate that even if our methods are different from those of other Christians, we will still strive to
have fellowship with all believers who have been bought by the precious blood of Jesus Christ."[279] God will use the body of Christ in all
its great diversity. When the Great Tribulation comes upon the earth,
we will not be overly concerned with various doctrinal opinions of
our brethren in Christ. Relational divisions will melt under the heat
of tribulation. We may as well get a head start on the road to unity
since we're going to end up there anyway. Living in anticipation of
Christ's return can help us walk in unity and proper relationship with
our brethren here and now. All benefit when we do.

Chapter 22

Overcoming by the Word of Their Testimony (Rev. 12:11)

And they overcame the devil, "because of the word of their testimony" (Rev. 12:11). The victorious Church will be faithful to share its testimony of faith. This Church is not only proclaiming the wonderful things of God behind church walls, but also to those on the outside. This reflects an overcoming Church obeying the Great Commission willing to verbally maintain its gospel testimony in spite of opposition, threats, persecution and even death. The Revelation of Jesus Christ begins with a declaration of God's love for us demonstrated in his blood sacrifice (Rev. 1:5). His revelation continues with the Church being faithful to proclaim his gospel and his wonders to all nations (Rev. 5:8–10). This faithfulness in making proclamation to all nations is followed by the complete revelation of Jesus Christ at his return to planet earth with his beautiful bride (Rev. 19:6–8).

Therefore, an essential characteristic of the overcoming Church is faithfulness to make disciples of all nations. Why has it been so important for the Church to be perpetually ready for the Lord's coming if the Lord knew it would be over two thousand years until his return? Because it produces an earnest desire to further the Kingdom of God in our lives and in the world. This in turn plays a role in unfolding the actual revelation of Jesus Christ to the world.

The Great Commission is a summary of the Church's purpose and mission before the Lord's return. Every ministry and calling of every individual in the Church must be seen within the larger context of this Great Commission. Everything revolves around bringing glory to God by being and making disciples.

Christ's purpose should become the bull's eye of our lives. Seeking first the kingdom of God releases a tremendous sense of purpose that invades every area of our lives, just as God intended it to (John 10:10). The Christian who feels spiritually apathetic and without direction can refocus on the Kingdom of God and the person God has called them to be in light of his coming. It is so important to God for us to be disciples and make disciples of all nations, he will literally not return to earth until we have adequately obeyed him in this.

Jesus commanded, "Go therefore and make disciples of all nations baptizing them in the name of the Father and the Son and the Holy Spirit, teaching them to observe all that I commanded you; and lo, I am with you always, even to the end of the age" (Matt. 28:19–20). It is a mistake to think the Great Commission is only for professional missionaries and evangelists. By relegating this to "professionals," the larger body of Christ misses the joy of an essential part of their calling in God.

Most people are not called to move to another culture to minister the Gospel. Thus, out of guilt, apathy or confusion, many Christians largely ignore missions. But the Great Commission is not meant to engender guilt, but bring motivation and purpose. Serving God should be purposeful and joyful. Finding our place in working to reach his goal is part of our preparation as the Bride of Christ. By faithfully taking up our assignment from God, we are preparing ourselves for the marriage of the Lamb.

So what is our role in the Great Commission? It is beyond the scope of this book to fully tackle these issues. The book and course *Perspectives on the World Christian Movement* can help every Christian find out what their role is in obeying the Great Commission. A list of resources has also been compiled in the appendix. Still, we'll touch on a few points briefly.

Being Disciples to All Nations

The command of the Great Commission to make disciples assumes an important premise. Making disciples must mean being disciples. We cannot reproduce what we are not ourselves. Being a disciple involves abiding in Christ. This is foundational, as Jesus stated, "Abide in Me and I in you. As the branch cannot bear fruit of itself unless it abides in the vine, so neither can you unless you abide in Me . . . for apart from Me you can do nothing" (John 15:4,5b). Abiding in Christ is not just something mystical, as we are sometimes tempted to make it out to be. Jesus taught that abiding in him means allowing his word to find a home in our hearts and affect everything we are and do. He summarized obedience to his command as being expressed by loving one another in the same way that he loved us.

If we are divisive, faultfinding hypocrites, we will make divisive, faultfinding hypocrites as disciples. Good trees produce good fruit and bad trees bad fruit. Many of us assume that not being called to a foreign nation exempts us from reaching out to distant nations. Nothing could be more untrue!

Reclaiming the Apostolic Mindset of the Early Church

Jesus distinctly said we must "go . . . and make disciples of *all the nations* . . ." (Matt. 28:19a). Most Christians will not be called to become full-time, vocational cross-cultural missionaries learning another language and spending years in a foreign land. However, before automatically dismissing such a calling, we should be absolutely sure we aren't called to go. After all, there is a crying need for more full-time laborers. There are still entire people groups without the Gospel. It is safe to assume that there are many more people called to physically go live in another culture than are currently on the field. The fact is, less than half of one percent of all true Christians are serving as missionaries. That means more than 99.5% are not. A doubling of the number of full-time missionaries is not an unreasonable goal.

Unfortunately, many doctors, teachers, construction workers and so on, often assume their lack of Bible School training or ordination certificates automatically disqualifies them from working on foreign church-planting teams. Nothing could be further from the truth. In reality, the remaining unreached people groups are found in nations mostly closed to traditional full-time missionary work.

In order to enter such places, it is often necessary to have professional skills to offer. Only then will many governments grant visas and residence permits. Most of these nations are desperate for trained doctors, nurses, English teachers, engineers, computer programmers and people with advanced construction skills. If you are from the West, they assume you are a Christian anyway, and it is generally not an issue. Anyone with a bachelor's degree in any subject area can obtain a certificate in Teaching English as a Second Language by taking six week crash courses at a number of different institutions around the world. We have listed some in the appendix. Within a matter of a few weeks you can have skills that much of the world is desperate to get, simply by teaching people your native language.

Far more importantly than training, the Chinese Church has "seen thousands of times that it does not matter that an evangelist or missionary is poor and uneducated according to the standards of the world. All that matters is whether the hand of God is on that person."[280]

Indeed many young people with only high-school degrees have found entry into supposedly closed nations by choosing to obtain college degrees at universities in those countries. Some of these colleges even teach some of their courses in English. Many times they are also much cheaper than universities in America. Other countries will grant retirement visas to individuals in their 50's or older. Such individuals can live much more comfortably on low retirement incomes in many of these countries where the cost of living and medications are often dramatically lower.

Although special skills are not necessary to enter some nations, they can prove valuable to stay long term in a country and gain credibility. While practically serving real needs in the local population, God gives opportunities for friendship and lifestyle evangelism. I have always found it far easier to gain opportunities to verbally share my faith with Muslims from the East than with the typical Westerner.

The Body of Christ takes Ownership of the Great Commission

We can also learn much from the Pauline example for those who stay behind. The whole Church embraced the Great Commission in his day. We see the entire body of Christ working hard with Paul to see the Great Commission become the great completion. Paul tells the Romans he had "for many years a longing to come to you whenever I go to Spain." Why? Certainly, they were brethren and he loved them and could help them. But also he says, "I hope to see you in passing, and to be helped on my way there by you" (Rom. 15: 23–24). Paul knew it was not enough for those who are called to go to leave. He needed help from the rest of the Church. We see that the wider Church practically helped him in a number of ways.

For one thing they were willing to send out additional laborers with him. In Acts, we see a church releasing Timothy, one of their best, to labor with Paul long term (Acts 16:1–3). The Jerusalem church sent out the short-term prophetic team of Judas and Silas to assist Paul and Barnabas, the long termers.

Interestingly enough, Silas the short termer felt called to stay longer after going on what was originally a short-term trip (Acts 15:22–34). He thus joined up with Paul and Barnabas in long-term ministry. God has surprised many long-term missionaries with their long-term calling while going on a short-term trip. This willingness to release people short and long term cannot be over-emphasized. It can be difficult for a local pastor to release some of his best people when he can so easily see the ongoing needs around him. It requires trust in God and a realization that it is God's kingdom he must seek to build first. God's kingdom is far bigger than a local community. As always, it takes real sacrifice to make real advancement.

The Chinese Church understands this principle. As one brother explains,

> The house churches of China will remain in revival as long as they remain obedient to the vision to preach the Gospel back to Jerusalem. If we lose our first love and start to focus on our own needs, our spiritual life will shrivel up and die. As long as we strive to obey God's call to take the Gospel to the Muslim, Buddhist, and

Hindu nations, he will bless our churches and revival in China will continue . . .

We encourage Christians and churches around the world not to focus on their own needs and desires! If you do you will surely shrivel up and die. God's principle is that when you seek to bring blessing to others, your own lives will be blessed. When you make missionary outreach to nations that have never heard about Jesus the priority of your church, you will not fail to be blessed . . .

Christians or churches that seek blessings for their own pleasure and enjoyment are in danger of idolatry . . .

When you are truly obeying the Lord's call you please God, and when you are in step with the work of the Holy Spirit you begin to feel the heartbeat of our loving Savior. Your work stops being a chore and starts becoming a natural overflow of the love of God that has been deposited in your heart.[281]

Short-term help

We can also not overstate the tremendous help believers from various professions can be to long-term workers. Sometimes they can assist long-term church planting efforts through emergency relief efforts. The aftermath of wars, earthquakes and famines often demand a temporary influx of huge numbers of short-term volunteers. Distributing much needed aid and assistance in a professional caring way, in the name of Christ, can open hearts and weaken prejudice. This can aid long-term workers in getting a fairer hearing from locals. It can generate fresh opportunities to explain the faith. Sometimes short termers can also engage in more risky outreach. If a long termer did it, they might be permanently kicked out of a country.

The Body Prays

Paul also coveted prayers and felt the prayers of Christians made significant differences in his ministry. He tells the Philippians he believes God will release him from prison in answer to their prayers (Phil. 1:19), not his! And we know from history, he was actually released, not long after that letter was crafted. The Thessalonians, Colossians and Ephesians were all asked to pray in specific ways for him. And most of these were churches he had planted as a missionary. Thus, right from their beginning these churches felt ownership of the Great Commission by assisting Paul through their prayers. Prayer is effective regardless of position, age, finances or experience. Any Christian can pray.

The Scriptures tell us we should pray frequently and with many requests. How should we pray for missionaries and the people amongst whom they work? Fortunately, the Holy Spirit has seen fit to give us many examples in the Bible as to how we can pray to assist the work. A list of Pauline prayer requests and one directly from the Lord Jesus include:

1) Praying for more Laborers (Matt. 9:36–38)
2) Praying for the Word of the Lord to Spread Rapidly and be Glorified (2Thess. 3:1a)
3) Praying for boldness for the missionaries and Christians in pioneering regions (Eph. 6:19)
4) Praying for the governing authorities (1Tim. 2:1–4)
5) Praying for the missionaries personal needs (1Thess. 5:25).

Certainly the Holy Spirit may give us other specific things to pray for, but here we have a good starting point when we pray for unblessed nations and those working to reach them.

The Body Gives

The Church willingly supplied Paul with financial support. It is often erroneously thought that Paul only worked as a tent maker. However, the Bible clearly shows us that at times he received financial support from the body of Christ (Phil. 4:16–18). Thus, in a very concrete way, the jobs and professions God has blessed us with can be instruments to further the Great Commission. In this way we can demonstrate Christ's love by blessing others. Again, we can learn from a rebuke from our Chinese brethren. One leader observed, "We have noticed that many Christians in the West have an abundance of material possessions, yet they live in a backslidden state. They have silver and gold, but they don't rise up and walk in Jesus' name."[282]

Pioneering missions work needs finances. Currently only one-tenth of one percent of all ministry funds are devoted to reaching the unreached. This must change. Where are the armies of Christian businessmen willing to plow large shares of profits into financing the Great Commission instead of ever-larger financial bonuses?

Touching the Nations Coming to Us

It's exciting to know that thousands and thousands of foreign university students from some of the least-reached people groups in the world still come to our universities every year. They are unaccustomed to an unwelcome culture of unfriendly Americans and lonely individualism. Most would be thrilled to be befriended by Americans and spend some time visiting with them. American college degrees are so highly valued in their nations that most will become the future leaders of their countries.

What a tremendous opportunity to touch an unreached people by loving a foreign college student! Muslim students especially receive the cold shoulder. What a unique opportunity to show them the love of Christ! They are often very inquisitive and curious about what we believe. Love them sincerely with friendship. Give them the freedom to criticize our country. Serve their needs and give them the good news of Jesus.

Strategically Loving the Nations in Missions Endeavors

Jesus said that the greatest commandment was to ". . . love the Lord your God with all your heart, and with all your soul, and *with all your mind*, and with *all your strength*" (Mark 12:30). We have already talked about our heart and soul being given over to God. We surrender to the Spirit of God and let the Word of God invade and affect every part of our emotions, attitudes and motivations. Now let's consider the latter two aspects of the greatest commandment: using our minds and strength to love him.

Since we are called to disciple all nations, and not just some, if we love God we will obey him in doing this. Since part of loving

God involves loving him with all our mind and strength, then it's reasonable to ask what nations, outside of our own, we are called to help reach. A single individual, a single church, and any finite group of churches cannot be everywhere at once. Learning to strategically funnel our mental and physical efforts is a way we can love God with our mind and our strength thereby increasing our impact and effectiveness.

Given the situation the Church faces regarding the unreached, what ought we to do? What would Paul have done? Paul writes to the Romans,

> I aspired to preach the gospel, *not where Christ was already named*, so that I would not build on another man's foundation; but as it is written, *they who had no news of him shall see*, and they who have not heard shall understand. For this reason I have often been prevented from coming to you but now, with no further place for me in these regions, and since I have had for many years a longing to come to you whenever I go to Spain for I hope to see you in passing, and to be helped on my way there by you . . . (Rom. 15:20–24a)

A general principle we learn from Paul is that apostles or missionaries sent out from the body of Christ to other regions of the world should especially target the unreached. He states in verse 20 that he didn't want to preach Christ where he was already named. Why? Was this evidence of an independent Spirit? Certainly not! In verse 21 he quotes Isaiah 52:15 "They who had no news of him shall see, and they who have not heard shall understand." He realizes God's heart is that those who haven't heard the good news would get to hear it. Because he has a heart after God, he longs to see God's desire satisfied.

Paul says, in effect, "Lord if you want the nations, then I want the nations too." Paul was so serious in this, he says, "I do not consider my life of any account as dear to myself, so that I may finish my course in the ministry which I received from the Lord Jesus, to testify solidly of the gospel of the grace of God." (Acts 20: 24). In effect, he is saying, "I have no agenda left anymore for my life except the agenda that Jesus gave to me."

What is needed today in foreign missions efforts, together with passion and godly character, is the Pauline strategy (itself birthed out of his passion for God) of going where the Gospel hasn't gone before. We must ask ourselves, "How can we better utilize the precious few laborers who feel the call to cross-cultural ministry?" Some great resources for planning can be found in the *Perspectives* reader, the book *Operation World*, and the CD *Countries and Peoples of the World*. There are also a number of networking ministries listed in the appendix that will assist churches in formulating a missions program to reach the least reached.

The blessed peoples of the world who have experienced the promise given to Abraham (Gen. 12:3) must be ready to give the blessing to those who have yet to be blessed. A *blessed people* are a people where the church is sufficiently large enough and healthy enough to effectively preach the Gospel and disciple its own people without outside assistance.[283] This does not mean a great deal of work doesn't remain to be done within a blessed people group. Jesus said to preach the Gospel to all (Mark 16:15) within our people group and outside it. It simply means blessed peoples have significant numbers of vibrant Christians in witnessing communities of believers. They are actively engaged in the task of making disciples. There will always be more work to do, but a *blessed people* already has a community of laborers with their hands to the plow. They are in sufficient numbers and reproductive health so that we can say, with some assurance, the next generation will continue to see an ongoing witness. This will happen with or without outside help. Some missiologists would call them a reached people. An example of such a people group would be suburban Americans, or Mohawk Indians, or Puerto Ricans.

With unblessed peoples, one cannot be assured the Christian community will be growing and healthy by the next generation without outside help. In fact, in some cases it doesn't even yet exist. These types of people groups are known as unreached peoples. This would include people groups like the Pashtuns of Afghanistan, the Laz people of Turkey or the Marsh Arabs of southern Iraq.[284]

Although it is impossible to pinpoint, a discipled population of at least 1–2% evangelicals will probably be able to maintain a significant Christian presence into the next generation. In most cases, groups with that percentage or higher will experience growth on their own.

What does this mean for us in mission strategy? After people groups pass a threshold, the fastest growing churches within those peoples tend to be those with indigenous leadership and a Christian subculture nearest to the native culture. Given these facts and our limitations as foreigners, it would be good stewardship to direct most funds and laborers away from blessed peoples, since Christian communities there are sufficient to carry on the task of making disciples. Additionally, they could probably do it far better than most foreigners could. Obviously it would be foolish to take away funds from fruitful missionaries currently working amongst such groups, just because they are reached peoples. However, when sending new missionaries, shouldn't we take a second look on just where someone is going to make sure the need really justifies the expense and effort? Most new laborers should be strategically placed.

Unlike foreigners, people in healthy native churches already know the language and culture of their people. They don't need to get visas or work permits. They don't need furloughs. And they can reach their own culture at a fraction of the cost required by the foreigner. Why send them more foreigners? It makes far more sense to allow locals to carry on this work. We can reserve the far more difficult and costly task of cross-cultural church planting to places where it is absolutely necessary. In reality, the Church in many missions-receiving lands in Latin America, parts of Africa and Asia (not just China) are themselves sending out increasing numbers of missionaries to unreached peoples.

The new frontiers remaining for the Church are those parts of the world most filled with unreached peoples. Currently only about 2.4% of the full-time missionary force are being used to reach this section of the world that makes up about thirty-percent of the world's population. Less than .1% of all mission funds are being allocated to outreach there. The time has come for a change.

Paul's Roman letter says he was long delayed in coming to Rome, but now he could finally come. Why? Paul essentially said there weren't any unblessed peoples left in that area. The area had been well exposed to the Gospel and the Church was growing rapidly

(Rom. 15:20–23). Once those regions had been well reached with the Gospel and growing churches established, Paul knew it was time to move on. He knew the established Church could carry on the Great Commission work of discipleship and witness to their communities. He knew God's heart was longing for those who had yet to hear, living beyond reach of any existing church.

The amazing fact of the matter is that God has chosen to largely limit himself to his Church in reaching the world. The prophetic fulfillment of the Scriptures is tied to the Church obeying the Great Commission and finishing the task of proclaiming the Gospel to all the nations (Matt. 24:14). Of course God is sovereign. Certainly the Father knows the day and the hour the job will finally be done. The specific time is in exact accordance with his will. Yet, that doesn't stop the Holy Spirit from exhorting us to be "looking forward to and speeding his coming" (2Pet. 3:12).

His sovereignty and our obedience in speeding his coming work hand in hand. When we preach the Gospel and assist in completing the Great Commission, we are in a real way literally speeding his coming! Is that exciting or what? We can actually be involved in the Second Coming instead of sitting around staring at Israel hoping for something to happen. Are we yearning to see the Lord return? Is anyone suffering from lack of vision in his or her Christian life? Let's give ourselves to living a holy life and making disciples among those who haven't heard from within our people group and outside it.

Chapter 23

Overcoming by not Loving our Lives Even unto Death (Rev. 12:11)

S tone him! yelled the crowds, "Stone him!" A calm young man was surrounded by a group of wild-eyed mad men. The would-be murderers were religious radicals. They were raving mad fundamentalists willing to die for their faith. They were dressed in flowing robes and loved to do their prayers and religious observances in public. They held a sham trial for the innocent Christian whose only fault was preaching the Gospel.

Forcefully, they shouted down the defendant before he had a chance to finish his defense. They dragged him out into the streets and pummeled him with stones until he died. However, they were not the only ones willing to die for their faith, so too was the young devout Christian man. And die he did, with dignity and a prayer of forgiveness for his enemies. Where did this story happen? Afghanistan? Saudi Arabia? How about Jerusalem in the first half of the first century! The man, of course, is Stephen, known as the first martyr of the Christian faith.

Stephen is among those who overcame Satan, because "they did not love their life even when faced with death" (Rev. 12:11b). Is God calling us to have this same attitude nowadays? Or has freedom of religion delivered us from the need of making sacrifice?

As we look at the list of peoples yet to be blessed with the knowledge of the Gospel, one can't help but quickly realize that in many cases the bulk of these people are found in "hard to reach" areas. Areas that in some cases carry risk to foreigners. Some places are riskier than others are. Many times risk is more imagined than real. Still, why can't God just supernaturally deliver the message to people in these places and *poof*, all done? Of course, he *could* do this, but the fact is, he largely hasn't and for the most part he won't. In the mystery of God, Jesus has delegated the completion of this task to the Church.

When we read chapter 10 of Acts, we discover God sent an angel to the gentile Cornelius in order to bring Peter to him so he could hear the Gospel. Why didn't God just use the angel to preach the Gospel? Why go through the elaborate trouble of getting Peter? After all, they would have to travel several days on dusty roads. Then Peter would have to return with them on the same dusty roads. Not only that, it would mean Peter would have to go to people he didn't understand or like very much.

What a hassle! Why the trouble? God had his reasons, and one of them is that God has chosen men and women, his men and women, to do the job. Paul tells the Romans, "How then shall they call upon Him in whom they have not believed? And how shall they believe in Him whom they have not heard? And how shall they hear without a preacher?" (Romans 10:14) Clearly God is interested in using his people.

Taking Risks

But what about taking the risks? Does God really expect us to take risks to make disciples? In a word, yes. God not only expects us to take risks to make disciples, he demands that we take the ultimate risk just to *be* a disciple.

Right after telling the disciples he would be rejected by the chief priests, scribes and elders and then killed, Jesus gave his disciples an important message.

> If anyone wishes to come after Me, he must deny himself, and take up his cross daily and follow Me. For whoever wishes to save his life will lose it, but whoever loses his life for My sake, he is the one

who will save it. For what is a man profited if he gains the whole world and loses or forfeits himself? (Luke 9:23–25)

Five more times, similar statements are recorded in the Gospels. We have grown so accustomed to allegorizing this message in the West that we forget that throughout most of the Church Age, in most of the world, that message has needed to be taken literally not just spiritually. The risk of dying for one's faith has been at least a slight possibility for many.

The problem with our human nature is that we would like to have it both ways. We would like to gain the whole world and be a follower of Jesus at the same time. Ironically, we will inherit the whole earth, but only if we first are willing to give up our lives. As a Zimbabwean missionary to Sudan once said, "The problem with the church in America is that it preaches a deathless gospel."[285]

Why was Stephen willing to die so calmly for the cause of the Gospel? Because he had already lost his life much earlier when he became a disciple. Jesus told his disciples quite plainly,

If the world hates you, you know that it has hated Me before it hated you.

If you were of the world, the world would love its own; but because you are not of the world, but I chose you out of the world, because of this the world hates you.

Remember the word that I said to you, 'A slave is not greater than his master.' If they persecuted Me, they will also persecute you; if they kept My word, they will keep yours also . . . . An hour is coming for everyone who kills you to think that he is offering service to God. (John 15:18–20, 16:2b)

Jesus again told his disciples quite plainly, ". . . they will deliver you to tribulation, and will kill you, and you will be hated by all nations because of My name" (Matt. 24:9).

Being his disciple entails risks, and in some cases may mean death. The apostle Paul stated, ". . . all who desire to live godly in Christ Jesus will be persecuted" (2Tim. 3:12).

Dealing with Threats and Persecution

How did Jesus tell us to behave in the face of the threat of death for the Gospel? Are we to fear? Are we to step back from preaching the Gospel due to a perceived threat?

Fortunately, Jesus directly addressed this very issue. He stated,

> . . . Do not fear them, for there is nothing concealed that will not be revealed, or hidden that will not be known.
>
> What I tell you in the darkness, speak in the light; and what you hear whispered in your ear, proclaim from the housetops.
>
> Do not fear those who kill the body, but are unable to kill the soul; but rather fear Him who is able to destroy both soul and body in hell.
>
> Are not two sparrows sold for a cent? And yet not one of them will fall to the ground apart from your Father. But the very hairs of your head are numbered.
>
> So do not fear; you are more valuable than many sparrows.
>
> Therefore, everyone who confesses Me before men, I will also confess him before My Father who is in heaven. But whoever denies Me before men. I will also deny him before My Father who is in heaven. (Matt. 10:28–33)

Thus, we learn from Jesus not to be afraid of those who can only kill our bodies. Furthermore, we are to be bold in confessing our faith. Jesus also told us, "Brother will betray brother to death, and a father his child; and children will rise up against parents and cause them to be put to death."

"You will be hated by all because of My name, but it is the one who has endured to the end who will be saved. But whenever they persecute you in one city, flee to the next . . ." (Matt. 10:21–23a). We learn also that when we are persecuted in one city we should flee to the next. Although persecution can take many forms, the form that Jesus refers to here is specifically martyrdom. Notice it is *after* martyrdom happens that the remaining believers are instructed to leave, *not before.*

What about Paul's example?

What can we learn from Paul in this? We learn in Acts that Paul specifically changed his plans in response to specific plans to kill him (Acts 9:24–25, 14:5–6, 23:12–24) but never in response to a general threat. General threats were considered normal. On the contrary, he went to Jerusalem *in spite of* a general threat declaring his willingness to die for Christ if that should happen (Acts 21:11–13). He also immediately returned briefly to Lystra *after* an unsuccessful attempt at killing him there (Acts 14:19–20). Although in that case, he did not stay.

Furthermore, a little while after the attempt on his life in Iconium and Lystra had passed, Paul returned to both of these cities to strengthen the church before returning to Antioch (Acts 14:21–22). His message to the newly formed churches there was "through many tribulations we must enter the kingdom of God" (Acts 14:22b). How different from the messages we usually share with new believers today!

What about the Example of Other Apostles?

In Acts 4 we see Peter and John arrested after healing the lame beggar. They are threatened and commanded to stop preaching the Gospel. They boldly declare, "We cannot stop speaking about what we have seen and heard" (Acts 4:20). Dumbfounded, the Jewish leaders have them released. In response to these vague threats, they do not leave Jerusalem! Instead the believers gather together and pray for greater boldness and more miracles. The Lord hears their prayers, the Gospel continues to advance and people continue to be healed.

In Acts 5, filled with jealousy at this growing following, the Sadducees have all the apostles arrested. An angel miraculously releases them all. The next day they are found not running away, but preaching in the temple. Arrested again, they declare to the Jewish Council that "We must obey God rather than men" (Acts 5:29b). They declare how God raised the man, Jesus, whom they killed from the dead and exalted him as Israel's Savior. The Jewish leaders are outraged and now intend to kill them. However, an influential member of the council, Gamaliel, recommends they be spared, having the wisdom to realize the council itself may be wrong in its assessment. Even so, they are beaten and ordered not to speak in Jesus' name.

Did they flee? No! Instead they rejoice at being found worthy to suffer for Christ. What an incredibly different mindset we have in the Western church about suffering! Once again, with the passing of the immediate threat on their lives they stay in Jerusalem and continue to preach the Gospel. They keep going from house to house and there is no record of any believers leaving.

What about the New Testament Church?

It is only after the actual death of Stephen and massive arrests of believers that we begin to see believers flee Jerusalem. When they left, did they decide to keep quiet about their faith? Let's face it, there were Jews throughout the empire. There was always the possibility relatives, friends or acquaintances of the Jewish Council might be found in one of the Jewish synagogues in another city. Saul himself was looking to go to other cities to round up these Christians. Did this silence them? On the contrary, ". . . those who had been scattered went about preaching the word" (Acts 8:4).

What can we learn from the New Testament Church in regards to risks for the sake of the Gospel? First, we can see they were quite willing to face general threats with boldness. They refused to allow a general threat to keep them silent about their faith, even though there was a possible threat of dying for the faith. Secondly, they only fled to other cities *after* somebody actually got killed or specific attempts were being made to kill them.

Had they kept silent in the face of vague, general threats, that held the possibility of death, the Church would have never taken off and probably would have died out. Why are there so few missionaries and believers in the Islamic world? Could it be, in part, because we are allowing vague and general threats of possible death to hold us back from proclaiming the Gospel to them? As one Chinese leader noted,

Many Western missionary organizations pull their workers out of a place as soon as there is any sign of trouble. Advance will be very slow with such a mentality! If self-preservation is that important, then there is no point in going in the first place. God looks for children who are willing to die for him if necessary.[286]

Living Free from the Fear of Death

Do we love our lives so much that we are unwilling to lose them? Where are the overcomers unafraid of "those who kill the body, but are unable to kill the soul" (Matt. 10:28a)? The only way the Church will overcome the devil and overrun his last strongholds is when we rise up, laugh death in the face and do not allow fear to control us.

And they overcame him (the devil) because of the blood of the lamb and because of the word of their testimony, and they did not love their life even when faced with death" (Rev. 12:11).

After all, didn't Jesus come to set us free from the fear of death?

". . . Since the children share in flesh and blood, He Himself like-wise also partook of the same, that through death He might render powerless him who had the power of death, that is, the devil, and might free those who through fear of death were subject to slavery all their lives. (Heb. 2:14–15)

As one wise Chinese leader stated,

One of the most powerful ways we can overcome the spiritual giants of Islam, Buddhism and Hinduism is by witnessing with our own blood and laying down our own lives. For each Christian that the devil tries to kill, the light of the Gospel will shine a little brighter and his hold on the people will loosen little by little.[287]

Fear of death leads to slavery. It can push us around and control us. We could end up disobeying the very things God commands us to do if we give in to fear. Such commands include taking the Gospel to Muslim people or being willing to maintain our Christian testimony during tribulation. Fear can actually be a form of worship. When we

allow fear of something other than God to rule our lives we are setting up an idol out of our lives and the ones whom we fear.

Jesus addresses this directly when he stated, "Do not fear those
who kill the body . . . rather fear Him who is able to destroy body
and soul in hell" (Matt. 10:28). Ironically, Jesus says the one who
loves his life will lose his life, whereas the one who willingly gives
it up will actually find it.

What this means for those called to cross-cultural ministry is crystal clear. But what does this mean for those staying behind? Recently,
as the clouds of possible war with Iraq were hanging over us, some
close friends of mine were preparing to go on a short-term outreach
to a Muslim country neighboring Iraq. Their trip would involve relatively open proclamation of the Gospel in public areas through the
vehicle of Western music. Interested individuals would be followed
up by long-term church planters. In the months leading up to their
trip, they and their pastors were literally besieged by well-meaning
individuals concerned for their safety and urging them not to go.

None of them felt personally worried. On the contrary, they all
felt a tremendous peace in their hearts about going. The long-term
workers actually living in the country were very enthusiastic about
their upcoming arrival and also reported they expected them to be
quite safe. This didn't stop people from worrying.

Fortunately, they chose to ignore those who feared for their death
and went on the trip. The trip was very fruitful and a number of individuals came to faith in Christ. Thousands of people got to hear the
Gospel and hundreds of fresh contacts were generated for long-term
church planters to follow up. Ironically, the only threat to their lives
came when they got in a car accident on a slippery road. The group
found the people overwhelmingly friendly and hospitable and very
interested in hearing about their faith.

Such stories have been repeated so many times, I lose count. Yet
some pastors and even some mission agencies continue to steer people
away from serving in Muslim nations because of perceived general
threats. Although there are danger spots, often threats are nothing
more than smoke screens the enemy has constructed to scare people
off. By the time the Beast rises to a prominent position of authority,

the threat against believers will rapidly spread throughout the world, and it won't matter very much where one is living.

In the meantime, we have a season of tremendous opportunity to get the Gospel out in the Muslim world. It requires prayer, sensitivity and creativity, but opportunities are real and all over the Muslim world. According to a major ministry in this part of the world, opportunities and openness among Muslims have never been greater.[288] We must take advantage of these opportunities while we have them. As Jesus said, "We must work the works of Him who sent Me, as long as it is day; night is coming when no man can work" (John 9:4).

In the Muslim country I worked in, there have been about four-thousand full-time long-term missionaries (who have served two years or more) spread out over the past forty years. During that entire time, a grand total of one missionary was killed. To this day, it is uncertain as to what the motivation behind the killing was. Specifically, it is unknown whether or not it was related to his faith. Furthermore, there have only been about a half-dozen physical attacks upon foreign missionaries during that entire forty-year period. Let's just assume for a minute that this missionary was killed for his faith. Then this is a rate of about twenty-five missionaries for every 100,000 spread out over a forty-year period.

Compare this with the fact that the annual traffic death rate in the United States in 1999 was 15.3 per 100,000.[289] That was over a one-year period! Thus, over a forty-year period your chances of dying from a car accident in the United States are more than 2,400% higher than is your chance of dying because of being a missionary in this Muslim country even if you had lived there for forty years! And yet we quite willingly take the risk of dying in a crash to drive to football games, go shopping, go on vacations, and go to work..

We are willing to pack up our families and take the risk of dying in a car accident to go to a basketball game. Yet are we unwilling to take the more remote risk of dying as a result of being a missionary to Muslim peoples! What's wrong with this picture? This is a question that those who don't go have to ask themselves also. Because it is those who stay who often prevent those called to go from going where they are needed. How many Christian parents have put pressure on their children to avoid such "risky" places in missions outreach?

How many pastors and missions leaders have counseled "wisdom" in response to vague threats?

Does this mean no missionary will ever die from a terrorist or be arrested? Of course, not. Real people also win the lottery. There will always be a threat and occasionally some deaths. But one thing 9/11 should have taught us is that attacks can happen anywhere.

We must ask ourselves, do we really believe in the Resurrection? Do we really believe we need to be willing to lose our lives to find them? Are we really obeying Jesus and not fearing those who can only kill the body? Do we really fear God whom the Scriptures say numbered our days before one of them ever started? (Ps. 139:16)

Might there be times when missionaries may have to leave or avoid a particular area because of specific death threats or the martyrdom of a colleague in the same city? Of course, there will be such times. But this mentality that says we must avoid even the *possibility* of trouble, does not match the teaching of the Bible or the example of the early Church. Indeed, it has not matched the example of the triumphant Church throughout the ages. We are kidding ourselves if we think this situation will change. Such obstacles will continue until Jesus returns.

The life of Paul, the testimony of the Scriptures, and the history of the Church testify to the fact that where the Church is being pioneered, demonic, and sometimes violent opposition will not be absent. We must courageously accept this fact and together with overcomers from throughout the ages arise and overcome Satan. We will overcome him because of the blood of the Lamb and the word of our testimony and because we refuse to love our lives even unto death.

If the Church is unwilling to risk its own in response to remote, vague threats, how do we think we will ever stand when we are face to face with the pervasive threat of the Beast? We must choose to only fear him who can kill soul and body in Hell. In the words of the old hymn, "Rise up O men of God, the Church for you doth wait! Give heart and soul and mind and strength to serve the King of Kings."

Chapter 24

Storing up Treasures in Heaven (Rev. 22:12)

A s we saw earlier, Paul recognized the need for the Church to give in order for the Gospel to spread. This giving can take the form of finances, but also time and service and hospitality. The greatest enemy of giving is self-absorption or self-centeredness. The opposite of self-absorption is a God-centered life. Living God-centered is important preparation for the Great Tribulation and the return of Christ. Especially in America, the enemy of our souls is trying hard to get us to turn inward into a little protective cocoon, concerned only with our personal well-being and the well-being of our immediate family.

Avoiding Getting Weighed Down with Life

In the West, we can ignore the outside world and wall ourselves off into our own little comfort zones, our own little Christian islands, trying to fend off and ignore the storm around us. Jesus warned us, "Be on guard, so that your hearts will not be weighed down with dissipation and drunkenness and the worries of life, and that day will not come on you suddenly like a trap; for it will come upon all those who dwell on the face of all the earth" (Luke 21:34–35).

This is a peculiar statement, for the dissipation and drunkenness are said to be *of the heart*, not the literal kind. Dissipation just means a nauseated feeling in the pit of the stomach caused from drinking. The warning is against our hearts being weighed down with this. It is a picture of a heart that is afflicted with a stupor. It envelops us with worry and care over the things of this life. It causes a spiritual paralysis and makes us unprepared for what is coming on the earth.

Our brethren in some parts of the world don't have the luxury of not facing persecution. Yet for us in the West, there is a danger that in our attempts to keep out the nastier elements of the outside world, we can become engrossed in the more comfortable things of the world. Of course, we will filter out the most obvious evils and avoid participating in obvious sin. We go to Church on Sundays and go about our time working our jobs and paying our bills, all necessary tasks.

The temptation of the world around us goes beyond this. It tempts us to become engrossed in saving money for new toys to keep ourselves entertained. There is an ever-present temptation to become occupied and numbed by the rat race of life. We are tempted to avoid involvement in the lives of others. There are always new products to capture our imagination, our pocketbooks and our time. New computers, new software, new web sites, new DVD players, new cars, better and bigger homes, bigger and better vacations, new televisions, new videos, the latest music CD's, increasing numbers of TV stations, and the like. They all vie for our affections and finances. In the pursuit of happiness through possessions, the world wants us to become burdened down in mountains of debts and expenses. Debt of course only increases our worldly worries and pressures, even as we try to escape them through yet more pleasure and comfort. What a vicious cycle!

The problem lies not with any single possession. Not one is sinful by itself. Anyone who judges someone using any combination of these products has fallen into legalism. The real temptation is for these things to engulf our affections, our thinking, ever-increasing amounts of time, and increasingly our very souls. As Paul stated,

> But this I say brethren, the time has been shortened, so that from now on those who have wives should be as though they had none;

and those who weep, as though they did not weep; and those who rejoice as though they did not rejoice; and *those who buy, as though they did not possess; and those who use the world, as though they did not make full use of it, for the form of this world is passing away.* (1Cor. 7:29–31)

Radical, but important advice for us today. The form of this world is passing away. The real danger goes beyond things. The danger involves becoming so engrossed in stuff that we fail to see its temporary nature and become the servant of stuff. Jesus warned us we cannot serve both God and mammon. Jesus said we will "either hate the one and love the other, or he (we) will be devoted to the one and despise the other."(Matt. 6:24a). We must take care to avoid devoting our lives to earning money and in the process end up despising (i.e. lightly esteeming) God. If the world chokes us, the kingdom of God will be given little weight and importance in our lives.

Most of us would probably say his kingdom is important to us. But do our lives give out a different testimony through our time investments, relationships (or lack of) and our financial investments? Living here in the affluent West, I am regularly challenged to examine my life for evidence of apathy and love for the things of the world.

I remember hearing testimony of a friend of mine who had recently returned from China on a short-term trip where she met with some Chinese Christians. She said she felt bad for them because of the continual danger and persecution they faced because of their faith. One Chinese sister said that was not a problem, for she felt privileged to suffer for Christ. On the contrary, she regularly prayed for the temptations faced by the American church. She said she felt bad for the American church because it must be so hard to live devoted lives for Christ given the temptation of great wealth and freedom. How perceptive!

Not Making Full Use of the Things of the World

Coming back to Paul's statement, we are clearly warned to avoid making full use of the things in the world. In other words, we shouldn't live as if things of the world are all there really is to life. We might have financial blessing in our lives and be able to spend large sums of money on things, but does that mean we should? Should we not keep a view to eternity and be making investments (financial and otherwise) in the everlasting kingdom of God to which we claim to be a part?

Paul states to Timothy at the close of his life, "Suffer hardship with me as a good soldier of Christ Jesus. No soldier in active service entangles himself in the affairs of everyday life, so that he may please the one who enlisted him as a soldier"(2Tim. 2:3–4). Paul again warns Timothy of becoming overly engrossed in temporal matters and temporal pursuits. Seeking first God's kingdom will at times involve some denial, some voluntary hardship on our part. Ultimately it could require the voluntary surrender of our life on account of our faith. Willingness to embrace voluntary sacrifices is what Jesus talked about when he said that unless we take up our cross daily and follow him we cannot be his disciple. Crosses don't feel nice and by definition they signify the death of someone.

Discipleship will mean voluntary hardships. Perhaps it may involve living in a house less perfect than what we desire, or driving a car of lesser quality or stature than we can afford so that we can have extra finances for eternal matters that advance the kingdom of God. Perhaps it may involve giving up or scaling back on a hobby that takes away too much time from more fruitful kingdom service.

Coming back again to the Corinthian scripture, Paul even warns against turning our own spouses into an idol or even allowing our own emotions or emotional condition to rule over us. ". . . The time has been shortened, so that from now on those who have wives should live as though they had none; and those who weep as though they did not; and those who rejoice as though they did not rejoice . . ." (1 Cor. 7:29b–30a). There is an urgent call to sober thinking here.

". . . Those who have wives should be as though they had none . . ." What's this? Is Paul suddenly contradicting his teaching in Ephesians 5 that husbands need to love their wives as their own bodies and as Christ loves the Church? Absolutely not! Most of us need to make greater strides toward living this laudable goal. What is he saying then? Simply that loving our wives, and our children for that matter, is not the end all, be all to life. Our families, as important as they are in the sight of God, are not to become our god.

Remember that the form of this world is passing away. Jesus even stated that in heaven we shall be like the angels and we shall no longer be given in marriage. There shall be no more husbands and wives. In contrast, the Mormons have made an idol out of marriage and family. According to their teachings, a Mormon husband and wife shall be married for all eternity and some of them shall rule over a planet one day as gods. We need to maintain a biblical perspective on our families.

Marriage on earth is to reflect the mystery of Christ's relationship to the Church; it is not a substitute for it, just a reflection. Marriage must be submitted to the higher purpose of glorifying Christ. The husband must take the lead with a sensitive and listening ear toward his wife. Yet, he may have to make decisions that, in a temporal sense, would appear to be inconsiderate toward his wife. We must recognize this if we are to be prepared for the Great Tribulation. How so?

What about the many thousands of married Christian men down through the ages, and even to this day, who have the choice of forfeiting their faith and denying Christ in order to avoid the hardship of imprisonment or martyrdom? Imagine the difficulties and suffering staying true to the faith imposes on their families. Some are pondering that choice as you are reading this. We mentioned in the introduction Pakistani brother, Ranjha Masih. He was imprisoned on May 8, 1998 as a victim of Pakistan's Law against blaspheming Muhammad. He has been told that all he needs to do to be freed from prison is become a Muslim.

By choosing to stay a Christian, he faces life imprisonment apart from his family while they struggle on his wife's $36 per month just to keep their one bedroom house and food in the mouths of their four children. If it came down to it, if it meant our families would suffer greatly, would we still be able to remain faithful to Christ? Some like brother Ranjha have realized this world in its present form is passing away. They have been able to make the right choice because they kept their eyes on the eternal prize. Whether we ever have to face the firing squad, or imprisonment, this attitude of considering eternity and the unshakable kingdom of Jesus needs to remain with us in our daily thinking. Such a mindset helps us keep things in their proper balance. It will help us be prepared for whatever lies ahead.

Paul states that "those who weep should be as though they did not weep and those who rejoice as though they did not rejoice" (1 Cor 7:30a). Again, what is he saying? Jesus said we are to mourn with those who mourn. In fact, he said we are blessed if we mourn with them. Paul himself exhorted us to rejoice always. What is Paul saying here? Is this another supposed contradiction in the Bible? Again, absolutely not!

Paul is addressing another temptation we must beware of if we are to properly not love our lives even unto death. It is a mindset that elevates our desire to feel in a good mood above everything else. This attitude allows our feelings to cloud our judgment and if we let it, rule our lives. The West has countless books analyzing and re-analyzing why we feel the way we do. Perhaps some of them do some good. But the temptation is to go overboard in trying to make ourselves feel good. We can become engrossed in trying to figure out all our psychosis. We are often preoccupied with self-fulfillment.

If we become too engrossed with ourselves, we don't have time to be concerned about others or serving in the kingdom of God. Paul warned Timothy that "in the last days difficult times will come. For men will be *lovers of self, lovers of money . . . lovers of pleasure* rather than lovers of God" (2Tim. 3:2a, 4b). This is especially startling because the context of the scripture indicates that Paul is talking about the Church, not the world.[290]

This is not to belittle legitimate trials, suffering and hardship that some are going through, perhaps even as they read these words. Only, there is a need again to put things in eternal perspective. Jesus said, "In the world you have tribulation . . ." How many of us want to claim that promise? But He continued, ". . . take courage; I have overcome the world" (John 16:33b).

On the opposite end there is a temptation to become so enthralled with feelings that come with rejoicing that we spend our time running from special meetings to special conferences in a frantic search for a "spiritual or emotional high." Again, the temptation is to have our emotions served rather than serve others. There is nothing wrong with desiring a touch from God. But emotional states are temporary. The form of things here is going to pass away. Certainly God is deeply concerned with our emotional well being, and he wants to help us in our emotions. But we have all eternity to enjoy the never-ending bliss of heaven. This can anchor our soul, freeing us from a need to pursue temporary spiritual or emotional fixes.

We can enjoy pleasant feelings when they come, and we should always have a rejoicing attitude. We'll be more likely to have both if we love God and others. The Scriptures exhort us to not get wrapped up in always needing some special experience. If we become addicted to pleasure, how will we respond when we have to face the unpleasant reality of the Great Tribulation?

Leaders from the Chinese house churches have an important message for us in the West. One said,

> God cannot use a person who wants a safe comfortable Christian life. If your only aim in life is to get yourself into heaven, then you are not likely to take many other people with you. Many Christians have somehow become deceived into spiritual selfishness, gorging themselves on the latest Christian teaching, books, seminars, music and fads. When we spend all our time edifying ourselves and not seeking to win the souls of lost humanity, we are in deep trouble! Ironically, the more we feed our souls without serving God's purposes in the earth, the more our souls get sick of the food and bloated with information.[291]

We must remember ". . . the time has been shortened . . . ." A new heaven and a new earth are on the way. Has the reality of this gripped our lives? Is it affecting the way I think and the way I live? It must. Jesus Christ is coming again and everything that can be shaken will be shaken. Are we getting ready? Are we letting this profound truth shape our lives?

This is the reality. Aren't you glad? The way things are is coming to an end. There is "a new heavens and a new earth where righteousness dwells" and it's on the way. No more children being kidnapped and abused. All evil and filth will forever be banished. No more conflict will go on in the Church. This is a place where righteousness reigns supreme. Yet this new heavens and new earth will not come without some travailing. Hebrews 12:26–29 makes it clear. God is shaking everything that can be shaken, including what's in the Church. God will shake out things in our lives and in the Church that need shaking. The Lord exhorts his own Church to come out of Babylon so that she will not share in its judgment.

The Warning of Lot's wife

When speaking of the end, Jesus warned us it would be like the days of Noah, everyone going about their business quite unsuspecting of the disaster that would soon hit. We are furthermore warned to remember Lot's wife (Luke 17:32–33). Why Lot's wife? The warning is clear.

Genesis tells us that Sodom and Gomorrah were nestled in a particularly beautiful part of the land of Canaan (Gen. 13:10). These cities had become home to Lot's wife. It's where her house was. It's where her shopping malls were. It's where all her fine jewelry and new furniture was. She had raised her children there. She had some pretty nice things there. It was comfortable there. The idea that she would suddenly lose all that was too much for her. The worries of this life overwhelmed her. How would she prepare her food? When would she be able to have her own kitchen again? Would this mean poverty the rest of their days?

Would we be willing to give those things up in faith to avoid denying Jesus Christ? Ironically, by loving the things of the world more than the things of God, Lot's wife ended up losing both of them. And so could we, if we respond as she did. Before we get too harsh on Lot's wife, think about what she faced. Suddenly and quite unexpectedly she had to leave all this stuff with only a few hours notice.

What would our answer be if we went home today and found out we had a few hours to leave, or we could deny Jesus Christ and follow the Beast and get to keep everything we have? What if the day came and we were called to surrender all of our things because of our faith in Jesus Christ? What if we were given the choice to follow Jesus and endure hardship like we've never known, or we could hang onto relative comfort by taking the mark of the Beast? Would we choose Jesus if it meant losing our homes, losing our jobs, losing most of our possessions, losing our freedom, losing our family and possibly losing our lives? Would our vision be so clouded by love of things in this world that we would make the wrong choice?

Would we have the faith to believe in God's eternal kingdom, or would we only see the temporal?

Would we try to hang onto that which we're going to lose anyway, or would we be willing to part with it to follow Jesus and keep that which matters? This is the dilemma that a generation of people is going to face. Some Christians even today have already been face to face with such choices. Not all have made the right choice. Will we? Joel saw multitudes in the valley of decision (Joel 3:14a), a day when the choice will be faced by all. What if we end up being that generation?

Whether or not we actually get asked to do this in our lifetimes is not the question for us right now. Certainly, we must be ready for that possibility should it come. Yet our spiritual well being for both today and the future depends on it. If our affections are being overwhelmed by worldly things, we will not be fruitful in the Kingdom of God today, whether or not we ever face serious persecution (Matt. 13:22). But worse yet, we could end up losing everything that truly matters.

On the other hand, we could finish our race in the words of Paul. We could say, "I have fought the good fight, I have finished the course, I have kept the faith; in the future there is laid up for me the crown of righteousness, which the Lord, the righteous Judge, will award to me on that day; and not only to me, but also to all who have loved his appearing" (2Tim. 4:8). Not long after penning these words, Paul gave up his head for Jesus. May we be ready to do the same!

How Can the Rich Overcome?

How can we, as wealthy Christians in the West prepare for the days ahead, whatever comes? What can we do to make sure we can finish our lives like Paul, having fought the good fight and not getting bogged down in the cares of the world? We may not consider ourselves very wealthy. However, the facts reveal that the average American is wealthier than nearly everyone else in the world. We are very rich.[392] There is no sin in that. But there is risk. Jesus said it would be difficult for the rich to enter the kingdom of God, not impossible, just difficult (Matt. 19:23–24).

The solution to overcoming the deceitfulness of riches is to vol-
untarily live a life of sacrifice for the sake of the Gospel. That was
the advice that Jesus gave to the rich young ruler. He advised him
to sell what he had and give to the poor. Would we be able to do
that? Are we willing to do that? The Scriptures are clear; it is when
the wealthy live a life of sacrifice they will take hold of real life. Paul
gave us wealthy people this instruction,

> Instruct those who are rich in this present world not to be conceited
> or to fix their hope on the uncertainty of riches, but on God, who
> richly supplies us with all things to enjoy. Instruct them to do
> good, to be rich in good works, to be generous and ready to share,
> storing up for themselves the treasure of a good foundation for the
> future, so that they may take hold of that life which is life indeed.
> (1 Tim. 6:17–19)

The challenge for us is take Paul's exhortation seriously. We
mustn't become proud, or place our hope in our wealth but use
wealth as an opportunity to do much good. By doing so, we will be
laying up treasures in heaven, and we will be prepared to give up all
our earthly riches for the sake of the kingdom, should things ever
come to that. As one Chinese leader stated, "The best way for a selfish person to be delivered from self-obsession is to start praying for
and meeting the needs of others . . . Evangelism is for the glory of
God. Worship is far more than just the singing of songs. Worship
occurs every time a believer does something that brings honor and
glory to Jesus."[293]

If we find ourselves standing face to face with the greatest tribulation the earth will ever know, what should we do? The discourse
recorded in Matthew is clear, "When you see all these things, recognize that he is near, right at the door" (Matt. 24:33).

We shouldn't look down in gloom, but wait in anticipation of our
Lord's return. We can endure knowing that the suffering will not last
long. "For momentary, light affliction is producing for us an eternal
weight of glory far beyond all comparison, while we look not at the
things which are seen, but at the things which are not seen; for the
things which are seen are temporal, but the things which are not seen

are eternal" (2Cor. 4:17–18). And we can be assured that we shall soon be face to face with that which is eternal.

As one of the Chinese Church leaders of the, "Back to Jerusalem" movement said,

> Pray that we will be fully prepared for a battle to the death. I believe that we are facing the greatest spiritual war the church has seen. The stakes are high! Success means nothing less than the fulfillment of the Great Commission and the return of our Lord Jesus Christ! The devil, who has kept Muslim, Buddhist and Hindu nations captive for thousands of years will not surrender without a strong and bloody fight . . . Pray that God will find his church faithful to obey the calling he has given us to take the gospel to all the unreached nations of the world.[294]

Of course, the battle will not end with the fulfillment of the Great Commission. The intensity of attack will heat up even more for the short season just before the Lord's return. But the Lord will be faithful to us. Together with Paul, as he faced possible execution, by the grace of God we will be able to say, "The Lord will rescue me from every evil deed, and will bring me safely to His heavenly kingdom; to Him be the glory forever and ever. Amen" (2Tim. 4:18). "Now may the God of peace Himself sanctify you entirely; and may your spirit and soul and body be preserved complete, without blame at the coming of our Lord Jesus Christ. Faithful is He who calls you, and He also will bring it to pass" (1Thess. 5:23–24).

Appendix A

Missions Resources

Great Web Sites:

General Information:

www.adoptapeople.org
www.everypeople.net
www.pioneers.org
www.calebproject.org
www.gmi.org
www.whorizons.org

Long-term opportunities

www.interserve.org
www.pioneers.org
www.gospelcom.net/awm/
www.om.org
www.gospelcom.net/send
www.antioch.com.sg/mission/asianmo/
www.wycliffe.com

Prayer Materials

www.global-prayer-digest.org
www.antioch.com
www.gospelcom.net/awm/

Mission Conferences /speakers

www.adoptapeople.org
www.calebproject.org

English Teaching Certificate Programs

Contact Youth With a Mission on the Internet at *www.ywam.org* for a schedule of classes and locations.

Missions Courses

Perspectives Study Program
1605 Elizabeth St.
Pasadena, CA 91104
1-626-398-2125
e-mail: *perspectives@uscwm.org*
www.perspectives.org
(This course is available at places all over the US and Canada throughout the year.)

Short-term opportunities

www.globalopps.org
www.frontiers.org
www.gospelcom.net/awm/
www.us.omf.org
www.gospelcom.net/send
www.wycliffe.com
www.calebproject.org

Strategic Networking Groups for Churches and Individuals:

Antioch Network
5060 North 19th Avenue, Suite 306
Pheonix, AZ 85015
USA
1-602-589-7777
Email: *info@antiochnetwork.org*
Website: *www.antiochnetwork.org*
(This group is an umbrella group for a number of smaller networks, such as the International Turkey Network and others.)

Adopt-a-People Clearinghouse
PO Box 28000
Chicago, IL 60628
USA
1-866-825-4636 (toll-free)
Email: *aapc@BibleLeague.org*
Website: *www.adoptapeople.org*
(Specifically geared toward helping churches take the next step in reaching the unreached. Their website has the most detailed information on unreached people groups that is currently available.)

Missions Publications and Missions Book Distributors:

Mission Frontiers, published by The United States Center for World Mission, 1605 E. Elizabeth St., Pasadena, CA 91104. Telephone: 1-626-797-1111 or *www.missionfrontiers.org* . 6 issues yearly, suggested subscription of $18 per year. This is a great magazine.

Mission World Catalogue (great resource for Mission books—call 1-8More-books or email at *gabriel@omlit.om.org*)

Great Reading about Missions

Countries and Peoples of the World CD, (ILS International, 2003). The purpose of this tool is to provide the most accurate up-to-date information on each of the 233 nations of the world and all of the ethnolinguistic peoples of the world. It also contains articles and contact information for adopting a people for outreach as well as an introduction to the Perspectives Study Program. It's a great resource! It can be purchased through YWAM's product catalogue at *www.ywam.org* . William Carey Library may also now have it available at 1-800-MISSION.

Loving the Church, Blessing the Nations, George Miley, (Gabriel Publishing, Waynesboro, GA 2003). A great book about networking and involving the whole Church in the Great Commission.

Missions in the Third Millennium, Stan Guthrie (Paternoster Press, Waynesboro, GA, 2001). He's a bit pessimistic in spots, but overall has some very helpful insights in missions trends.

*Operation World, Patrick Johnstone and Jason Mandryk, (Paternoster Publishing, Waynesboro GA 2001). An awesome prayer guide and spiritual overview of all the nations in the world. It's unbeatable for what it does. A great way to help evaluate the needs of different nations for foreign mission outreach. Each country has a section which details who the least-reached people group in a nation happen to be.

Penetrating Missions' Final Frontier, Tetsunao Yamamori, (Intervarsity Press, Downers Grove, 1993). A little bit dated, but he still has some good practical insights on reaching the unreached.

*Perspectives on the World Christian Movement, Third Edition, Edited by Ralph D. Winter, Steven C. Hawthorne (William Carey Library, Pasadena, CA, 1999). *This is the single most important book on missions that anyone could read!* It is the core text in the well-known "Perspectives" course and it is actually a collection of writings and excerpts of books and speeches. Some areas that are covered include: The Biblical Perspective for Missions, The Historical Perspective including the birth of the World Christian Movement, The Cultural Perspective including culture and communication and the Gospel as it relates to culture, the Strategic Perspective, Strategy for World Evangelization, Strategies for Development, Strategies for Church Planting and Case Studies of Pioneer Church Planting, World Christian Discipleship and World Christian Partnership. It is a tremendous reference book, it is very practical and it is very

inspirational. It's a must for anyone serious about finding their place or their churches' place in completing the Great Commission. You can purchase the text most inexpensively through the William Carey Library by calling 1-800-MISSION.

Revolution in World Missions, K.P. Yohannan (gfa books, Carrollton, TX, 1998). A radical challenge to the Church in the West to use our wealth to further the Great Commission.

The World of Islam, Resources for Understanding CD, (Global Mapping International, Colorado Springs, CO, 2000). This is a priceless resource filled with direct source documents of authoritative Muslim teachers as well as valuable articles on understanding and reaching Muslims for Christ. This may be your single best investment for learning about Islam and reaching Muslims. It is available from Global Mapping International, email: *info@gmi.org* or by calling 1-719-531-3599.

Appendix B

The Beast (the AntiChrist) & the Islamic Jesus.

- Muslims believe that Jesus will return to establish Islam in all the Earth:

Biblical Description of the Beast (Anti-Christ)	Islam & the Islamic Jesus
• The whole world will be stunned and amazed and will fall into line after the Beast. (Re 13:3)	• If he comes as an Islamic Jesus, radical and religious Muslims will rejoice at what they see as the fulfillment of Islamic prophecy. It will not be hard for them to follow after him.
• Some will follow out of devotion, but many will follow him out of fear saying, "Who is like the beast and who is able to wage war with him?" (Re 13:4)	• Islam demands that all means of weapons, including WMD, should be used to advance Islam, and to die for Islam is the only way to insure going to heaven. (Su 9:41, 47:8, 4:74)
• Worship the Dragon & the Beast (Re 13:4)	• Muslims & subdued peoples are commanded to bow down to Allah at the reading of the Koran. Loyalty and obedience to Allah's apostle is equal to obeying Allah. (Su 32:15,48:8-10, 64:12).
• Those who don't worship the Beast will be killed. (Re 13:15)	• Those who don't worship Allah and accept his religion will be killed and thrown to hell at the coming judgment. (Su 77:49, 9:3-5, 9:29-34, 9:123, 27:82-86, 98:1-7)
• There will be a great apostasy. (2 Th 2:3)	• "True" Christians will acknowledge Mohammed and the Koran. (Su 29:47-48)
• He will come with satanic false signs and wonders. (2 Th 2:9)	• The Koran states that Allah's apostles *always* come with signs. (Su 5:110, 43:63-64).
• He will be a man of lawlessness. (2 Th 2:3)	• Allah's apostle is accountable only to Allah. (Su 48:8-10, 64:12, 59:8).
• He will worship a god of fortresses. (Da 11:38)	• Jihad, or holy war, is a key tenet of Islam. (Su 2:216, 9:29).
• He will have "no regard for the desire of women." (Da 11:37)	• Islam is inconsiderate of women's needs and wants. (Su 66:1-5, 4:34, 64:14-15).
• He will have no regard for any other god and will exult himself above all others. (Da 11:37)	• Allah is the only true god to be worshiped. Allah's apostle and the Koran supercede all other revelations. (Su 48:28
• He will use wealth and riches to advance the cause of his god. (Da 11:38)	• The Koran commands Muslims to use their wealth for Islam. They have much oil wealth. (Su 9:44, 57:10).

• He will destroy many while they are at ease.(Da 8:25)	• There is more wealth and riches in the world than ever before. The Koran says unbelievers are often wealthy and comfortable and will be punished. (Su 34:34-38)
• He will utter great boasts and blaspheme the God of heaven. (Da 7:8,11,20, Re 13:6)	• Muslims believe that when Jesus returns he will quote from the Koran a verse that exhorts Jews and Christians to accept Islam and mocks Christians for believing in his divinity. (Su 4:171-172).
• He will blaspheme those who dwell in heaven. (Re 13:6)	• The Koran teaches that Gabriel revealed the Koran to Muhammad. (Su 81:22)
• His number is a man's number and is 666. (Re 13:18)	• There are either 6616 verses in the Koran or 6666 verses, depending on which scholar you talk to. The Islamic Jesus is the word and spirit of Allah. (Su 4:171)
• He will make war on the saints and overcome them. (Re 13:7)	• Muslims believe that Jesus will break all crosses at his return and destroy all who will not convert to Islam.(Su 72:18, 9:123, 27:82-86)

"We have sent you (Muhammad) forth as a witness and as a bearer of good news and warnings, so that you (the Meccans) may have faith in Allah *and* His Apostle and that you may assist Him (Muhammad), *honour Him, and praise Him morning and evening*."

"Those that swear fealty to you (Muhammad), swear fealty to Allah Himself" (Surah 48:8-9).

Appendix C

The False Prophet and the Islamic Mahdi.

- Muslims, especially many Shiites, believe that a 12th century Imam, Imam Mohammad Al-Mahdi never died and is in hiding on the earth. He will eventually reveal himself and establish Islam in all the earth.

The False Prophet of Revelation	Islam and the Islamic Mahdi.
• The False Prophet will rise up from the earth. (Re 13:11a)	• The Islamic Mahdi is believed to be on the earth waiting for Allah's time to reveal himself and establish worldwide Islam.
• He performs false signs and wonders. (Re 13:13-14).	• Allah's apostles always come with signs. (Su 26:100-186)
• He forces the whole earth to worship the Beast. (Re 13:14-15)	• To show their loyalty and true submission to Islam, all Meccans had to bow down at the reading of the Koran, praise Muhammad twice a day and obey Muhammad in all things as Allah's apostle. (Su 64:12, 32:15, 58:8-9,12-13)
• He will force all to take the mark of the beast or the number of his name or they cannot buy or sell. (Re 13:16-17)	• Islamic Sharia Law demands that all non-Muslims must receive a mark and pay the jizya (infidel tax) to prove that they have submitted to Islamic rule. In the future, when the Islamic Jesus comes, the option of paying the tax will be removed and the only options will be conversion or death. Only converts will be able to conduct economic transactions.

"The Jizyah (infidel tax) … is specifically a punishment for "infidelity" - i.e. for not being a Muslim. It is levied only on non-Muslims. The aim of the tax is not to safeguard the rights of the payee, but to demonstrate the superiority of one religious confession over another. *Often when paying the tax, the dhimmi was struck on the head or the neck, and had to wear a parchment proving payment or face sanctions.*" *

* source is the World of Islam CD-ROM

One of Mohammed's followers quoted him saying that when Jesus returns to establish worldwide Islam, "He (the Islamic Jesus) will break the Cross, and kill the swine, and *take away the poll-tax*… and fight for the religion of Islam until Allah shall destroy in His (Jesus') day the people of every other faith except Islam, and worship shall be Allah's alone."[1]

Unlike past practice where infidels were allowed to pay the *jizyah* (the poll-tax) in place of converting to Islam, the Islamic Jesus will bring an end to all other religions except Islam. He will "take away the poll-tax" since there will not be need for it. The only choices will be conversion to Islam or death. The inability to buy and sell without the mark will be one mechanism used to force all to make a choice.

---

[1] Samuel Zwemmer, *The Moslem Christ*, (New York: American Tract Society, 1912) as found in *The World of Islam*. CD-ROM. (Colorado Springs, CO.: Global Mapping International, 2000).

General Index

wormwood 94

Y

Yugoslavia 38, 67

Z

Zakaria, Fareed 50, 146, 230
Zechariah 47, 48, 49, 50, 51, 53,
54, 55, 99, 107, 108, 230,
231, 240, 251, 262, 263,
264, 270
Zionism 31, 123

Index of Scripture

Endnotes

[1] "Behold Your Family," *Voice of the Martyrs* Magazine, July 2003, p. 3.

[2] I capitalize the word *church* whenever I refer to the whole body of Christ. Also the term *Church Age* refers to the period of time from the Resurrection of Jesus Christ to his return.

[3] Some have suggested that these "angels" may have been the human couriers who would take these messages to the churches since the Greek word simply means messengers. Others feel these "angels" may have possibly been the leading elder or pastor of these seven churches. However, there is nothing in the text to support this latter position.

Chapter 1: The Islamic Beast is Revived

[4] *The Rock Star and the Mullahs Debate: Islam and Democracy, Individual Rights* PBS. Wide Angle —Web site. 17 July 2003 <*http://www.pbs.org/wnet/wideangel/shows/junoon/debate_4.html*>.

[5] Christopher Dickey and Carla Power. "Rethinking Islam," *Newsweek* Sept. 15, 2003, p. 51.

[6] Paul Berman, "The Philosopher of Islamic Terror," *The New York Times* Magazine, March 23, 2003, p. 25.

[7] *Views of a Changing World 2003*. 3 June 2003. Pew Center for the People & the Press. 7 July 2003 *http://people-press.org/reports/display.php3?ReportID=185.*, p.36,39.

[8] ibid., p.34,35

[9] *Talk of the Nation*. NPR. WSLU. Canton, NY. 1 June, 2004.

[10] *Avoiding Armaggedon Part III*. PBS. WPBS. Watertown, NY. 16 April 2003.

[11] ibid., p.34.

[12] "The Rock Star and the Mullah." *Wide Angel.* PBS. WPBS, Watertown, NY. 3 July 2003.

[13] David E. Kaplin with Aamir Latif. "Are We Safer? —Where's Osama?," *US News & World Report*, Sept. 15, 2003, p. 24.

[14] "The Hunt for Bin Laden." *US News and World Report* 10 May 2004, p.32.

[15] Morgan Norval, *The Fifteen Century War* (Indian Wells, CA.: McKenna Publishing Group, 2002) p.97.

[16] "The Rock Star and the Mullah." *Wide Angle.* PBS. WPBS, Watertown, NY. 3 July 2003.

[17] ibid., p.3.

[18] ibid., p.28.

[19] ibid., p.71.

[20] Berman, p.27.

[21] ibid, p.28.

[22] *Avoiding Armageddon Part III.* PBS. WPBS. Watertown, NY. 16 April 2003.

[23] *Morning Edition.* NPR. WSLU. Canton, NY. 16 Oct. 2003.

[24] "The Rock Star and the Mullah." *Wide Angle.* PBS. WPBS. Watertown, NY. 3 July 2003.

[25] ibid.

[26] Islamist groups are Islamic political parties and organizations which desire to see the re-establishment of Sharia Law as the law of the land. They are also philosophically supportive of Islam taking over the world.

[27] "Terror and Tension in the Middle East." *The Connection*, NPR. WSLU. Canton, NY. 14 May 2003.

[28] Dr. Daniel Pipes, The Rock Star and the Mullahs Debate: Islam and Democracy, Individual Rights PBS/Wide Angle —Web site.

[29] "The Rock Star and the Mullah." *Wide Angle.* PBS. WPBS. Watertown, NY. 3 July 2003.

[30] Fareed Zakaria. "Our Last Real Chance." *Newsweek* 19 April 2004, p.46.

[31] Steve Hagerman. *TWOsh@onlinecol.com*. TWO News forwarded article by Deborah Sontag, "The Erdogan Experiment" *New York Times Magazine* Web Site, 11 May 2003. E-mail to the author. 29 May 2003.

[32] Ibid.

[33] ibid.

[34] "Turkey," *Go magazine*, first quarter of 2004, p.12.

[35] Dr. Muqtedar Khan, *The Rock Star and the Mullahs Debate: Islam and Democracy, Individual Rights* PBS/Wide Angle —Web site.

[36] The idea of MAD (mutually assured destruction) was that neither the communists nor the democracies would be willing to risk nuclear war because it would inevitably lead to the utter destruction and devastation of both sides.

[37] Norval, p.106.

[38] ibid. p.66–67.

[39] D.E.K. "Are We Safe? —Target: Al Qaeda," *US News & World Report*, Sept. 15, 2003, p.25.

[40] Norval, p.144–145.

[41] Ahmed Rashid, *Jihad* (New York: Penguin Books, 2003), p.9.

[42] ibid. p.4.

[43] Paper printed from Christar Web site, *www.christar.org*, 2000.

[44] Patrick Johnstone & Jason Mandryk, *Operation World* (Waynesboro, GA.: Paternoster Publishing 2001) p.393.

[45] Rashid, p.228.

[46] ibid., p.223.

[47] ibid., p.225.

[48] *Morning Edition.* NPR. WSLU, Canton, NY. 22 Sept. 2003.

[49] Frank Viviano. "Kingdom on Edge," *National Geographic*, Oct. 2003, p. 12.

[50] "Saudi Voices of Dissent." *The Connection*, NPR. WSLU. Canton, NY. 28 Oct. 2003.

[51] Ibid.

[52] Ibid.

[53] "*Morning Edition.*" NPR. WSLU. Canton, NY. 1 June, 2004.

[54] "Interview with Dr. Fuwaz Gerges" (author of *Islamists and the West* and professor at Sarah Lawrence College) *Newshour*, PBS Watertown, NY. 19 May 2003.

[55] Rashid, p.222.

Chapter 2:

[56] Merrill C. Tenney, *Interpreting Revelation* (Peabody, Massachusetts.: Hendrickson Publishers, 2001), pp.190–191.

[57] The Father stated prophetically through the Psalmist, "You are my Son… Ask of Me, and I will surely give the nations as Your inheritance, the very ends of the earth as Your possession. You shall break them with a rod of iron, You shall shatter them like earthenware" (Ps 2:7b–9).

[58] Charles Caldwell Ryrie, Th.D, Phil..D., *The Ryrie Study Bible New American Standard Bible* (Chicago, Moody Press), p. 1902.

[59] Ergun Mehmet Caner and Emir Fehti Caner, *Unveiling Islam* (Grand Rapids, MI.: Kregel Publications, 2002), p. 194.

[60] Ibid., p. 185.

[61] There's a good reason they have been called fundamentalists. They are returning to the fundamentals of the faith.

[62] Some theologians believe that Antiochus IV, the King of the Seleucid Empire who captured Jerusalem and desecrated the temple back in 167 B.C, is a typing of the Beast who is to come. It is interesting to note that in his case, he too came to power illegitimately and he seized the kingdom by intrigue (Dan. 11:21) even as Daniel prophesied he would.

[63] Surah 9:73 and several others plainly state this. Surah 4:89 is especially blunt, "If they (hypocritical Muslims) desert you (faithful Muslims), seize them and put them to death wherever you find them…"

[64] Albert Hourani, *A History of the Arab Peoples.* (New York, NY.: Warner Books, 2003), p. 144.

[65] Omestead, Thomas. "A fast-spreading Conflagration." *US News and World Report* 10 May 2004, p.24.

[66] "Kingdom on Edge," *National Geographic*, Oct. 2003, p. 26–27.

[67] "Video of bin Laden shown on Al-Jazeera," *Watertown Daily Times*, 11 Sept. 2003, sec. A:1,7.

[68] Fareed Zakaria. "America's New World Disorder," *Newsweek*, Sept.15, 2003, p. 47.

[69] "Live Radio News coverage of Kofi Annan's (Secretary General of the United Nations) speech to the United Nations General Assembly" *NPR*. WSLU, Canton, NY. 23 Sept. 2003.

[70] This restrainer may have been identified in Daniel 12:1 as Michael the archangel. For it is after Michael arises that a "time of distress such as has never occurred since there was a nation until that time" will happen, probably referring to the Great Tribulation. In any case, the restrainer will ultimately be under God's control.

[71] "Kingdom on Edge," *National Geographic*, Oct. 2003, p. 11.

[72] Appenzeller, Tim. "The End of Cheap Oil." *National Geographic* June 2004, p.108.

[73] ibid. p. 90–91.

[74] "Attack on Saudi Foreign Compound." *USA Today Online*. 30 May 2004. <http://www.usatoday.com/news/world/2004-05-29-saudi-attacks_x.htm?csp=24>

[75] *"All Things Considered."* NPR. WSLU. Canton, NY. 1 June, 2004.

[76] Appenzeller, p. 88.

[77] Michael Youssef, *America, Oil and the Islamic Mind*, (Grand Rapids, MI.: Zondervan, 1991), p. 131.

Chapter 3: The Great Completion and the Transition to Christ's Return

[78] This is a true story adapted from a newsletter. The names and setting have been changed to protect the individuals.

[79] The NASB translators translate the word as *book*, but include the word *scroll* in the margins. Book is more understandable to the modern ear, but since books were only newly invented in the first century and not widely used, this is quite likely a scroll. For the rest of the book, I will use the word *scroll* in place of book. Even the NASB translators felt this was a very valid way to translate this word. Indeed many translations (KJV, NKJV, etc.) use the word *scroll*.

[80] Many books have been written on this topic. Probably the most famous classic is *The Genesis Flood*. However, I can remember sitting in a linguistics class at Albany State University with an evolution-believing professor stating calmly that the evidence was very strong that there was almost certainly originally a single language in the earth. Furthermore, we learned that there was an ancient "flood" tradition found in the folklore of many language families all around the earth.

[81] Paul Hattaway, *Back to Jerusalem*. (Waynesboro, GA.: Gabriel Publishing, 2003), p. 110.

[82] Again, this wasn't an isolated doctrine of a few churches. Paul writes to an established church in Rome explaining why he hadn't been able to visit them yet. What was his reason? He stated plainly, *"I aspired to preach the gospel, not where Christ was already named*, so that I would not build on another man's foundation; but as it is written, *'They who had no news of Him shall see* and they who have not

heard shall understand.' For *this* reason I have often been prevented from coming to you..." (Rom. 15:20–22). He informs them the only reason he can see them now is because *there are no places remaining* in the regions between Jerusalem and Rome that haven't heard the Gospel. So he plans on going to Spain. Why go to Spain? They hadn't heard the Gospel yet. He knows it would be convenient for him to pass through Rome now. The church at Rome could help him along in his ministry to the unreached. They would refresh him as he refreshed them (Rom. 15:23–24).

Chapter 4: Tracking the Great Completion
[83] Ralph Winter, "The Kingdom Strikes Back." *Perspectives on the World Christian Movement*, Eds. Ralph Winter and Steven Hawthorne, (Pasadena, CA., William Carey Library, Third Edition, Fourth Printing, 2000) pp. 195–213. The article can also be found for free at *www.mission1.org.*
[84] For a quick overview of the spiritual progress and continued need in these countries I would recommend the book *Operation World* or the web sites of *www.peopleintl.org , www.calebproject.org , www.gmi.org* or *www.adoptapeople.org* .
[85] as reported to me by a Bosnian missionary in 2001.
[86] I cannot name this organization because they officially operate in some "closed" nations as a secular company.
[87] Patrick Johnstone and Jason Mandryk, *Operation World* (Waynesboro, GA.: Paternoster Lifestyle, 2001) p. 451.
[88] About 100 years ago South Korea had virtually no known Christians. Some of the early missionaries were greeted with arrows. After a slow fifty years and the establishment of a tiny church, the Church finally began to take off following the Korean War. Today, more than one-third of the people are Christian and more than half of these people are born-again. In the past 15 years or so, South Korea has become a major missionary-sending nation.
[89] *Countries and Peoples of the World,* CD-ROM, ILS International, 2003.
[90] Patrick Johnstone, "Covering the Globe" excerpted from *The Church is Bigger than you Think* (Great Britain, Christian Focus Publications, 1998, Chron. 21–22) used by permission in Winter and Hawthorne, p. 544.
[91] Winter and Hawthorne, p. 521.
[92] ibid.
[93] ibid.
[94] "Turkish World Outreach Newsletter," July, 2003, p. 1.
[95] *Frontiers* missions agency brochure
[96] "Turkish World Outreach Newsletter," p. 1.
[97] ibid.
[98] For example, although they lie within the 10/40 window, the majority Han Chinese people and the South Korean people have huge thriving and growing evangelical churches and communities and a vibrant missions movement. The largest church in the world is in Seoul, South Korea. Pastor Yonghee Cho's church has well over 100,000 members. However, virtually the entire remainder of the people in the region are grossly underrepresented in the worldwide Church.

[99] Johnstone used in Winter & Hawthorne, p.543.

[100] This information comes from a report filed by this Bible Correspondence Course in 2002, which I received in the spring of 2003.

[101] *Turkey AfriAsia Creative Outreach.* Videocasette. TACO, 2000. 15 min.

[102] Arab World Ministries 2003 annual report. (Upper Darby, PA.: Arab World Ministries, 2003) p. 2.

[103] Johnstone & Mandryk, p.374.

[104] This information comes from a prayer letter of a Christian working in this nation.

[105] This is taken directly from an agency report on Indonesia by Pioneers.

[106] Winter & Hawthorne, p.261.

[107] Hattaway, p. 13.

[108] Ibid., p.2.

[109] Ibid., p. 20.

[110] Ibid., p.69.

Chapter 5: The Great Tribulation: The Jihad against the Bride

[111] Ibid., p. xi.

[112] Ibid., p.97.

[113] The only missing tribe is Dan. Joseph is split into his two sons, Ephraim and Manasseh giving us 12.

[114] If forced to guess, it would not be surprising one bit if at least some of those who will "follow the Lamb wherever He goes" don't find themselves working among the last, scattered, hard-to-reach people groups yet to hear the Gospel. As we have already seen, few things resonate more in the heart of God than rescuing people for himself. He desires a kingdom representing every tribe and tongue and nation. However, that would be nothing more than a wild guess. The Scriptures nowhere specifically indicate they will be involved in evangelism any more than any other spirit-filled Christian.
Certainly the 144,000 will not be some special group of people to get the rest of the Church off the hook from completing the Great Commission. There is another interesting fact. The scriptures indicate the Lord will re-gather Israel to himself (Is 60:4). Undoubtedly, much of the Israelite Diaspora is made up of descendants who have long since lost track of their roots. Many have become completely unaware of their Israelite heritage. Perhaps these devoted individuals will be from the tribes of Israel chosen as "first fruits" by God from among the scattered Diaspora of Israel and not even know it. These may be what is meant by the "first fruits" of the ultimate turning to God of the remainder of Israel which is to follow shortly. In any case, believing Israel (aware of its heritage or not) is spiritually one with the Church. Neither is excused from this Great Commission task. Together we make up the Church, the body of Christ.
Another speculation some have suggested is that the number of 144,000 is actually symbolic. It is representative of something not literal. This possibility has some merit for the following reasons. The first four horses are clearly spiritual symbols of what will be physically manifested on the earth. The statement of the martyrs in

the fifth seal probably captures a collective thought rather than something literally spoken by all of them simultaneously. The sixth seal also has a statement made by all the unbelievers of the world, which is probably not literally stated. Their statement captures the attitude they will all possess at the Lord's return.

Could it be these 144,000 are merely a numerically tidy number representing the initial down payment of that final turning to Christ of Israel? The Scriptures say it will happen to all of Israel at Christ's return (Zech. 12:10–13:2, etc.). The Scriptures say this turning to Christ by Israel will follow the time when "the fullness of the Gentiles has come in" (Rom. 11:25b). This will follow the completion of the Great Commission, which itself immediately precedes the Great Tribulation. Who knows? Perhaps they will be involved in helping to evangelize Israel during the final three and one half years before Christ's return (Matt. 10:16–23). In any case, we can only speculate.

[115] Once the world is conquered the Beast will rule over the entire world, including the saints (Rev. 13:7). It is at this time that multitudes of saints will be slaughtered (Rev. 13:10,15). The fifth seal signifies more slaughter.

[116] Perhaps these seven angels are the same seven angels for each of the seven churches. Of course, if the seven angels for the seven churches were actually earthly messengers then these would be different heavenly angels.

Chapter 6: God Responds to the Jihad Against His Bride
[117] Iraneus (written between A.D. 182 and 188), *Ante-Nicene Fathers, Book 1* (Peabody, MA.: Hendrickson Publishers, second printing, 1999) p. 557.

[118] In Noah's case, not only did he have to build an ark; he had to witness the destruction of his house and many of his possessions and indeed the entire world he had known. He lost virtually everything he had. He had to endure living with all the animals of the world in tight knit, rather stinky quarters, for over a year. However, there is no sign that Noah complained. Instead, when he left the ark, he offered thanks to God.

In the case of the sacking of Jerusalem, Ezekiel declares that the righteous will have a mark put on their forehead, and they would be spared their lives from the judgment of God. Physically spared from God's wrath, they still, undoubtedly, suffered the loss of much property and possession. Most had to endure exile to a foreign country, which didn't speak their language. Many never got to see their homeland again. There was hardship to be endured, but God's protection from his judgments on earth extended to their lives.

In the case of Sodom and Gomorrah, the judgment of God meant the destruction of Lot's property and even his wife, who apparently loved her property and possessions more than her life. He had to spend a time living and roaming in the mountains. Again, the pattern is repeated, much discomfort and dislocation, but God's protection from his judgments on earth extends to the lives of the righteous. Unfortunately, for our flesh, this doesn't guarantee freedom from death at the hands of human enemies of God. The Scriptures and history up to our current day are filled with the testimonies of those that have died and are currently dying at

354

the hands of God's enemies. Revelation makes it clear, that that pattern will also continue and indeed intensify.

[119] "Meteor." *Funk & Wagnalls New Encyclopedia*, (New York: Funk & Wagnalls Inc., 1973) 16: p. 212.

[120] "Incoming!" *Popular Science*, Sept. 2003, p.79–80.

[121] The largest meteorite discovered on land made a crater 2 $\frac{1}{2}$ miles in diameter containing a lake and surrounded by concentric piles of shattered granite (*Funk & Wagnalls New Encyclopedia*, 16: p. 212). There may, in fact, be the remnants of others undiscovered on the ocean floor. In any case, there is no rule limiting or defining the size of a meteorite or a shower of meteors and meteorites. Furthermore, evolutionary scientists have even speculated that perhaps a massive meteor shower and/or volcanic activity led to massive blocking out of the sun and subsequent radical environmental change on the planet. Although I don't agree with evolution, this particular notion of meteors causing massive problems is considered viable, even by secular, unbelieving scientists.

[122] "Incoming!" p.80.

[123] ibid.

[124] ibid.

[125] ibid., p.110.

[126] "Comet." Funk & Wagnalls New Encyclopedia, 6: p. 329.

[127] ibid.

[128] ibid., p.331.

[129] It could even be this is what happens should the great "star" of the third trumpet finally slam into planet earth. If so, the beginning results of this trumpet would also be tied to the earlier four trumpets. Perhaps it is simply the strategic and direct impact of this "star" which opens the bottomless pit. Interestingly, there is smoke like the smoke of a great furnace rising from this pit when it is opened. This may indicate the deep impact of an object from space slamming into the earth. All around this pit the sun and air are darkened and obscured by the smoke rising from this pit. This is similar to what happens during the fourth trumpet when one-third of the sun, moon and stars are darkened. Perhaps the opening of the pit in the fifth trumpet is just another result of that same event which also caused the darkening of the sky announced by the fourth trumpet.

[130] Perhaps this sixth trumpet is related to the sixth bowl of wrath since the Euphrates River is mentioned in both cases. If so, then the releasing of these four angels might be connected with the releasing of the three spirits that come out of the mouth of the dragon, the Beast and the false prophet in Revelation 16:14,16. These spirits are identified as "spirits of demons, performing signs, which go out to the kings of the whole world to gather them together for the war of the great day of God, the Almighty… and they gathered them together to the place which in Hebrew is called Har-Magedon" (Rev. 16:14, 16).

In that case, the destruction poured out on the remaining unrepentant people of the world may involve these troops as they move toward Israel. Whoever they are, they will be inspired to kill one-third of the earth's unrepentant population along the way, perhaps by simple rape and pillage. As evil as they are, these armies seem to be physical instruments of God's wrath. Maybe just as the Babylonian army—and later the Roman army—were used as instruments of judgment in the previous sackings of Jerusalem, these too will be instruments of God's wrath. It is likely that by this time, Christians have already been killed, imprisoned or dispersed in the mountains and remote places of the world. If so, they would be avoided by these marauding armies. When we discuss the likely nature of the Beast's kingdom and the identity of the Beast and the Prophet, we will come back to this idea and discuss it more fully.

[131] Given his description, "clothed with a cloud, and the rainbow was upon his head, and his face was like the sun, and his feet like pillars of fire and he had in his hand a little book (scroll) which was open" (Rev. 10:1), some suggest this is the Lord Jesus as described in chapter 1. Others suggest he is the seventh and final angel preparing to blow his trumpet (see Rev. 10:7).

[132] What are these fourteen different mysteries? Twelve relate to things in God's kingdom, while two involve evil. Nine have already found their fulfillment. They are: 1) the mystery of the kingdom being given to the Church, (Mark 4:11) 2) the mystery of the gospel of Jesus Christ (Rom. 16:25, Eph. 6:19) 3) the mystery of God's hidden wisdom revealed to the Church (1Cor. 2:7) 4) the mystery that Gentiles are fellow heirs together with believing Israel (Eph. 3:3–7) 5) the mystery that a husband and wife are like Christ and the Church (Eph. 5:32) 6) the mystery that Christ in you (the believer) is the hope of glory (Col. 1:26–27) 7) the mystery of Christ Himself (Col. 2:2, 4:3) 8) the mystery of the faith (1Tim. 3:9) and 9) the mystery of the seven stars (Rev. 1:20). The two mysteries relating to evil are the Beast and Babylon (Rev. 17:5, 7, Dan. 2:18–19, 27–30, 47). These will become clearer in the future, but also prior to the last trumpet being blown. Two of the mysteries, the mystery of the Rapture (1Cor. 15:51–52), and the mystery of all of Israel getting saved (Rom. 11:25–29) have their timing identified by scripture elsewhere. The Rapture will happen right at the last trumpet call (1Cor. 15:51–53) as we shall see later. The repentance of Israel will immediately follow the Rapture as the Lord appears on the clouds (Zech. 12:10–13:2). That leaves one mystery to take place immediately prior to the last trumpet call and the return of Christ to the earth. It is this mystery which is addressed in the text.

Chapter 7: Great Signs in the Heavens

[133] Some have suggested they simultaneously represent the twelve apostles of the Lamb and the Church. Together with spiritually born-again Israel, the Church will rule the nations under the authority of Christ. Although the identity of the twenty-four elders is uncertain, some believe the twenty-four elders of Revelation (Rev. 4:4, etc.) also signify Israel and the Church. Specifically, there are twelve elders representing the twelve tribes of Israel and twelve elders representing the twelve apostles of the Lamb.

[134] This does not negate the sovereignty of God over the timing of these events. This is merely an acknowledgment of the role of suffering and the struggle both the Church and Israel have endured in the process of being God's instruments in seeing God's purposes fulfilled.

[135] Perhaps it also is symbolic of the seven continents, since the dragon will rule all of the earth through this beast.

[136] Some feel these "angels" of Revelation 1:20 are only earthly messengers delivering the prophecies to the Church.

[137] The fifth-century Church Historian Eusebius writes, "...the people of the church in Jerusalem, were commanded by oracle given by revelation to those in the city who were worthy of it, to depart and dwell in one of the cities of Perea, which they called Pella." Eusebius (in the early 5th century), *Ecclesiastical History, Book 3, v.5 in.3–4* as quoted by Ellis Skolfield in *Sozo: Survival Guide for a Remnant Church* (Fort Myers, FL.: Fish House Publishing, 1995) p. 56.

[138] Daniel was given a glimpse of this spiritual battle over governments and rulers in Daniel 10:20–21.

[139] Hattaway, p.90.

[140] Even though the threats are there, in too many cases, the perceived threat is often greatly blown out of proportion by the devil, the news media, and our own imaginations.

[141] Isaiah 2:1–4, Acts 1:6–7,11–12 are a few of many scriptures that refer to this.

[142] Romans 11:25–27, Zechariah 12:9–13:2, and Ezekiel 37:1–28 are just a few of many scriptures that describe this.

[143] *Views of a Changing World*, p.6.

[144] ibid., p.5.

[145] Caner & Caner, p. 69.

Chapter 8: The First Six Heads of the Beast's Kingdom

[146] Since the waters mentioned in Revelation 17:1 are identified in verse 15 of chapter 17 as being "peoples and multitudes and nations and tongues," seeing these waters as people is a consistent interpretation.

[147] We will talk about this more when we discuss the sixth kingdom.

[148] "Pharaoh." Funk & Wagnalls New Encyclopedia, 19: p.8.

[149] J.D. Douglas organizing Editor, *New Bible Dictionary* (Wheaton, IL.: Tyndale House Publishers, second edition, 1982) p. 923.

[150] Ryrie, p. 91.

[151] "Alexander III." Funk & Wagnalls New Encyclopedia,1: p. 407.

[152] Notes on 1st Maccabees, *New American Bible* (Chicago, IL.: Consolidated Book Publishers, 1976) p. 381.

[153] Douglas, p. 53.

[154] This information can be found in a variety of Church History books. I compiled the information from Michael Collins and Matthew Price, *The Story of Christianity* (New York: DK Publishing, 1999).

Chapter 9: Muhammad, Islam & the Seventh & Eighth Kingdoms

[155] Caner & Caner, p. 41–42.

[156] Hourani, p. 28.

[157] Caner & Caner, p. 70.

[158] Bruce Farnham, *My Big Father* (Waynesboro, GA.: OM Literature, 1985) p. 41.

[159] *Why We Fight?: Prelude to War.* Videocasette. (Part One of a Seven Part Documentary) USA, 1942. 52 min.

[160] Johnstone & Mandryk, p. 3.

[161] In fact, it may be this signifies that the primary makeup of this Beast will involve all of the beasts, but the former Roman Empire least of all.

[162] There are exactly the same number of beasts mentioned here, as the ones named in chapter 2. Due to this and the descriptions given, Biblical scholars have felt these describe the same kingdoms found in chapter 2, namely Babylon, Medes-Persia, Greece, and Rome, and in that order.

[163] The first kingdom of Daniel chapter 2, who is also the first kingdom in Daniel chapter 7, is named as Babylon.

Chapter 10: The Beast's Islamic Empire
[164] This figure was arrived at through my personal study of the Koran. I made a careful tally of all separate commands for Muslims to use violence for Allah.

[165] Daniel eventually calls the little horn, a beast (Dan. 7:8–11). Thus, the horns are probably identified here as connected with the beasts.

[166] Hourani, p. 29.

[167] Although there were several other Islamic dynasties during these years, none lasted as long, and this one had the longest running claim to the Caliphate until its demise.

[168] Hourani, p. 33.

[169] ibid., p. 58.

[170] ibid., p. 228–229.

[171] ibid., p. 83.

[172] ibid., p. 96.

[173] ibid., p. 159.

[174] ibid.

[175] ibid., p. 256–257.

[176] Abul Ala Mawdudi, The Punishment of an Apostate According to Islamic Law as quoted by Colin Chapman, *Islam and the West* (Carlisle Cumbria, UK.: Paternoster Press, 1998) p. 130–131.

[177] Caner & Caner, p. 50.

[178] ibid.

[179] ibid., p. 52.

[180] Joshua Hammer. "In the Hands of the Insurgents." *US News and World Report* 24 May 2004, p. 35.

[181] The word *time* signifies a year, *times* signifies two years, and *a half time* is a half-year. Thus, the total is 3 1/2 years.

[182] Mauritania, Morocco, Algeria, Tunisia, Libya, Egypt, a sliver of northwestern Saudi Arabia, Jordan, Lebanon, Syria, Iraq, Turkey, Northwestern Iran, Azerbaijan, Bosnia-Herzegovina and Albania are all regions predominantly Muslim in their populations that were also part of the Roman Empire.

[183] I have talked with writer and missionary to Sudan, Michael Howard and others as well who have voiced such an opinion.

[184] According to the Museum of Civilization in Ottawa, Canada, more than 40,000 loyalists fled to Canada after the Revolutionary War.

[185] Evan Thomas. "The Vietnam Question." *Newsweek* 19 April 2004: 32.

[186] ibid.

[187] Fareed Zakaria. "Our Last Real Chance." *Newsweek* 19 April 2004: 46.

[188] Norval, p. 197–198.

[189] Ibid., p. 180.

Chapter 11: The Apostles of Islam: The Beast and the False Prophet

[190] Caner & Caner, p.221.

[191] ibid., p.63.

[192] ibid., p.193.

[193] Hourani, p.157.

[194] ibid., p.284, 294, 313.

[195] ibid., p.153.

[196] ibid., p.144.

[197] ibid., p.145,146.

[198] ibid., p.145.

[199] Iraneus, p.559.

[200] Caner & Caner, p.134.

[201] ibid., p.137.

[202] I remember reading in a newspaper of the relatively liberal "progressive" Muslim country I was living in, that a study had been conducted showing that approximately 75% of the men in that nation beat their wives. It said that the few women who bothered to try to report this to the police were often harassed and sometimes beaten by the police as well!

[203] Caner & Caner, p.189.

Chapter 12: The Sign of the End: The Beast Rears His Ugly Head

[204] "Back on Iraq at the U.N.," *The Connection* , NPR. WSLU. Canton, NY. 22 Sept. 2003.

[205] *Avoiding Armaggedon Part III*. PBS. WPBS. Watertown, NY. 16 April 2003.

[206] For an overview of how this has happened in history, read the article "The Kingdom Strikes Back" in Winter and Hawthorne, p.195–213.

[207] Paul referred to this temporary separation of God from Israel when he said, "A partial hardening has happened to Israel until the fullness of the Gentiles has come in, and so all Israel will be saved; just as it is written, 'The Deliverer will come from Zion, He will remove ungodliness from Jacob.' 'This is my covenant with them when I take away their sins'" (Rom. 11:25b–27).

[208] "Old Testament History Chart," *Thompson Chain Reference Bible*, for the New American Standard Bible, (Indianapolis: B.B. Kirkbride Bible Company, Inc., 1993) p.1890.

[209] If one multiplies this 69 times 7, we arrive at 483 Jewish years of 360 days. To

convert that into Gregorian years of 365.25 days, we must first multiply 483 years times 360 days to arrive at a total of 173,880 days. Then we divide 173,880 into 365.25 years to equal 476 years.

[210] It is important to realize that these desolations in this context are spoken of as coming after the destruction of the city and the sanctuary and after the Messiah had been cut off. Antiochus IV never completely destroyed the temple, but merely desolated it by ransacking it and by sacrificing a pig on the altar, thus, desecrating it. Furthermore, he attacked, but never leveled the city of Jerusalem, and he did all of this in 169 and 167B.C, long before the coming of the Messiah. Although Daniel also clearly prophesied the coming of Antiochus in Daniel 8:11–14 and 11:21–35, Jesus was of necessity referring to the other desolations of Daniel that would come in the future *after* his earthly ministry. These future desolations, following the cut-off of the Messiah, are the ones referred to in the scriptures we are looking at here.

[211] Antiochus IV ruler of the Seleucid Dynasty desolated the temple in 169 and 167 B.C. He was a prophetic type of the post-Roman latter prince who is to come.

[212] Some believe the prince should refer to Emperor Vespasian's son General Titus, since he would literally be as a prince in the more traditional meaning of the word. Of course he operated under the orders and general direction of his father and both he and his father had the same goals and both were in authority over the people. Thus, either could be considered the prince who fulfilled this prophecy.

[213] Josephus (written late in the 1st century) *The Wars of the Jews*, (Grand Rapids, MI.: Kregel Publications, 1981) Book 3 Chapter 1 section 3, Book 3 Chapter 2 Section 4, & Book 3 Chapter 4 Section 2, p.502–504.

Chapter 13: On the Wing of Abominations

[214] Additionally Daniel 12:11 reads, "From the time that the regular sacrifice is abolished and the abomination of desolation is set up, there will be 1290 days." This may mean that the abolishment of the regular sacrifice and the setting up of the abomination of desolation will be followed by 1290 days of abomination. This setting up of the abomination of desolation may also refer to the setting up of the image of the Beast (Rev. 13:14–15). Interestingly, the Hebrew word *tamid* which is used there for regular sacrifice is *not* the same as the word used for a slaughtered sacrifice which is *zabach*. The only place *tamid* is translated as a reference to a regular sacrifice is five times in Daniel. Interestingly, in Daniel 9:27 when Daniel talks about the sacrificing and grain offerings being brought to a halt, he uses the normal Hebrew word for sacrifice *zabach*. *Zabach* is used in most other Old Testament scriptures when referring to Temple sacrifices. This makes sense because the literal animal sacrifices and grain offerings that were being given to God would cease in A.D. 70. Daniel 9:27 refers directly to that. So then why does Daniel use the word *tamid* and not *zabach* in these other verses?

The word *tamid* is used 98 other times in the Old Testament. The word *tamid* is actually derived from an unused word that literally means "continuity." In all the other instances in the scriptures it is translated as the word(s), all times (1), always (4), constantly (2), continual (26), continually (52), continuously (2), ever (2), perpetual (1), regular (3) and regularly (5). In none of these cases does it mean, "sacrifice." Yet in the context of the five verses where it is used in Daniel, the context makes it clear that it will involve the removal of something regularly presented to God. But, again, the specific word for animal sacrifice predominantly used in the Old Testament is *not* used in any of these cases. Perhaps that is because it is not referring to animal sacrifices. Perhaps it simply means the continual sacrifice and/or act of worship that Christians are accustomed to giving regularly every Sunday. (See Heb. 13:15). Perhaps this is the regular presentation of corporate worship to God that will suddenly cease on a given day. This could very well happen around the time that the Beast seizes power. Perhaps immediately prior to his takeover and afterward, all church buildings and Christians are threatened with destruction and bombing if Christians should enter these places for worship. This view is entirely within the realm of possibility and once again, a reconstructed temple need not be manufactured for this text to be literally fulfilled if we understand that this could very likely not signify the cessation of animal sacrifices. If so, the Beast, who reigns for 1260 days, may freeze worship (perhaps by threats) about 30 days before his world rule is completely established.

[215] Daniel further prophesied of this event in Daniel 11:31 when he stated that "Forces from him will arise, desecrate the sanctuary fortress, and do away with the regular sacrifice. And they will set up the abomination of desolation." This section of scripture from Daniel 11:21–45 is another example of a multiple fulfillment of prophecy as portions of this clearly referred to Antiochus, a typing of the latter prince. The Seleucid Dynasty, ruled by Antiochus, had its power base in Syria, but also gathered troops from throughout the Empire. Again we see the "forces from him" which were dominantly Syrian, trampled the holy people, desecrated the sanctuary fortress, and did away with the regular sacrifice from about 171 B.C. to 165 B.C. (about 2300 mornings and evenings). However, the Roman soldiers came later and did the same thing with greater devastation, destroying, not only desecrating, the sanctuary, and putting an end to sacrifice. They too were led dominantly by Syrian forces together with Arabs, Egyptians and surrounding peoples. All are dominantly Muslim today. Amazingly, at the beginning of his reign, the power center of Abd al-Malik was also dominantly Syrian with a smattering of other Middle Eastern forces (Hourani, p.64). Thus, "forces from him" eventually "set up the abomination of desolation" not only for Antiochus (a statue of Zeus), but also, via Abd al-Malik, for the Beast (the Dome of the Rock).

[216] Josephus, *Wars of the Jews Book VI*, Chap 6 Sec 3, p.584–585.

[217] Ibid., *Book IV*, Chron. 2, Chron.. 3, p.525–530.

[218] Ibid., *Book VI*, Chron.. 2, p.574–577.

[219] Only after finishing the Luke discourse does Luke declare that Jesus went up to Mount Olivet after teaching the people in the temple during the day (see Luke 21:37–38). Of course it is also possible that Jesus gave this initial discourse to the questioners as he was leaving the temple and heading toward Olivet. Then later while on Mount Olivet with his disciples, he would then give a greater clarification concerning some of the issues he had just touched on earlier.

[220] In fact, in recent peace proposals, the Temple Mount has been turned over to the Muslim authorities.

[221] If one compares the passages in Luke 21, Mark 13 and Matthew 24, one is struck by the very close parallels of the Mark and Matthew passages, but significant differences when compared to Luke's discourse. Here is a quick summary: 1) Luke records the story of the poor widow and her two small copper coin offering followed immediately by him overhearing people talking about the temple's beauty. He then makes his statement about its destruction. Matthew and Mark make no mention of the widow's offering. 2) There is no mention of him ever leaving the temple in Luke when he begins talking about the temple's destruction as there is in Matthew and Mark. 3) The people talking about the temple's beauty do not have their identity revealed in Luke. Thus, these may or may not have been disciples. They may have been any nearby Jews whereas in Matthew and Mark it is the disciples who are mentioned as coming to him privately. 4) The Matthew/Mark passages are described as taking place privately on the Mount of Olives. Luke makes no mention of this. 5) Luke talks of the need to leave the city when it is surrounded by armies. However, Matthew/Mark make no mention of this. 6) Luke speaks of this destruction as being a judgment and wrath upon the Jews for rejecting Messiah. He makes no mention of a great tribulation. 7) Only Matthew/Mark mention a great tribulation. They make no mention of a specific judgment on the Jews. 8) Only Luke mentions the scattering of the Jews and Jerusalem being trampled by the Gentiles until the times of the Gentiles are fulfilled. Matthew/Mark make no mention of this or the times of the Gentiles. 9) Luke makes no mention of the completion of the Great Commission as the Matthew/Mark passage does. 10) There is also no mention of the ingathering of the Church in Luke whereas there is in Matthew/Mark.

Even if the Luke passage was also spoken only to the disciples, there is still no reason to believe it was not a separate discourse from the Matthew/Mark passage. It may be that Jesus began his Luke discourse in relation to the future of the Jews as he was leaving the temple building. Then he later gave the clarification about the sign of his coming and the end of the age and the future of the Church after the disciples asked him to clarify this while sitting on the Mount of Olives.

[222] Also, the end of the discourse in Matthew 24:31 and Mark 13:27 speak of the ingathering of the Church. However, Luke does not speak of this ingathering. In the case of Luke, Jesus is addressing the Jews who will *not* be raptured to meet the Lord in the air. Instead he tells them to look up, when they see this happening for their "redemption is drawing near" (Luke 21:28b). For it is at this time when the Lord returns in the sky that the Jews will repent as they see their Messiah coming. He will return and wash them from their sins and redeem them (Zech. 12:10–13:2).

[223] The passage that parallels this account is given in Mark 13:1–37.

[224] *Ryrie Study Bible*, p.1443.

Chapter 14: The Islamic False Prophet: The Chief Enforcer

[225] Shiites are in the majority in both Iran and Iraq. Shiites believe that Ali, the son-in-law of Muhammad, who was murdered, was the rightful Caliph of Islam. Unlike the majority Sunni Muslims, they believe that only blood descendants of Muhammad should be Caliphs. They also tend to be somewhat more into mysticism than most Sunni Muslims.

[226] Caner & Caner, p.164.

[227] "AL-HEDAYA, Vol. 2 from the Hanafi Manual" as found in *The World of Islam.* CD-ROM. Colorado Springs, CO: Global Mapping International, 2000.

[228] Samuel Zwemmer, *The Moslem Christ,* (New York: American Tract Society, 1912) as found in *The World of Islam.* CD-ROM. (Colorado Springs, CO.: Global Mapping International, 2000).

[229] Caner & Caner, p.114–117.

[230] ibid., p.83.

Chapter 16: The Destruction of Babylon

[231] *Avoiding Armeggedon* (Part III). PBS. WPBS. Watertown, NY. 16 April 2003.

[232] "Interview with Mark Sageman, former CIA agent and author of *Understanding Terror Networks.*" *Fresh Air.* NPR. WSLU. Canton, NY, 27 May 2004.

[233] The 144,000 showing up in heaven in chapter 14 may symbolize this.

[234] Matthew Benjamin, "China Conundrum," *US News & World Report,* 15, Sept. 2003, p. 38.

[235] ibid.

[236] China's official economic figures place it as the world's number-two economy. Most economists feel the numbers are greatly inflated. According to the article, "China Conundrum" in the September 15, 2003 issue of *US News & World Report,* China is the sixth largest world economy.

[237] *World Almanac and Book of Facts,* 2003, p.108.

[238] ibid., p.160.

[239] ibid., p.223.

[240] "The Center of the World." *The Connection* NPR. WSLU. Canton, NY. 9 Sept. 2003, as quoted from Guy Prezol, President of the World Trade Association.

[241] "Conflict and Character: George W. Bush." *The Connection* NPR. WSLU. Canton, NY. 28 May 2003 as quoted from Richard Brookheiser, Senior Editor of *The National Review.*

[242] ibid.

[243] ibid.

[244] "Conflict and Character: George W. Bush." *The Connection* NPR. WSLU. Canton, NY. 28 May 2003 as quoted from David Gergen, Director of Center for Public Leadership, Harvard University.

[245] Views of a Changing World, p.71.

[246] ibid., p.73.

[247] ibid., p.73, 78.

[248] ibid., p.78.

[249] ibid., p.88.

[250] Malcom Dale. <*mgdale1@earthlink.net*>. "ABC TV —please read." 14 June 2003. E-mail to the author. 14 July 2003.

[251] Lynn Elber. "Gays give advice on style." *Watertown Daily Times* 12 July 2003, sec. B: 1.

[252] ibid., sec. B: 6.

[253] *Views of a Changing World*, p.114.

[254] ibid.

[255] *World Almanac Book of Facts, 2003*, p.80.

[256] "Barna Identifies Seven Paradoxes Regarding America's Faith," *Barna Updates*. 17 Dec. 2002. Barna Research Group. <http://www.barna.org/FlexPage.aspx?Page =Barnaupdate&BarnaUpdateID=128>

[257] ibid.

[258] (Revelation 18:11–19)

[259] ibid., p.19.

[260] *Views of a Changing World*, p.5.

[261] Fareed Zakaria. "The Good, the Bad, the Ugly," *Newsweek*. 31 May, 2004, p.33.

[262] ibid.

[263] *Statue of Liberty*. Videocasette. Florentine Films, PBS Home Video, 1985. 58 minutes.

[264] R.A. Coombes, *America the Babylon, America's Destiny foretold in Bible Prophecy* (Liberty MO.: Real Pub. 1998) p.132, cited in Mark Hitchcock, *Is America in Bible Prophecy?* (Sisters, Oregon: Multnomah Publishers, 2002) p.32.

[265] Hitchcock, p.32.

[266] In July 2003, the United States Supreme Court overturned Texas' anti-sodomy law, effectively overturning all anti-sodomy laws still on the books anywhere in America.

[267] Senator Ted Kennedy made Ashcroft's Pentecostal faith a central point in his grilling of Senator Ashcroft during his confirmation hearings for Attorney General. Kennedy openly questioned whether or not Ashcroft would be able to abide by the laws of the country due to his Christian faith! Ashcroft was approved by a razor-thin margin. Similar questions have been raised in many judicial hearings of judicial nominees. A number have never even been allowed to come up for a vote.

[268] "Kingdom on Edge," *National Geographic*, October 2003.

[269] ibid.

[270] ibid.

Chapter 18: Closing in on the End: Six Bowls of Wrath and Har-Mageddon

[271] In the *New Bible Dictionary* we learn that "the only reasonable identification of Gog is with Gyges, king of Lydia in 660 B.C." (*New Bible Dictionary* —NBD- p.432) whose land was located in what is now western Turkey. Magog could be Assyrian for *ma gugu* or 'land of Gog.' It is further stated that "the popular identification of Rosh with Russia, Meshech with Moscow and Tubal with Tobolsk in Siberia has nothing to commend it from the standpoint of hermeneutics..." (NBD, p.432). On the other hand, Josephus identified it as the land of the Scythians which was

to the north and northeast of the Black Sea in what are today the Muslim Russian Republics of Dagestan and Chechnya. Charles Ryrie identifies Rosh, Meshech and Tubal as the area of modern Turkey (Ryrie Study Bible notes, p.1286).

The *New Bible Dictionary* states that most Bible scholars identify Rosh with the Assyrian word *Rasu*. *Rasu* was located on the northwest border of Elam in Media. If that were the case, it would place it in the modern country of Iran. Persia, at the time of Ezekiel, included most of Central Asia, including Pakistan, Turkmenistan, Afghanistan, Uzbekistan, Kyrgyzstan, western China, and southern Kazakhstan. Ethiopia may have only referred to that portion of old Ethiopia that recently became the independent nation of Eritrea. Put is of uncertain origin, but the NBD says it is certainly African and likely includes what would today be either Libya or Sudan. Given that they border one another, perhaps it is meant to refer to both. Gomer is probably a reference to the ancient Gimirrai (Cimerians) an Aryan group originating in the Ukraine who eventually conquered what is today parts of Armenia and eastern Turkey. The Cimerians of Turkey have long ago converted to Islam. Charles Ryrie identifies beth-Togarmah as the part of southern Turkey that borders Syria and, interestingly, is made up of predominantly the descendants of Syrian Arabs. Once again, we see that the predominant troops all come from Muslim nations, with the possible exception of the Cimerians, but even they can now be most identified with Muslim eastern Turkey.

Chapter 19: The Harvesting of the earth and the Return of Christ
[272] Notice that he doesn't say we who are alive and remain until the Lord's coming will not precede those who were earlier raptured.
[273] The fact that the rest were killed by the sword that comes from the mouth of him who sat on the horse seems to suggest that although he will come with his army, he himself will actually slay the Beast's armies.

Chapter 20: The Millennial Kingdom of Christ on earth and the Judgment
[274] Here are just a few scriptures which describe the millennium: (Zech. 8:4–5), (Isa. 65:19–25), (Isa. 11:6–9), (Isa. 60:10–18) and (Isa. 51:4–5).
[275] (see Zeph. 3:19, Isa. 24:1,6, Isa. 13:12)
[276] To read more on the evidences for the Resurrection consider these few of many great books on the subject, *More than a Carpenter* or *The New Evidence that Demands a Verdict*, both by Josh McDowell.

Chapter 21: Overcoming by the Blood of the Lamb
[277] There is a list of mission networks, organizations and materials given in the Appendix A.

Chapter 22: Overcoming by the Word of their Testimony
[278] Hattaway, p.108.
[279] ibid.
[280] ibid., p. 89.
[281] Ibid., p. 104–105.

[282] Ibid., p. 89.

[283] George Miley in his book, *Loving the Church, Blessing the Nations,* uses this term and talks about this more extensively.

[284] The CD-ROM, *Countries and Peoples of the World* can help you identify who the least reached peoples are.

Chapter 23: Overcoming by not Loving our Lives even unto Death

[285] I heard him say this while he was preaching.

[286] Hattaway, p.99–100.

[287] ibid., p.90.

[288] The source is from an annual report of a missions agency operating in the region. The name is withheld to protect our innocent brothers and sisters laboring in the region.

[289] Source is DWI Resource Center, 9/12/00, *www.accountablegovernment.org* using 1999 statistics from the National Highway Traffic Safety Administration.

Chapter 24: Storing Up Treasures in Heaven

[290] (see 2Tim. 3:5–9)

[291] Hattaway, p. 125.

[292] According to *Operation World,* 2001, US per capita income is higher than any other nation except Japan and a couple tiny places like Liechtenstein. Only a handful of other countries such as Canada, Great Britain, Germany, and France come within or higher than 50% of our per capita (per person) income levels. Most countries are dramatically lower than 50%. Some examples we could give would be Barbados, at 21% of the US level, Portugal 35%, Hungary 14.3% and Turkey 10%, but most countries are lower than even levels like this. For example, China's per capita income is 2.7% of the level of the average American. Kyrgyzstan is 1.5%, and a Tajik in Tajikistan makes just 1% of what the average American makes in income.

[293] Hattaway, p.126.

[294] ibid., p. 69–70.

Printed in the United States
28436LVS00001B/133-178

9 781414 102627